A NUMISMATIC HISTORY OF THE BIRMINGHAM MINT

A late 19th century view of The Birmingham Mint

A NUMISMATIC HISTORY OF THE BIRMINGHAM MINT

By
James O. Sweeny

THE BIRMINGHAM MINT LTD.
Icknield Street, Birmingham B18 6RX, England

First published 1981 by
The Birmingham Mint Ltd., Icknield Street, Birmingham B18 6RX, England
© 1981 by J. O. Sweeny

All rights reserved

No part of this book may be reproduced by any means, nor transmitted, nor translated into a machine language without written permission.

British Library Cataloguing in Publication Data

Sweeny, James O.
 A numismatic history of The Birmingham Mint.
 1. Birmingham Mint
 2. Mints—England—Birmingham
 I. Title
 332.4'6'942496   HG950.B

 ISBN 0-9507594-0-6

Typeset in Bembo by Pintail Studios Ltd.; and
printed in Great Britain by Pardy & Son (Printers) Ltd.,
both of Ringwood, Hampshire

Contents

Author's Preface	....	vii
Prologue	The First Ralph Heaton	ix
Chapter I	Development of a Business	1
Chapter II	Ralph Heaton & Sons – Until 1862	8
Chapter III	The Proprietorship of Ralph Heaton III	17
Chapter IV	The Stewardship of Ralph IV	26
Chapter V	The Nadir – 1923–35	32
Chapter VI	The Modern Era – 1935 to Date	35
Chapter VII	The Heaton Mintmarks	45
Chapter VIII	The Manufacture of Blanks	57
Chapter IX	Advertising Pieces	63
Chapter X	Minting Equipment	71
Catalogue	Coinage Issues of The Birmingham Mint	86
Appendix I	The Marseilles Affaire	223
Appendix II	Edward Wyon	227
Appendix III	The Heaton Family	230
Appendix IV	The Soho Sale of 1850	232
Appendix V	The Ubiquitous "H"	234
Appendix VI	Australasian Tokens	240

Plates

Frontispiece	A late 19th century view of The Birmingham Mint	
I	Where it all started	x
II	Ralph Heaton (II) and his second wife, Mary Ann Proud	2
III	Title page of Soho Mint auction catalogue	6
IV	The Imperial Mint, Marseilles, 1856	10
V	Ralph Heaton (II) in older age	14
VI	Page from the *Illustrated Times*, May 10th, 1862	18
VII	Product catalogue issued between 1860 and 1889	21
VIII	Ralph Heaton (III)	24
IX	Ralph Heaton (IV)	28
X	Managing Directors of The Birmingham Mint since 1920	36
XI	The Birmingham Mint in 1980	42
XII	Heaton casting and rolling plant of the 1880s	58
XIII	Heaton coining machinery	60
XIV	Architect's drawing of the Canton Mint	72
XV	The Birmingham Mint's engineer, Edward Wyon, at one of the Chinese Mints, ca. 1900	79
XVI	Heaton presses newly installed at the Royal Mint, Bangkok, 1903	83

Author's Preface

It all started out as a simple exercise in applied curiosity — a desire to find out something about those intriguing little H mintmarks on some of the coins in my collection. But what began as a spark eventually became a conflagration, and so now — ten or more years later — this book.

Along the way a great many people have contributed to the accumulation of facts and suppositions presented herein, but certainly none more than Mr. W. R. P. King, former Chairman of the Board of The Birmingham Mint. Ray King, as he was affectionately known to his many friends, spent many hours digging out facts and data from the musty files of his nearly two century old company, and with his lovely wife Joyce gave me the hospitality of his home while I was undertaking research in Birmingham. I am in his debt. His successor at The Mint, Mr. Colin Perry, has also been most helpful in resolving many of the dilemmas that have arisen due to the inevitable conflicts in available data.

Outside of The Mint, Mr. Graham P. Dyer, Curator of the Royal Mint, has graciously allowed me to use information he has painstakingly accumulated, particularly regarding the output of The Mint for British West Africa, East Africa, and England itself. His data regarding the production of English coinage by The Mint during the 1850–70 period, as well as his study of Heaton's participation in the token coinage for the Bank of Upper Canada, provide hitherto unpublished information in these interesting areas.

Two other English numismatists have also been most generous in sharing their time and their specialized knowledge. They are Commander Richard Wright, who has made an in-depth study of the contributions by The Mint to the modernization of China's coinage at the turn of the century, and Major Fred Pridmore, whose knowledge of British Colonial coinage was without peer.

Too many others to name individually have also helped, but I must not forget one who has been an ever-present source of encouragement in my many frustrations. It is to her that I dedicate this book – my wife Ginny.

The reader will note two subjects that are conspicuous by their absence in this edition. They are The Mint's contributions in the areas of medals and tokens, time and opportunity not having been available for the research necessary to include them herein.

Prologue

The First Ralph Heaton

The Birmingham Mint, described by Thomas Becker[1] as "...the finest example of a private mint (in Europe)...", as a mint dates back to the year 1850, when Ralph Heaton II, diesinker and brassfounder, acquired the minting equipment originally used in Matthew Boulton's Soho Mint. Thus equipped, he added coining to the business known then as Ralph Heaton and Son, and the Heaton Mint was born.

His father, Ralph I, has usually been credited with founding the business that is today known as The Birmingham Mint, but the available facts do not support this. True, Ralph I did provide space in his own shop for his son's entry into the business world as a diesinker, and he did later give Ralph II land and buildings nearby to enable him to operate independently of Ralph I's quite different kind of business, but this was the extent of his involvement. Nevertheless, his own history deserves more than passing comment, as it did provide a backdrop against which the history of The Birmingham Mint unfolded.

And so, to begin at the beginning —

Ralph I was born in 1755 "...of good family in the town of Birmingham ... and bred to the trade of brassfounder..."[2] As was common with sons of middle class families in those days, his principal education came from being apprenticed to the owner of a brass foundry. This would have been around 1769 — a period of explosive progress in the mechanical trades — and near the beginning of the great Industrial Revolution. It was also near this same time that Matthew Boulton, a noted Birmingham industrialist, established his Soho Manufactory, teaming up in 1775 with James Watt to produce a radically improved version of the steam engine. The entrepreneurial spirit and an infectious sense of challenge pervaded the community; inventions,

---

[1] Thomas A. Becker, *The Coin Makers* (Garden City, N.Y., Doubleday & Co. 1970), p. 168.
[2] This and other recollections are contained in a letter dated 29 April 1880 from Thomas Gutteridge Cheselden to Ralph Heaton III.

x Prologue

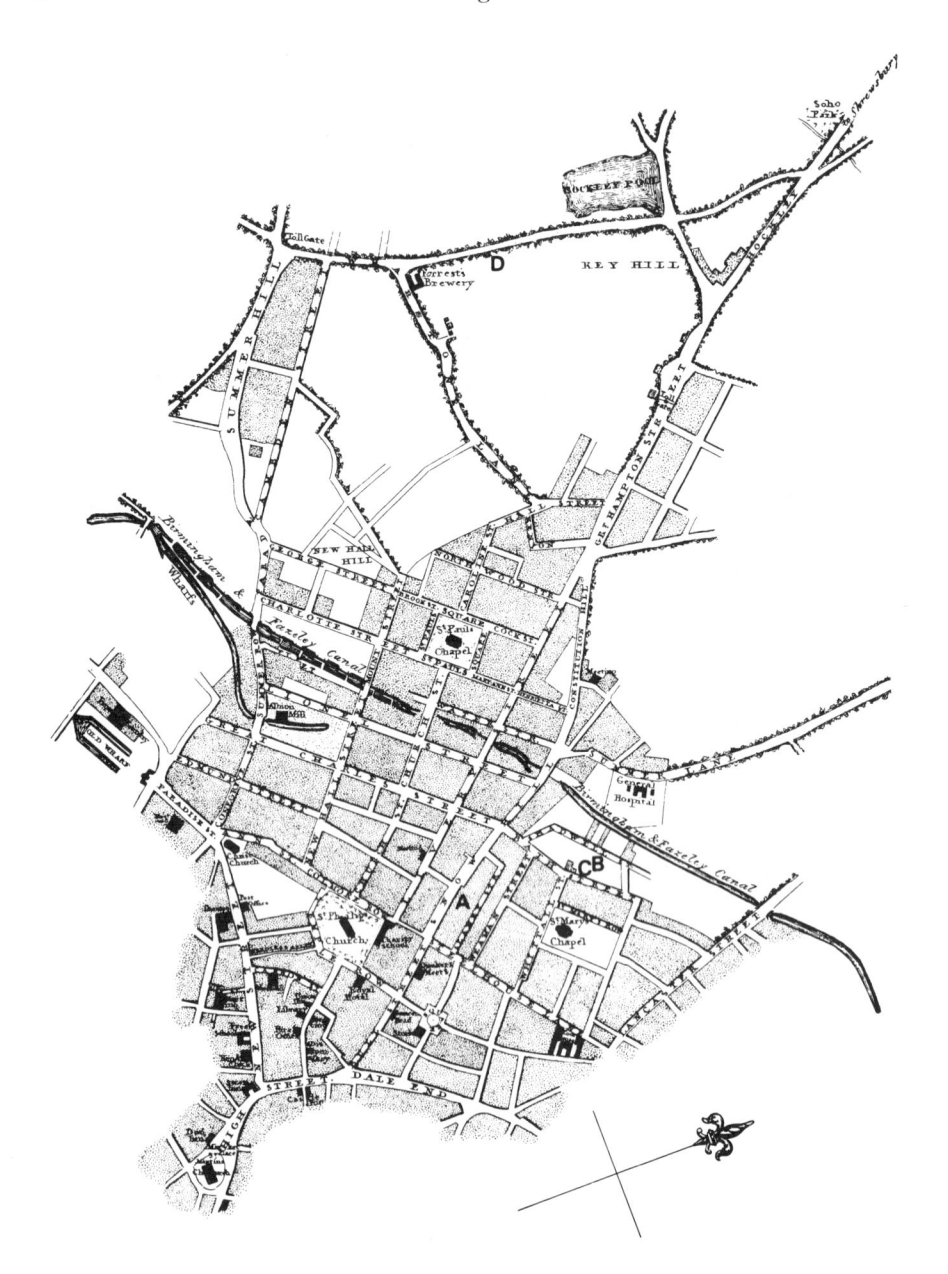

Plate I. Where it all started – taken from an 1808 map of Birmingham in the possession of the City Museums and Art Gallery.
Key:-
A. 27 Slaney Street – Ralph Heaton (I), Jobbing Smith, 1794–ca. 1804.
B. 48 Shadwell Street – Ralph Heaton (I), ca. 1804–27; Ralph Heaton (II), Diesinker, 1816–17; Heaton Bros., 1827–47; George Heaton & Co., 1847–ca. 1852; Heaton & Dugard, ca. 1852–1923.
C. 71 Bath Street – Ralph Heaton (II), 1817–47; Ralph Heaton & Son(s), 1847–60.
D. Eventual site of The Mint, Icknield Street, from 1860 to present day.
Note: The Soho Mint was located until closure in 1850 near Soho Park at the top right corner of the map.

machines, and manufactured goods were pouring out of Birmingham in great degree — and it all must have had a profound effect on one young apprentice.

But like his illustrious contemporary, James Watt, Heaton also elected not to serve out the full seven years of his apprenticeship. Apparently due to a dispute, he left his employer and entered the Army. At least part of his military service was spent at Gibraltar, and some sources[3] credit him with conceiving the plan that saved the day when Gibraltar was under siege in 1782.[4] As the story goes, a combined Spanish and French Command had amassed a huge attack fleet, including ten enormous floating batteries constructed with timber walls some seven feet thick, which was wreaking havoc with close-in fire on The Rock. Heaton suggested firing white-hot shells at the batteries, using wads of turf to isolate the shells from the powder charges in the guns. The plan was completely successful; the floating batteries were all set afire, and the back of the offensive was broken. Eventually the Spanish and French gave up, and peace returned to The Rock. And eventually young Heaton was mustered out and returned home to Birmingham.

An account from a Birmingham journal[3] of 1886 picks up the story with Heaton's Army discharge:

> "...Ralph Heaton returned to Birmingham and took a situation. He soon afterwards invented a machine for ornamenting buttons, and having sold it, commenced business with the proceeds, as a machinist in Slaney Street, where he became famous for making rose engines for ornamenting various articles. He also produced a machine for drilling four holes in buttons simultaneously, and invented all kinds of tools used in manufactories, and in 1790 [sic] he patented[5] a machine for making button shanks, which after the lapse of so many years, and the great advance in mechanical services, has never been superseded, being still used for its original purpose at Shadwell Street Mills."

The Slaney Street operation apparently started in a modest way in about 1792. Sometime in the period 1808–12 Heaton moved his manufactory to larger quarters on Shadwell Street. The business prospered, and its scope continually expanded as four of his sons (John, William, George, and Reuben) joined the company. The Birmingham Directory of 1812 listed Heaton as a "Jobbing Smith, Roller of Metal, Buttonshank and Engine Maker." A decade later the Directory attested to a considerable expansion,

---

[3]"Edgbastonians Past-Present No. 66" *Edgbastonia*, December 1886.
[4]Cheselden suggests the more plausible story that Heaton was assigned responsibility for building and operating the furnaces used for heating the shot — a not inconsiderable contribution to the success of the defence of Gibraltar.
[5]The patent was in fact dated 1794.

then reading "Jobbing Smith, Manufacturer of Brass and Copper Wire, Plain and Ornamented Gilding and Dipping Wire, Button Shanks, Rolled Metal, etc."

Ralph I retired in 1827, turning the business over to the four sons who had joined him earlier. One of their interesting sidelines at this time was the manufacture and operation of steam tractors, one of which towed 34 passengers between Birmingham and Wolverhampton at an average speed of 8 miles per hour on test runs.[6] The business was listed simply as Heaton Bros. until 1847 when, with the other brothers dead or retired, it became George Heaton & Co. Sometime in the next ten years George took in a partner, and the name of the firm became Heaton & Dugard. It continued under this style, and at the Shadwell Street location, until well into the twentieth century. Finally, in 1923, Heaton & Dugard became an affiliate of the Delta Metal Co. Ltd.

Ralph I died in 1832, leaving the major portion of his personal estate to sons George and Ralph II. In his will he described himself as a Button Shank Maker, an activity in which he certainly excelled. His gravestone, still to be seen in St. Paul's Churchyard in Birmingham, reads as follows:

"Sacred to the memory of Mary, wife of Ralph Heaton, who died Feb. the 13th 1816, Aged 61 years, and of the above named Ralph Heaton, who died July 14, 1832, Aged 77 years. He was the inventor of the Button Shank Engine and various other machines and for 40 years a very extensively known and useful engineer."

[6]Stephen Chaplin, "Inter-City 1830", *Delta Review*, Winter 1975–6.

Chapter I

Development of a Business

That corner of the world into which Ralph Heaton II was born in about 1794 had a distinctly numismatic flavour. Matthew Boulton, with six presses of his own design in operation, was busy turning out coins for the East India Company and various countries of the world, as well as medals for presentation at home in England. Other less well-known entrepreneurs in this centre of manufacture of non-ferrous goods were involved in the production of tokens – both legitimate and otherwise. Indeed, Birmingham at the time was probably the leading British city insofar as counterfeiting was concerned.[1] Finally, the extensive button manufacturing trade required die making and metal stamping of a high order, as did the large local manufacture of stamped brass ornaments.

Little is recorded of the early years of Ralph II. It can be reasonably speculated that, as with other lads of his time and circumstances, his formal schooling ended at age twelve, at which time he was apprenticed to some local diemaker. It was certainly not his father to whom he was apprenticed, because that particular skill was not practised in his father's company. He does appear to have been a boy with an independent turn of mind, because he alone of the five Heaton sons pursued a course separate from the family business.

The first record of his post-apprentice period is to be found in the Birmingham Directory[2] of 1816–17, which contains the following two entries:

Heaton, Ralph (Jobbing smith, roller of metal, buttonshank and engine maker) Shadwell Street.
Heaton, Ralph jun. (Die sinker) Shadwell Street.

These two separate entries suggest that father and son were set up in the same shop, but with each pursuing his own trade independent of the other.

---
[1]H. W. Dickinson, *Matthew Boulton* (Cambridge University Press, 1937), p. 135.
[2]*Holden's Biennual Directory*, Reference Section, The Birmingham Public Library.

2   *Chapter I*

Plate II. Ralph Heaton (II), 1794–1862, and his second wife, Mary Ann Proud (courtesy G. Howard Heaton).

This conclusion is further reinforced by the 1818 Directory, which shows the senior Heaton still at the Shadwell Street address, but Ralph II relocated to a Bath Street site. On 2 December 1817 Ralph I conveyed by deed to Ralph II a parcel of land $16\frac{1}{2}$ feet on Bath Street and extending 81 feet toward Shadwell Street, containing a tenement and shop. It was here that son Ralph set up the business that was eventually to become the world's largest private mint. Continuing Directory listings over the course of the next quarter century support and add finality to the conclusion that Ralph II's business operated independently of that of his father. Ralph I's business, under his own name until his retirement in 1827 and thereafter under various other names, remained at the same 48 Shadwell Street address; Ralph II's business continued at the 71 Bath Street location. From these and other points of fact, it can be confidently stated that the firm known today as The Birmingham Mint was founded by Ralph Heaton II in about 1817.

Ralph I died in 1832, leaving his business to his sons John, Reuben, William, and George, and leaving property on Bath and Shadwell Streets to Ralph II. This additional property was very soon used for Ralph II's growing business, which by now included the closely related brass founder and stamping and piercing trades. With that, all the skills needed to conduct minting operations had been acquired by the company, and it only needed certain specialized equipment (coining presses, punch presses, etc.) in order to enter that business. But this was not to be for several years yet.

Meanwhile, both his business and his family were growing. Ralph Heaton III was born in 1827, and received his early education under Mr. Thomas Aston of Rose Hill School, Handsworth, Birmingham. Later he became a private pupil of Mr. E. Jackson of Aldridge Free Grammar School, and following that, at age twelve, he entered his father's business as an apprentice. George Heaton was born in 1833, and followed along in his brother's footsteps. In all, there were five sons and five daughters, but only Ralph III, George, and Harry made their careers in the business.

The business continued to expand. The advent of gas lighting provided special opportunities for the company's skills, and full advantage was taken of it. Chandeliers using brass sheet metal stampings of leaves, scrolls, and filigree work, and carrying up to fifty lights, were produced in great quantities. These were typically finished with a very attractive white and gold effect. A white enamel was applied to the ornamental parts and then removed from the high spots, which were hand burnished to yield the gold appearance.

The Heatons patented a brass gas burner which produced a so-called "bat's wing" flame. These were made by the millions and wholesaled to itinerant hawkers who specialized in door-to-door sales. An improvement on this burner, involving a steatite tip to eliminate the corrosion of the brass tips, was later invented by the Heatons, and this method became the industry standard until the advent of the incandescent mantle.

Products such as these, and ornamental brass stampings such as ceiling "roses", were the mainstay of the Company while Ralph III was serving his apprenticeship. His graduation to a position of responsibility was formally recognized by the name of the firm becoming Ralph Heaton and Son in about 1847. Brother George's participation was similarly recognized in about 1853 with the change to Ralph Heaton and Sons, which name continued to be used until 1889.

On Monday, 1 April 1850, a notice appeared in the local newspaper that caused great excitement at the Heaton firm. That day, Aris's *Birmingham Gazette* announced the auctioning of the equipment of the defunct Soho Mint that had been established by Boulton[3] in about 1788. One can imagine the questions that were discussed by the Heatons during the next few weeks. What equipment would be needed to enter the minting business? How much would it cost? How could it be financed? Where would it be placed? Who else might be competing for it? And most important of all, how could one be assured of enough contracts for coinage to justify the expenditure?

Their decisions were made, and when the doors of the Soho Mint were opened for the auction at eleven o'clock on the morning of 29 April, the Heatons were there. First to be auctioned were the four screw presses. These had been made by Boulton in the Soho Foundry, and were of the same type as those in the Royal Mint in London. Indeed, the wooden patterns that had been used for casting the iron parts of the Royal Mint presses were also among the items auctioned that day. In the auction catalogue the screw presses were described as follows:

> "Pneumatic Coining Press with 5 inch plunger and gun metal guide nut with gripping and quadrant gear, cast iron weight shaft, 12 inch and 15 inch air cylinders with trip and slide valves, cast iron balance weights and levers, cast iron trip sway bar and buffer, cast iron standards and bed plates."

These were steam-powered presses, operated through a master gear driven by a ten horsepower steam engine. Though they were made in the period 1790–1810, they were still reasonably modern in 1850; similar machines were the mainstay of the Royal Mint until 1880. A brief description of the latter facility from an 1832 visit is recorded as follows:[4]

---

[3]Dickinson, *Matthew Boulton*, p. 138.
[4]Eugene S. Ferguson, *Early Engineering Reminiscences (1815–1840) of George Escol Sellers*, by permission of the Smithsonian Institution.

NOTE: From the same source we get an impression of the state of the then Philadelphia Mint. Mr. Eckfeldt, Chief Coiner at Philadelphia, is quoted as follows:

Development of a Business

"In the fall of 1832 I visited the Royal Mint, but I was hurried through as sightseers generally are. At that time there was in the coining room a row of screw coining presses similar to those in our home mint (Philadelphia), save that they were driven by steam power, though the driving power was not visible in the room. The top of the screw still carried its heavily weighted balance lever, from the momentum of which the coin impression was made; the weighted lever end striking a wooden spring block was thrown back by the recoil, operating the dies for thrusting out the piece coined and inserting a fresh planchet. The power was given by a shaft through the ceiling from the power room above, which by a clutch box, took hold of the top of the screw; this clutch was automatically engaged and disengaged."

The presses were the key items in the auction. The other equipment would be of only limited value without the presses, as there were no minting facilities in Birmingham worthy of the name (or elsewhere in England, except for the Royal Mint itself). Whoever acquired the presses would have little difficulty acquiring the related equipment. The Heatons' main concern was probably that either the Royal Mint or the firm of James Watt & Co. would be competing for the presses. It is not recorded how active was the bidding, nor the prices, but the Heatons' bid was successful.

Next to be auctioned were six "cutting-out presses" for producing planchets from rolled strips. These were also bid in by the Heatons, as was most of the remainder of the available minting equipment. Now at last the Heatons had most of the equipment necessary to complement the skills they had already developed, the combination of which would enable them to enter the coining business. Certain additional equipment (engine, shafting, and sundry machinery) was soon thereafter procured from Joseph Taylor, whose firm is known today as Taylor and Challen.

All of this equipment was set up in the Heatons' Bath Street shops and made ready for coining. One formality remained; the British Foreign Office had to check them out.[5] It did so by soliciting a letter of recommendation from Richard Spooner, a member of Parliament from Birmingham. His letter was acknowledged as follows:

"If Mr. Peale (then Assayer, later Chief Coiner) had full swing he would turn everything upside down; why he even talks of throwing away our costly coining presses that have done and are doing such good service, dispensing with manpower, and yet he won't hear of applying steam power to our old screw presses, which has been successfully done in the Royal Mint, London."

[5] Whether this was really a requirement of the Foreign Office, or a device initiated by Heaton as an advertising aid, is not definitely known. The correspondence, however, did take place.

THE SOHO MINT, NEAR BIRMINGHAM.

A CATALOGUE
OF
THE VALUABLE MACHINERY AND PLANT
OF
THE SOHO MINT,

long celebrated and in high repute with the Government of Great Britain, as also with Foreign powers in Europe, Asia and America, the East India Company, and with mercantile and other firms of eminence in all parts of the world.

THE MACHINERY

may be pronounced as the most perfect of its kind in existence, having been constructed entirely under the personal superintendence of the late proprietor, whose genius and great mechanical skill are too well-known to render further allusion necessary; it includes

FOUR COINING PRESSES,

highly finished and worked by Pneumatic Apparatus. Each Press is constructed in a massive iron frame, with 5½-inch screw, working in a heavy metal nut; the dies are placed in a steel collar, which rises as the blank is struck, thereby preserving a square edge to the Coin. It is fed by a self-acting layer on, so formed as to reject an imperfect or improper Blank, and requiring merely the attention of a child in order to the efficient operation of the Machine. The speed varies from 60 to 80 blows per minute, according to the size of the Coin.

SIX CUTTING OUT PRESSES,

worked by the Steam Engine with pneumatic balance pumps; they are highly finished and erected in a circular iron frame, with fly-wheel and gearing, and capable of cutting 300,000 Blanks per day.

THREE MILLING MACHINES;

2 Shaking Machines, with Drying Stoves; Washing and Pickling Cisterns; Annealing Furnaces and Muffles;

A POWERFUL MEDAL OR MULTIPLYING PRESS,

to work by hand, with 5½-inch screw, and metal nut, in massive iron frame; several smaller Punching Presses;

A 10 HORSE POWER CONDENSING STEAM ENGINE;

2 Steam Boilers: 2 Timber Beam Condensing Steam Engines, *one of which will be considered highly interesting from the fact of its being the first erected by James Watt*; 2 powerful Vacuum Pumps; 700 feet Iron Shafting; 100 pair Plummer Blocks and Brasses; self-acting Screw-Cutting Lathe; 1 self-acting Turning Lathe; 8 Engine and Foot-turning Lathes; Drilling Machines; an assortment of Taps and Dies, Stocks and Steel Tools; 50 dozen Files;

EIGHT PLATE AND BAR ROLLING MILLS,

the Rolls by "Wilkes;" Driving Pinions and Apparatus; the iron frame work for a Water Wheel; 100 Spur, Rigger and Pinion Wheels; Cutting Shears; Tilt or Stamping Hammer; Smiths' Forges, Bellows and Tools; Box, Beam and other Scales; 2 tons Weights; Crab Crane; Machine Crane and Jib; Grindstones and Frames;

AN ASSORTMENT OF EXPENSIVE PATTERNS,

including those of the Royal Mint and the East India Company's Mints at Bombay and Calcutta, also of the various Machines at the Soho Mint;

12 TONS OF THE FINEST DIE STEEL,

made expressly for the late Mr. Boulton, under his personal directions, and acknowledged to be the best Die Steel in the Kingdom; 2 tons Shear and Scrap Steel; 7 tons of best Die Iron; 6 cwt. forged Dies and Collars;

5 TONS OF COPPER AND LEAD,

in sheets and Scrap, Cisterns, Pipes, &c.; Swedish Copper for Alloy; 50 Brass Cocks;

THE EXTREMELY VALUABLE COLLECTION OF DIES

for the Coins and Medals, well-known as the Soho Collection, most beautifully executed, principally by the celebrated Kuchler, and by Droz and Philpp, also the Dies for many rare Coins, hitherto considered as almost unique, including a Dollar George III., 1798, a Britanniarum Penny, many specimens of proposed Coins, of various dates, and of the French Republic, 1790 to 1792, a pattern Half-penny George III. by Droz, and Provincial Tokens; also

A CABINET OF COINS AND MEDALS,

embracing 4 sets of the Soho Collection, and many others extremely rare.

THE OFFICE FITTINGS AND FURNITURE,

including 2 Iron Strong-room Doors, an Iron Safe, Wainscot Presses, Desks, Copying Machines, Office Stove, and a large variety of miscellaneous property.

Which will be Sold by Auction, by Messrs.

FULLER AND HORSEY,

On MONDAY, APRIL 29, 1850, and following days, at 11 o'Clock,
AT THE WORKS, NEAR BIRMINGHAM. IN LOTS. BY DIRECTION OF THE EXECUTORS OF THE LATE M. R. BOULTON, ESQ.

The Machinery may be seen in motion, and the other effects Viewed, on Thursday, Friday, and Saturday prior to the Sale. Catalogues, without which no person can be admitted, may be obtained at One Shilling each, of Messrs. FULLER & HORSEY, Billiter Street, London.

Plate III. Title page of Soho Mint auction catalogue (courtesy Birmingham Reference Library).

>   Foreign Office
>   7 November 1850
>
> Sir,
>   I am directed by Viscount Palmerston to acknowledge the receipt of your letter of the 31st ultimo, vouching for the respectability of Mefs^rs Heaton and Son, who state that they have purchased the Coining Prefses of the Soho Mint at Birmingham, and that they expect to be employed by Foreign Governments.
>
>   I am,
>   Sir,   Your most obedient
>   humble Servant,
>   /s/ Stanley Alderley
>
>   Richard Spooner Esq. M.P.
>   Birmingham

Now it but remained for orders to be received, and the Heatons would be in the coining business. They had not long to wait.

Chapter II

Ralph Heaton & Sons – Until 1862

It was a propitious time for the Heatons. The British Empire was in an expansionistic mode, particularly in a commercial sense, and the need for minor coins was great, both at home and in the colonies. And the Royal Mint was not quite up to the need. In 1850 the Government made the decision to abandon the old system of *contract* coinage under which England's needs had been but poorly served, and to restructure all Royal Mint functions under a Deputy Master of the Mint.[1] The purposes of this reorganization were several, especially including control, cost, and efficiency, but even thereafter the Royal Mint was still unable to respond fully to the nation's coinage needs. For one thing, two metals could not be processed through the metallurgical phases simultaneously, and so any time gold or silver coinages were required, copper coins could not be made for want of the means of producing copper blanks or bars.

Elsewhere in the world there were similar problems. In Central and South America the developing nations had only the heritage of the old Spanish American mints upon which to rely for their growing coinage needs – and these mints were grossly inadequate. They had been equipped to produce relatively small quantities of silver and gold coins, whereas the need now was for relatively large quantities of minor coinage.

Against the background of a proliferating demand and an inadequate supply of copper coins, Ralph Heaton & Sons' new project was launched with great promise. It is likely that from far-away Australia came the first order – for trade tokens for the mercantile establishment of Messrs Annand Smith.[2] In Australia in 1850 there was no indigenous coinage to meet the needs of commerce, and so tokens developed as the inevitable substitute, just as they had in England in the latter part of the eighteenth century. The Annand Smith company led the way, but this was their second issue of

---
[1] *First Annual Report of the Deputy Master of the Mint*, London 1870, pp. 15–17.
[2] See Appendix VI.

tokens, the first probably having been supplied by the Soho Mint as one of its last orders before having been shut down by the executors of the Matthew Boulton estate.

The next year, Heatons' first full year of minting operations, things picked up very gratifyingly. Their first foreign order came from Chile through the firm of Henry Van Wart, agent for the Government of Chile.[3] These were copper centavos and medio centavos, and on the centavos of 1851 Heaton proudly applied the now-familiar H mintmark for the first time.

Of great importance to Heatons that year was an order from the British Royal Mint. According to Mr. G. P. Dyer, presently Librarian and Curator of the Royal Mint,

> "Heaton's received a contract to supply the Royal Mint with copper blanks for pence, halfpence, farthings, half-farthings and quarter-farthings. Deliveries stretched into 1852 and it looks as if Heaton's may have supplied blanks for most of the coins of these denominations struck by the Royal Mint in 1851 and 1852."

This was the beginning of a long and mutually profitable association with the Royal Mint, an association which continues to this day.

One other emission in 1851 is to be noted. The Crystal Palace Exhibition in London that year provided Heatons with an opportunity to do a bit of advertising, which they responded to by striking a medal – their first – commemorating the exhibition. Other even more imaginative advertising pieces were struck from time to time, and will be mentioned later.

In 1852 Heatons' coinage was entirely for the Americas. From South America came an order from Venezuela, and from North America an order for the Province of Canada. Two other events occurred of more than passing significance to the firm. The first was an invitation to participate in a major recoinage of French money. This opportunity was especially welcome because it would introduce Heatons to the intricacies of working with bronze – a metal not then in general use for coins. Even the Royal Mint had not yet struck bronze coins; the English change from copper to bronze was not to begin until late in 1860.

The contract with the French, dated 27 October 1852, called for Heatons to re-equip the mint at Marseilles and carry out a coinage operation there under the supervision of the Director of the Marseilles Mint. Ralph III

---

[3]Great Britain at the time was one of the most highly developed countries of the world. From her workshops in the industrial cities poured a flood of goods that were needed by – but not locally available to – most of the less-developed countries of the world. Consequently, it became the practice of many countries to name British firms as their agents for the purchase of British goods. These agents became the medium through which coinage orders were placed.

10	Chapter II

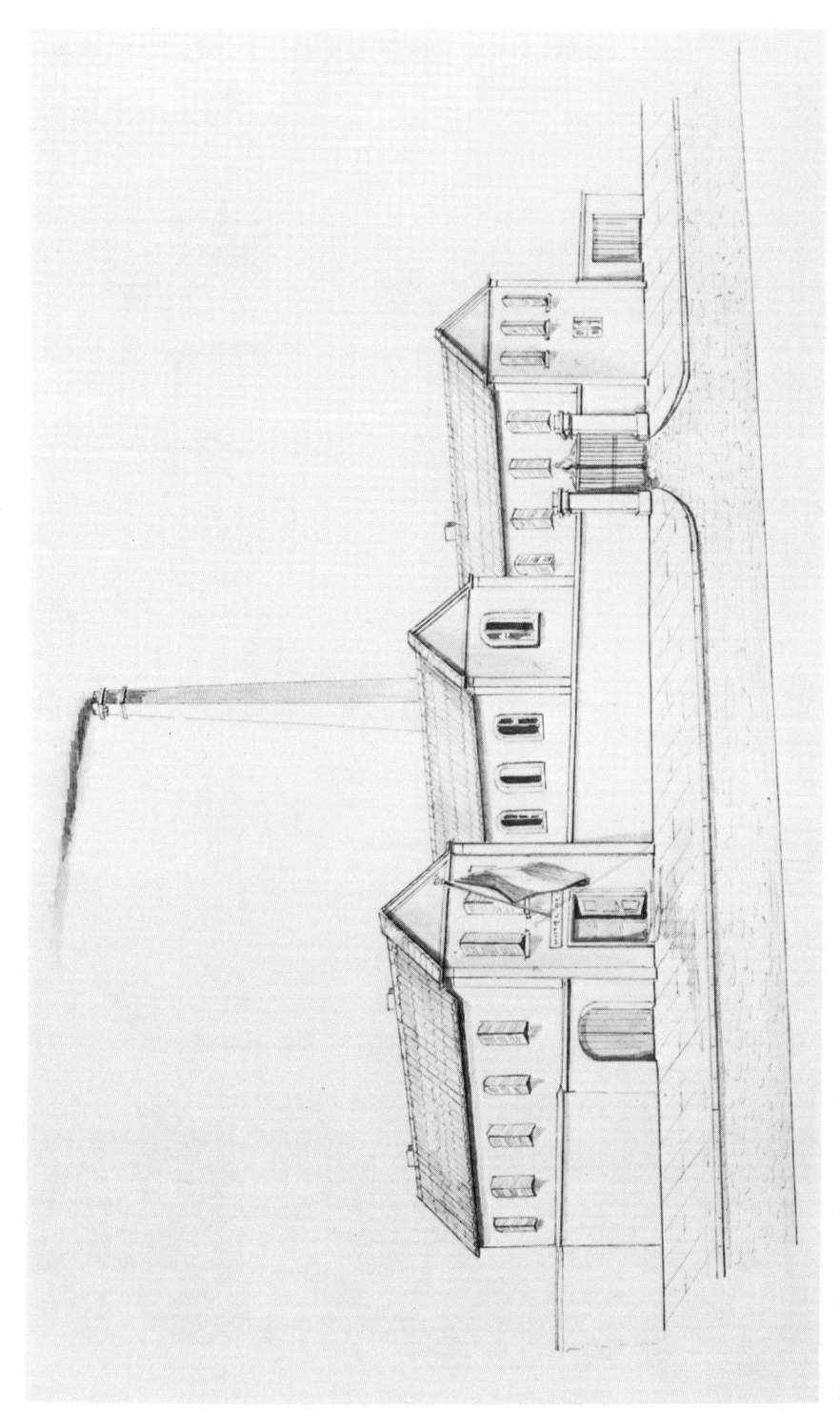

Plate IV. The Imperial Mint, Marseilles, 1856. From a sketch by Leonard Brierley, Heatons' Mint manager (courtesy Birmingham City Museums and Art Gallery).

selected key workers from The Birmingham Mint, and with this able cadre moved to Marseilles for the duration of the contract. A more detailed description of this operation will be found in Appendix I. Suffice it to say here that during the period 1853–7, Heatons produced about 750 tons of Napoleon III bronze coinage with an MA mintmark. At the conclusion of the contract the Birmingham cadre packed up and returned home, and the Marseilles minting equipment was sold to a French manufacturer for £1080.

The second event of significance in 1852 took place after Ralph III had departed for Marseilles. In England the need for copper coins continued to be acute. The Royal Mint was busy responding to the heavy demands for gold and silver coinage, and so could not take on this additional requirement. Accordingly, they advertised for bids to produce the copper coinage.

This opportunity was made to order for the Heatons, and they responded with enthusiasm. In a letter from France to his father, Ralph III observed:

> "We certainly have the advantage over anyone in England for the manufacture, having all the machinery ready. What a thing if we should be made coiners for the two greatest nations under the sun" [meaning, of course, France and England]. "I am convinced this is only the commencement of another Soho" [obviously a reference to Boulton's great Soho Mint].

He went on to suggest the arrangement that has ever since governed the contracts between The Birmingham Mint and the Royal Mint. Concerned about the increasing price of copper, he proposed:

> "If Sir John" [Herschel, Master of the Royal Mint] "will take a price for manufacture, in addition to that of the day's price of metal when deliveries are made, it will be a rather less speculative affair."

The contract between Ralph Heaton & Sons and the Royal Mint was signed on 30 March 1853. Mr. G. P. Dyer kindly supplied the following account of the execution by Heaton of the contract provisions:

> "In 1853 a new and far greater contract for a total of nearly 500 tons of these denominations (pence, halfpence, farthings, half-farthings and quarter-farthings) was placed with the firm, but this time for coins, not blanks. Delivery began in August 1853 and the contract was completed in August 1855, to be followed in 1856 by a much smaller order for 50 tons of pence, halfpence, farthings and half-farthings. This new order was completed in December of 1856. Our records are not as clear as they might be, but basically I think that it might be said that of the 550 or so tons of [these denominations] struck for circulation from 1853 to 1856 inclusive, Heaton's apparently produced all but three tons of pence, 18

hundredweight of halfpence, and 7 tons 5 cwt of farthings. This small quantity of 11 tons 3 cwt was struck by the Royal Mint in 1854."

These coins bear no distinguishing marks to identify them as Heaton issues, and so have been generally and mistakenly attributed to the Royal Mint.

At the height of activity on the English coinage, Heatons were producing in Birmingham on the four original screw presses about 25 hundredweight of coin per day. This was equivalent to about 110,000 pieces per day, a very large output for the times.

The conclusion of the 500 ton contract was the occasion for a celebration. The *Birmingham Journal* of 18 August 1855 noted:

> "Mr. Ralph Heaton of Bath Street, having on Wednesday completed his contract with the British Government for the coinage of 500 tons of copper coins, commemorated that event on Thursday last by inviting all his workpeople to dine with him at the new 'Rose and Crown', Lickey. Three vans were provided for the workpeople (and band) and a sumptuous dinner was served to 96 persons."

Following the small contract for the Royal Mint in 1856, it was several years before English coinage was again required of The Birmingham Mint. Nevertheless, foreign contracts continued to keep The Mint fully occupied, to the extent that expansion was a continuing necessity. As of February 1855 the Heatons had added a fifth press – a lever press of the type then being used in the Marsailles Mint. Further additions were made until finally the available space in the Bath Street shop no longer sufficed. The event that finally forced the issue was a huge order for India, for which production started in 1858 and continued well into 1862.

In 1860 the Heatons acquired a one-acre property on Icknield Street, Birmingham, and construction of a new three-story red brick factory was begun. The rectangular structure housed offices, counting rooms, and warehouses along the front; in the far rear were the coining and die rooms; along the sides were the operations required for the other trades in which the firm participated. In the centre of the rectangle were located the casting shops, rolling mills, and power house. In addition to the equipment moved from the Bath Street shop, several new presses and other machines were supplied by the Birmingham firm of Joseph Taylor. When the new mint was completed in 1862, over three hundred employees were required to handle the work that Heatons were enjoying, and The Mint had by then become the largest private mint in the world. Indeed, a newspaper article of the time claimed Heatons' capabilities to be six times those of the Royal Mint – although this undoubtedly somewhat of an exaggeration. The Birmingham Mint has remained to this day on the same site (though now covering a much larger area), and the original façade of the 1862 building still survives.

Meanwhile, there was considerable agitation in England for a decimal coinage, which would no doubt have created a need beyond the capacity of the Royal Mint. To this point, hearings were held by a Decimal Coinage Commission, and the Master of the Royal Mint, Mr. Thomas Graham, testified as follows on 30 July 1857:

Q. Where were your contracts made?
A. At Birmingham.
Q. Had you any difficulty in obtaining a supply of copper coinage that way?
A. No difficulty.
Q. If the public service required it, could you, through additional contractors, increase your supply of copper coin to any considerable extent?
A. It could be very easily extended, for large orders would induce the temporary establishment of private mints for the purpose of coining copper.
Q. From your vast experience in those 20 years, had you any reason to suppose that there was danger of a private contractor taking into account the difference of the actual value of the copper contained in the coin and its value in circulation; had you any reason to suspect fraud?
A. No reason to suspect fraud on the part of the contractor; indeed, the coin though struck in Birmingham, was struck under the surveillance of Mint officers, who retain possession of the dies.
Q. Have you more contractors than [the] one in Birmingham?
A. The coin has been executed by one contractor for the last five or six years.

Graham also presented to the Commission the results of a questionnaire circulated in England, Ireland and Scotland by Heatons. The questionnaire, which went mostly to tradespeople, sought reaction to the decimalization proposal. The response was generally favourable; only a small number of the respondents felt that the "inconvenience would be greater than the advantage", as one expressed it.

The intent of this testimony was to reassure the Commission that means existed to handle the huge requirements that would follow the adoption of a decimal coinage. Despite these assurances, however, the decision to change was not made – neither then in 1857 nor within the next hundred years. Thus for the rest of that decade, the Royal Mint was able to take care of the

Chapter II

Plate V. Ralph Heaton (II) in older age, from a photograph (courtesy G. Howard Heaton).

Empire's needs within itself, but it would not be long before **Mr. Graham's** testimony was fully verified.

Another success story of the period involved an interesting contract that Heatons signed with the Government of the newly unified Kingdom of Italy. This was for a coinage – to be produced in the Milan Mint – of a large bronze issue to replace the coins of the independent states and the provisional coins that had been circulating. Some of this same new issue was to be produced by the Government Mints at Bologna and Naples, but Heatons assumed responsibility for the operation of the Milan Mint. George Heaton was sent to Italy to supervise the work there, again taking along key people from Birmingham – some of whom had participated in the Marseilles adventure. Equipment had to be procured; George bought sixteen lever presses in Amsterdam, and brother Harry obtained the remaining nine presses in Paris. The first contract, for twelve million lira of fractional currency, was signed on 19 January 1861 and completed in about July of 1862. A second contract was signed on 11 August 1862 and completed later that year. The coin blanks for both contracts were sent out from Birmingham, but the actual coinage was entirely carried out in Milan. At the conclusion of the contracts, the equipment was sold to the Italian Government, and George and his Birmingham cadre returned home.

Despite these many successes, the period was not without its disappointments. In 1859 Great Britain made the decision to convert to a bronze coinage. The Royal Mint was again unable to produce the great quantity required, and so a contract for 1720 tons of Imperial bronze coinage was put out for bids. Just as the Master of the Royal Mint had testified in 1857, the opportunity attracted other bidders. Probably to the surprise of the Royal Mint, and certainly to Heatons' surprise, this very desirable contract was bid in by the firm of James Watt & Co., a derivative company of Boulton & Watt's enterprises of the preceding century, and a complete newcomer to the minting business. Watt had some trouble getting started, so Heatons received a small contract and supplied some forty-one tons of the bronze coins in 1861, but other than this their participation was limited to contracts for dies, bars and strips, and possibly for blanks. The most significant outcome, however, was that thereafter Heatons did not take its close relationship with the Royal Mint for granted – it was many years before another major contract was lost to a competitor.

Ralph Heaton II died in October 1862, ending a distinguished career that began as a diesinker's apprentice and culminated as a respected Birmingham industrialist. His minting achievements were significant indeed. Coinage operations were begun in late 1850, and during the next twelve years Heatons established itself as a major supplier to the Royal Mint of both coins and blanks. Major contracts were completed for the governments of France and Italy. Coinages were produced for many countries, including such diverse lands as the Ionian Islands, Venezuela, and India. An 1862 article[4] summed up the coinage of the period as follows:

"They were first employed in 1851 by the English Government and subsequently by Foreign Powers, and during the last ten years have executed

---

[4] "The Workshops of England", *Illustrated Times*, Birmingham, May 10, 1862.

for different States no fewer than 1050 millions[5] of coins, weighing upwards of 5260 tons, and which, if placed side by side, would extend over 14,800 miles."

A major new minting facility was planned, begun and completed. The Mayor of Birmingham[6] summed up the firm's accomplishments and capabilities very well in a testimonial[7] letter in 1861:

> "I, Arthur Ryland, Esquire, Mayor of the Borough of Birmingham, in the County of Warwick, do hereby certify that Messrs. Ralph Heaton & Sons, of the Mint, in the said Borough of Birmingham, are able, from the excellence of their machinery and the extent of their trading operations, to execute any amount of coinage that may be required either by the British Government or any foreign state.
>
> "The firm is well known in Birmingham as a house of high commercial standing, and is distinguished alike by the magnitude of its transactions and the integrity and skill with which they have conducted them."

It was most fitting that in his last year, Ralph Heaton's company was awarded an International Exhibition Medal for "Excellence of Manufacture of Coins".

---

[5]Note that the Catalogue section of this book accounts for only two-thirds of the above total of 1050 million coins.

[6]It is interesting to note that the Mayor also happened to be the personal solicitor to Mr. Heaton, whose will was prepared by Mr. Ryland.

[7]In about 1879 Heatons published an interesting little book, apparently for advertising purposes, which contained much information valuable to this research. There were a number of letters testifying to Heatons' overall competence as well as to the excellence of specific emissions, and sixteen plates showing coins produced either by Heatons or by other mints using blanks, dies, or machinery furnished by Heatons. A second edition was published in about 1886, expanded to include additional letters and twenty-one plates. Three subsequent editions, dated 1891, 1895, and 1904, also appeared. In all these, a total of some twenty-six plates of excellent coin photographs has provided important clues to the early workings of this minting establishment.

Chapter III

The Proprietorship of Ralph Heaton III

When Ralph Heaton III assumed control of the family enterprise in 1862 at age 35, he was already a veteran of twenty-two years service with the company. He had been thoroughly trained in all phases of coinage manufacture, having personally managed the Marseilles operation for nearly three years. He had cut his eye teeth on the old screw presses that were the mainstay of the company, but also had extensive experience with the European types of lever presses that had been adopted by the Paris Mint in about 1848. Indeed, he and his brother George had patented improvements to the lever press,[1] and his plan for modernizing The Mint involved a gradual transition to that type of equipment.

The new mint on Icknield Street had started out with one lever press and eleven screw presses. An 1862 print in the *Illustrated Times* shows these huge screw presses, fastened down to two immense balks of timber running the length of the press room. The machines were noisy, inefficient in their use of power, and occupied a large amount of space. In contrast, the lever presses were relatively quiet, efficient both as to power and space, and yielded greatly improved die life. By 1866, The Mint was equipped with twelve lever presses in addition to those eleven screw presses. Gradually, the screw presses were retired from use, the last one (and one of the original Boulton presses) continuing in service until 1882. The lever presses were made in Heatons' shops, and the experience gave rise to a new business opportunity – that of the manufacture of coining presses and other equipment.

Their first major contract for equipment came in 1864. It was an order for an entire minting plant for the Government of Burma. The contract called for Heatons to supply buildings, equipment, and start-up supervision, for which they received the following testament to the quality of their performance:

---

[1] British Patent No. 1855, dated 11 August 1859, described an invention for feeding blanks, moving the dies, and removing the finished coins automatically.

18   *Chapter III*

Plate VI.   Page from the Illustrated Times, *May 10th, 1862. The casting shops and rolling mills were located within the quadrangle and served the finished product departments in the peripheral building. The rolling mills and coining presses were powered by steam.*

"You, the Trader William Wallace, and the Agent Zan-ta-wut, acting on the order of His Most Glorious Majesty, procured the purchase of a Mint and arranged its delivery at the Court.

The Mint reached the royal capital Mandalay during the month of February 1865, and has been operating smoothly and efficiently since 11 November 1865 under the supervision of the Engineer Za-twe, whose services were provided by the said Trader and the Agent.

His Most Glorious Majesty and the Ministers of his Court are extremely pleased that Za-twe, the Engineer who has been provided, has proved to be capable and efficient in operating the Mint and demonstrating its working.

It will be of great benefit if you are able to serve His Most Glorious Majesty in the future as well as you have served him in the matter of the purchase and delivery of the Mint."

/s/ Min-gyi-min-hla-maha-si-thu, Chief Minister, Commander of the Ye-bet Cavalry, Lord of Yaw.

In addition to all the equipment, Heatons also produced 1200 dies for Burma's Peacock coinage. These were sent out with the machinery, but proof strikings from these dies exist in The Mint's coin cabinet.[2]

During the first few years of Ralph III's stewardship, the coinage requirements of the Empire were all produced by the Royal Mint and its branches in Hong Kong, India and Australia. Nevertheless, Heatons' coinage output continued at a very high level as a result of several important foreign orders. The first of these came about as a result of the excellent reputation that Heatons had established with the Italian Government during the operation of the Milan Mint in 1861–2. This was for the production, in Birmingham, of some ninety million 10 centesimi of King Victor Emanuel. There were actually two contracts, dated 14 June 1866 and 31 January 1868, for forty and fifty million pieces respectively. These latter, though struck in 1868, were dated 1867. For carrying out these contracts in an exemplary fashion, Heatons were given special recognition by an appreciative Italian Government. George Heaton, who had earlier supervised the work at the Milan Mint, was appointed a Knight of the Order of the Crown of Italy.

Also swelling the output of the 1860s was an 1865 order for forty million 1 mil pieces for Hong Kong. Another order, for twenty million 1 mils, was completed in 1866. A Romanian contract for 1, 2, 5, and 10 bani was received in 1867 totalling over fifty million pieces. This placed quite a strain on Heatons' mint, and so part of the order was subcontracted to James Watt & Co.

---

[2]For an interesting study of the beginnings of the Mandalay Mint, see: M. Robinson, "The Mandalay Mint", *Coins and Medals*, February 1969, pp. 19–21.

Chapter III

After the Italian order for fifty million pieces was completed in 1868, things settled down to a somewhat more restrained pace, if *pace* can be used to describe the rather drastic ups and downs that characterized Heatons' production. Ralph III commented on this in an 1866 article in a Birmingham publication:[3]

> "From the peculiar nature of this article of manufacture, it is obvious that the trade must be quite exceptional in its character. Coin, of course, can be legally made only under very special and stringent restrictions; and, again, a coiner, though at times he may be working to the utmost capabilities of his machinery, at other times must be content to see it all standing still, and unprofitable it may be for many months together."

From these comments it must be obvious that coinage was by no means the only product of Ralph Heaton & Sons. An advertising circular, issued sometime between 1860 and 1889, showed an impressive list of metal products (Plate VII). Note the inclusion of blanks for coining. This had already become an important sideline for the company. The production of blanks involved every stage of the coinage process with the exception of the final imprinting, and so entailed a high contributed value. It was a good way to keep much of the specialized equipment busy when there were no coinage contracts, and Heatons worked to build up this product line. Over the years it became a very important part of The Mint's activities. Just how important can be seen from the fact that between 1850 and 1866 Heatons produced 6000 tons of coins and 4100 tons of blanks.

During the next several decades, Heatons' coinage business was very much a reflection of the current state of the Royal Mint. The last major improvement to the Royal Mint had been in 1805–10 when it was completely re-equipped by Matthew Boulton's Soho Manufactory. At that time eight screw presses were installed, all powered from a huge cog wheel which in turn was steam driven. These were ultra-modern when they were installed, but sixty years later had long since become obsolete – and rickety. The Deputy Master of the Royal Mint, Charles Fremantle, complained loudly and frequently in his annual reports – decrying the fact that he was obliged to observe closer tolerances than other nations required, while at the same time having worse equipment than most national mints. This was all too true, and the result was a happy one for Heatons, who had added new strip mills and casting shops in 1871, and whose physical plant exceeded that of the Royal Mint, both in coinage capacity and in the quality of its equipment.

The decade of the 1870s was a period when this situation was especially

---

[3]Ralph Heaton, "Birmingham Coinage", *Industrial History of the Birmingham and Midland Hardware District*, Timmons, London, 1866, p. 555.

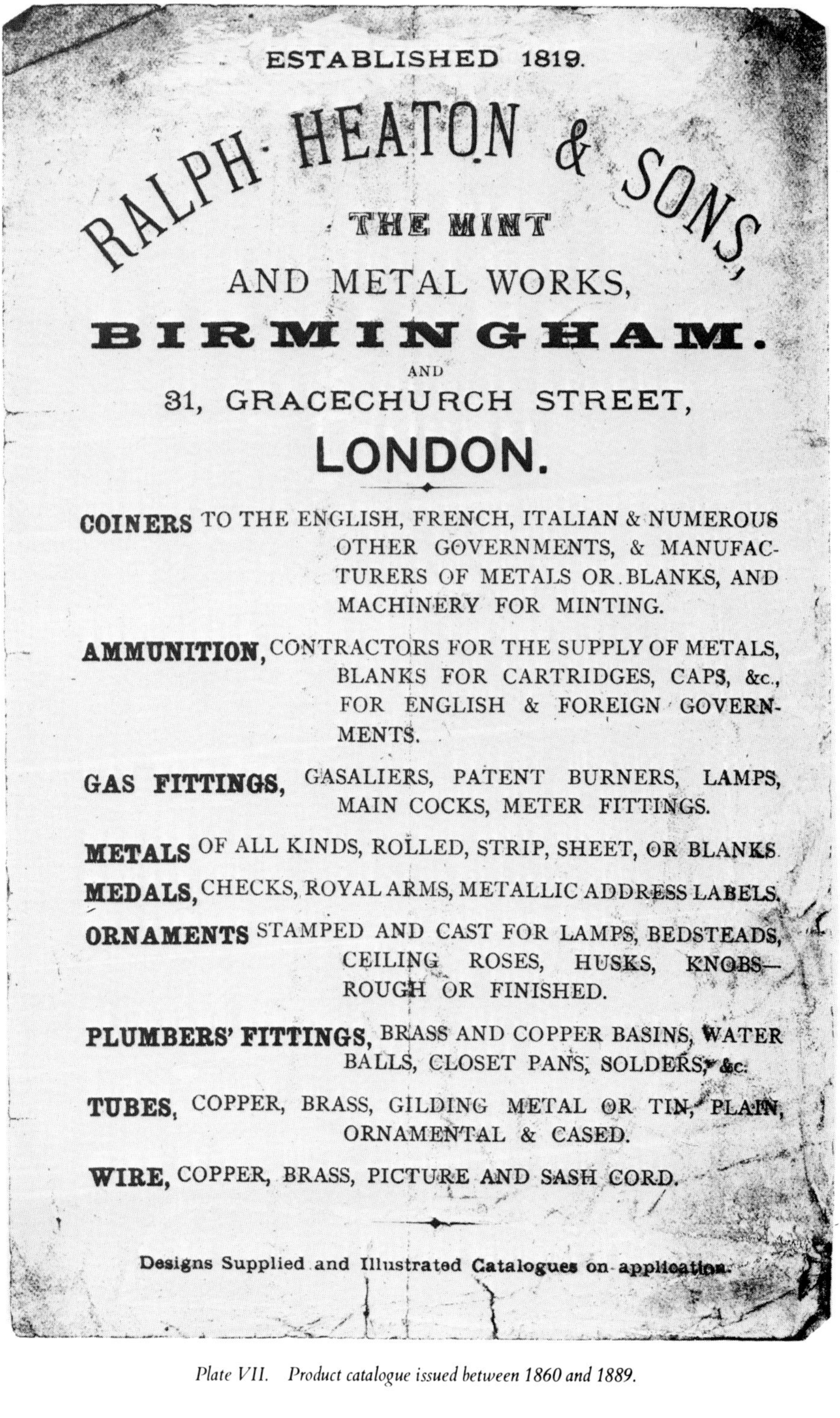

ESTABLISHED 1819.

RALPH HEATON & SONS,

THE MINT
AND METAL WORKS,
BIRMINGHAM.
AND
31, GRACECHURCH STREET,
LONDON.

COINERS TO THE ENGLISH, FRENCH, ITALIAN & NUMEROUS OTHER GOVERNMENTS, & MANUFACTURERS OF METALS OR BLANKS, AND MACHINERY FOR MINTING.

AMMUNITION, CONTRACTORS FOR THE SUPPLY OF METALS, BLANKS FOR CARTRIDGES, CAPS, &c., FOR ENGLISH & FOREIGN GOVERNMENTS.

GAS FITTINGS, GASALIERS, PATENT BURNERS, LAMPS, MAIN COCKS, METER FITTINGS.

METALS OF ALL KINDS, ROLLED, STRIP, SHEET, OR BLANKS.

MEDALS, CHECKS, ROYAL ARMS, METALLIC ADDRESS LABELS.

ORNAMENTS STAMPED AND CAST FOR LAMPS, BEDSTEADS, CEILING ROSES, HUSKS, KNOBS—ROUGH OR FINISHED.

PLUMBERS' FITTINGS, BRASS AND COPPER BASINS, WATER BALLS, CLOSET PANS, SOLDERS, &c.

TUBES, COPPER, BRASS, GILDING METAL OR TIN, PLAIN, ORNAMENTAL & CASED.

WIRE, COPPER, BRASS, PICTURE AND SASH CORD.

Designs Supplied and Illustrated Catalogues on application.

Plate VII. Product catalogue issued between 1860 and 1889.

important to Heatons. At first, orders from the Royal Mint came mainly because they lacked the basic capacity to meet the coin requirements of the Empire. In consequence, a general practice was adopted of placing major portions of the Colonial coinages with Heatons, while concentrating the Royal Mint capacity on Imperial coinage. Initially this arrangement applied only to Colonial bronze coinage, but it soon became necessary to contract out the silver Colonial coinage as well. The first silver coinage struck by Heatons was an order for Canada in 1871. Thereafter, silver became commonplace at Heatons as more and more Colonial coinage orders were received. In fact, Heatons even received a contract in 1872 for silver blanks for use in the Royal Mint for Imperial and Colonial coinages.

The Royal Mint's capacity problem was relieved somewhat in 1872 when they rented four lever presses from Heatons. It was still necessary for them to purchase blanks, however, due to limitations in melting and rolling equipment. Even this relief was short-lived, as a rash of equipment failures began to plague the Royal Mint. They were out of commission for twelve weeks in 1873, another six weeks in 1874, four weeks in 1875, and finally for four-and-a-half months in 1876. During these difficult times, Heatons provided strong back-up support to the Royal Mint by furnishing bronze bars and blanks, striking a major portion of the Imperial bronze coinage, and carrying a heavy load of Colonial coinages. Another order which came Heatons' way due to the Royal Mint's difficulties was the minting of South Africa's first gold coin – the famous 1874 Burgerspond. Eight hundred and thirty-seven gold coins were produced from dies engraved by Leonard Wyon, the Royal Mint's engraver.

These circumstances were good for the Heaton firm – but too good to last. In fact, Heatons played a large role in bringing them to an end. In 1881 the British Parliament approved funds for refurbishing the Royal Mint. All new equipment was purchased, of which ten lever presses and a sixth cutting-out press were manufactured by Ralph Heaton & Sons. With this, the Royal Mint was once again in a position to take care of the Empire's coinage needs, and so for the next ten years Heatons had to rely on foreign orders to keep The Mint going.

Early on, there was one interesting exception. Most of the Colonial coinages were handled through the Crown Agents, but Canadian orders were handled by the High Commissioner for Canada, who evidently did not get the word that the Royal Mint was ready to assume responsibility for all coinages for the Empire. At any rate, Heatons received an order for Canadian coinage in 1883 from the High Commissioner, and the Royal Mint Report for that year noted it with this rather pointed entry:

"This coinage could have been undertaken by the [Royal] Mint, but it was found that the High Commissioner in London had made arrangements with Messrs. Heaton and Sons for the purchase of silver, &c., as on many previous occasions, immediately after receipt of instructions from Canada, and on my representing that considerable trouble and expense would be entailed upon the Canadian Government if these arrangements were set aside, their Lordships were pleased to authorise the execution of the work by Messrs. Heaton. An intimation was at the same time conveyed to the Colonial Office by their Lordship's directions that for the future all coinages for Colonies would be undertaken by this Department."

And so they were for the remainder of the decade, save for those portions of the Empire which enjoyed some special status. The British North Borneo Company continued to patronize the Heaton Mint, as did the "White Rajahs" of Sarawak. Coinages were also produced for Brunei, Zanzibar, and Guernsey. In total, however, the foreign coinages Heatons struck slightly exceeded those for countries under the British influence. Orders for blanks also continued to be an important source of revenue for Heatons, as did machinery orders. In fact, in 1887 and 1888 Heatons provided a complete mint for the Chinese in Canton which, with ninety presses, was the largest mint in the world at the time.

During the whole period from 1862 to 1889, the coinage output of The Mint had been as shown in the graph below. Over the three decades, an average year involved eight to ten issues struck for three or four countries. Some years were duds – only about a half million coins were produced in 1873, and *no* coins were struck in 1878. A recession was the cause of that unhappy circumstance, as witness the following comment from the 1878 Royal Mint Report:

"In consequence of the continued depression of trade, the demand for

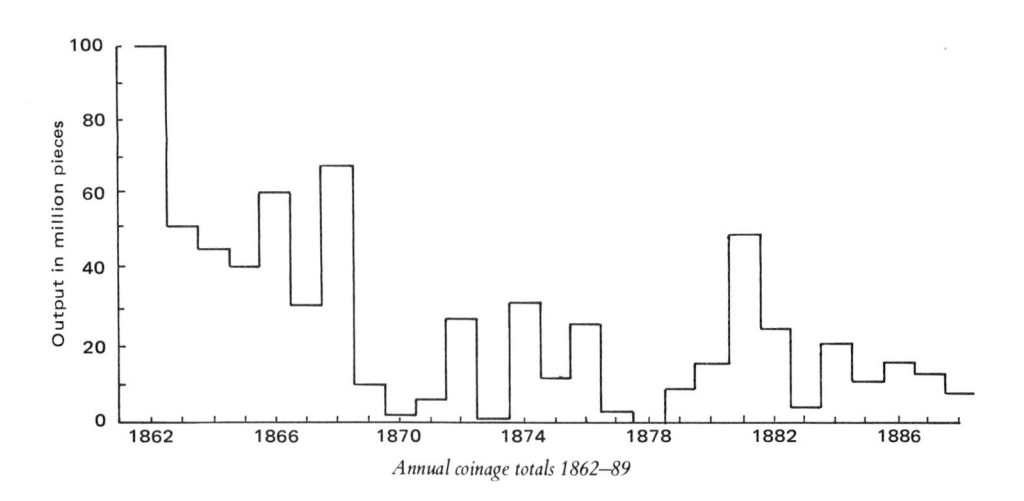

Annual coinage totals 1862–89

coin during the year 1878 has again been below the average, and for the first time since 1870 the Mint has been able itself to meet all demands for imperial coin, and to undertake the execution of the Colonial coinages required, without having recourse to contracts with private firms."

Some years were real bell-ringers. In 1872 five countries ordered nineteen

MR. RALPH HEATON, J.P.
(Knight of the Italian Order of St. Maurice and Lazarus.)
(*From a Photograph by H. J. Whitlock, New Street.*)

Plate VIII. *Ralph Heaton (III), 1827–91. Taken from a photograph and reproduced in* Birmingham Faces and Places, *April 1st, 1889.*

issues totalling 27 million coins; in 1882 eleven countries ordered thirty-two issues, again totalling about 27 million coins. This was the year the Royal Mint was being refurbished, and Heatons produced all the Colonial coinages and all the Imperial bronze.

As he approached the time when he would like to retire, Ralph Heaton III decided to convert the family business into a publicly held limited liability corporation. In due course a Prospectus was published, and shares were offered to the public. Finally, on 22 March 1889, an agreement was signed between Ralph Heaton and the new company, called The Mint, Birmingham, Limited, whereby control passed over to the new company.[4] Heaton received £110,000 plus £10,000 worth of copper (which would be sold back to the company over a period of time), plus an annual rent of £2000 for lease of the property to the new company. One term in the contract required the company to employ Ralph Heaton IV as General Manager, Gerald Heaton as Works Manager, and Walter Heaton as Secretary. Ralph III retired from active management, but continued to serve as a Director, from which position he could oversee the work of his three sons.

During his active business career, Ralph III had found time to participate also in public service. In 1867 he was elected a member of the Town Council, from which he resigned in 1884 for health and business reasons. While on the Council, he served on the Public Works Committee, being particularly active in connection with road construction in the City of Birmingham. He was also a magistrate for the County of Stafford and the City of Birmingham. In addition, he was a Trustee of several charitable organizations. His retirement years were cut short by his death at the age of 64 on 10 November 1891.

---

[4] An interesting result of the change to public ownership was that some shares in the new company were acquired by two members of the Royal Mint staff. This embarrassing fact was revealed in Parliament in 1890, and only shortly thereafter the Deputy Master of the Royal Mint issued instructions that the shares be disposed of – which they speedily were.

Chapter IV

The Stewardship of Ralph IV

In terms of both age and experience, Ralph IV was by far the youngest Heaton to take over the leadership of The Mint. When he became General Manager in 1889, he was only twenty-four years of age, and had only seven years of service with the company. So long as his father was on the Board of Directors, young Heaton had plenty of back-up support, but he was quickly thrust on his own by his father's untimely death in 1891. The Board apparently had no reservations about his ability, however, for he was elected Managing Director only a few months after his father's death. And as the record shows, he did indeed carry out his duties in an exemplary manner.

He had one very important thing going for him, which was a long history of very fine relations between the Royal Mint and The Birmingham Mint. As far as the record goes, there had been few untoward incidents to mar this relation.[1] On the contrary, the Deputy Master in his annual reports of the operation of the Royal Mint had often been quite complimentary regarding The Mint's performance. It certainly was no disadvantage that Ralph IV's maternal uncle, Mr. R. A. Hill, was the Superintendent of the Operative Department of the Royal Mint from 1869 to 1897. The evidence confirms, however, that The Mint earned every piece of business that the Royal Mint placed with it.

None had come for quite awhile, however. Since 1882 the newly refurbished Royal Mint had been able to handle all the coinage requirements for England as well as for the Colonies. Finally in 1889 the accelerating coinage needs of the Empire forced the Royal Mint again to seek outside help. Coinages for Hong Kong and Mauritius, as well as thirty tons of bronze

---

There was one unhappy occasion when Heatons were removed from the approved list of Public Department contractors. This took place in 1873, apparently as a result of Ralph Heaton's offer of money to the Deputy Master. In early 1874 the Royal Mint transmitted a memorial by Heaton to the Treasury, whereupon the firm was immediately returned to the bidders list.

blanks for English pence, were contracted out to The Birmingham Mint. Once again the Empire's needs had surpassed the capability of the Royal Mint, and for the next thirty years this was to work to the advantage of The Mint. Changes in the Royal Mint to improve its coinage capability were made in 1900, 1904, 1909–10, and 1912, but nevertheless it was only occasionally able to handle the total of the Empire's requirements. As a result, The Birmingham Mint continually enjoyed orders for Colonial coinages and for blanks and bars. In addition, orders were received for 16.8 million English pence in 1912, and for 7.1 million pence in 1918 and 1919.

As far as The Birmingham Mint was concerned, the lack of capacity in the London Mint was not without its drawbacks. In 1912 the long monopoly The Mint had enjoyed came to an abrupt end. That year the King's Norton Metal Co. Ltd. shared in an order from London for some 315 tons of bronze blanks. King's Norton again shared in an order for blanks in 1913, and finally in 1914 broke through with an order for Colonial coinages. Never again was The Birmingham Mint to enjoy a sole source relationship with the Royal Mint. Thereafter, King's Norton was a permanent fixture in private minting in England, first under its own name, then later (from 1926) as part of Imperial Chemical Industries Ltd. In 1962, ICI reorganized its metal division, including the minting activities, which became the now-independent IMI Ltd. IMI has since continued to participate in private minting, along with The Birmingham Mint, as part of a consortium with the Royal Mint.

Other private mints came – and went. Forrer[2] records that in 1895 the firm of James Watt & Co. went into bankruptcy, and that their minting equipment was acquired by The Birmingham Mint. It will be remembered that this was the company that received the major contract for minting England's new bronze coinage in 1860. Since then Watt had participated in several coinage contracts with Heatons, the most notable being the Romanian coinage of 1867–8. In 1920–1 Acroyd & Best Ltd., of Morley (near Leeds), produced a small part of the East African coinage, using an A mintmark. This was apparently their only venture into the coining business. Also in 1920 J. R. Gaunt & Sons, badge makers and military medallists of Birmingham, and located in a factory adjoining that of The Mint, shared with The Mint the coinage contract for British West Africa. This also was their only experience in minting for the Empire. Gaunts became a part of The Birmingham Mint Group in 1973.

During this period there were some interesting foreign orders produced by The Mint. In the years 1896–8 The Mint struck the whole of Russia's requirements for copper coins, amounting to an average of over 110 million

---

[2]L. Forrer, *Biographical Dictionary of Medallists*, Vol. II, 1904.

Plate IX.   Ralph Heaton (IV), 1864–1930 (courtesy Ralph Heaton V).

coins per year. It is undoubtedly safe to say that no other foreign mint, government or private, has struck so many coins for Russia.

In 1901 Brazil contracted with various world mints for a new coinage of 100, 200, and 400 reis pieces. Some 121 million pieces were produced in 1901–2 by mints at Vienna, Brussels, Paris, and Birmingham. The Mint's share was about 33 million coins, second only to Brussels' production of 40 million pieces. Again, it can be said that no other *private* mint has ever produced coins for Brazil.

Mexico became a customer of The Mint in 1906, on the occasion of a major currency reform. The Mint thus became the only foreign mint, aside from the U.S. Government mints, to produce coins for Mexico. The new coinage included pure nickel 5 centavos, of which the great majority was produced by The Mint in the period 1906–14. Thereafter, Mexico was self-sufficient insofar as her national coinage was concerned (except for occasional orders for blanks).

Of a more lasting character, however, was the relationship that was developed with Egypt, at that time aligned with Turkey but nevertheless issuing its own metal and paper currency. In 1904, after many years of placing its coinage needs with the Berlin Mint, Egypt placed the first of many orders with The Mint. For the next forty years there was scarcely a year when The Mint did not strike Egyptian coins.

Two other long-lasting relationships began in the period. Coinage for both East Africa and British West Africa was executed by The Mint in 1911, the first of a succession of orders that continued through the many realignments which finally culminated in their becoming several independent nations in the years 1957–65.

In 1914 World War I began in Europe. In various ways The Mint was kept busy supporting the war effort. In particular, brass strip and cold-drawn copper tubing were supplied to England's munitions works. Copper tubing had long been an important speciality with The Mint. Their manufacture grew out of an agreement with a Scots inventor who had developed a method for piercing copper billets to prepare them for cold drawing. The seamless tubing that resulted was a great advance over seamed tubing, and found major use in water and gas piping. A lively trade also developed in supplying tubing to the Midland Railway's locomotive works at Derby for use as boiler tubing.

The effect of the war on The Mint's coinage activity was mixed. Orders slowed, and even a portion of the Egyptian mintage was shifted to the Bombay Mint. But the manufacture of blanks for the Royal Mint rose to very high levels, including a not inconsiderable quantity of silver blanks for Imperial coinages.

Having brought his company safely through the travails of the war years, Ralph IV retired in 1920. His successor as Managing Director was Mr. W. E. Bromet, the husband of Heaton's sister Constance. Mr. Bromet came in on a high note – the coinage in 1920 was the second greatest on record at 142 million pieces, thanks to a huge mintage for British West Africa.

In 1922 Ralph Heaton V joined the firm. He was the eldest son of Ralph IV, was born in 1896, served as a Lieutenant of Artillery during World War I, and afterwards attended Birmingham University for three years, taking a Commercial course. His years with the firm were spent in commercial rather than management activities.

In 1923 The Mint came to the end of an era. Throughout its history it had been relatively free from domestic competition in minting for foreign

Annual coinage totals 1889–1923

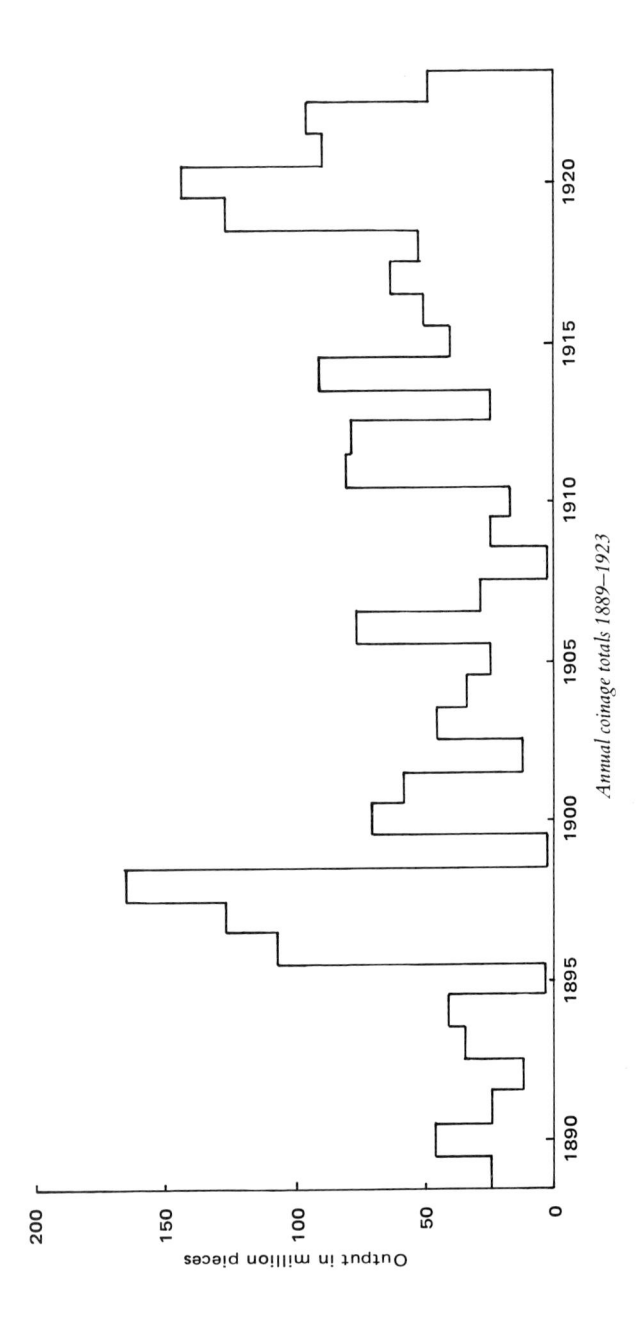

governments, but this finally ended in 1923 when the Royal Mint accepted an order for an Egyptian coinage. Never before had the Royal Mint sought foreign business. On a few occasions[3] it had accepted orders as a convenience to friendly foreign governments, but generally it had all it could manage to provide coinages for the Empire. In 1870 it entered into a negotiation with a foreign government, with the express approval of the Treasury, to provide a coinage of gold, silver, and bronze. Although the negotiations fell through, the Royal Mint had considered the propriety of such an action, concluding "that no private firm would be found willing to undertake the execution of a coinage of the precious metals."[4] The error of this conclusion was proved the very next year when The Mint struck for Canada its first silver coinage.

Since 1870 the Royal Mint had confined its operations to minting for the Empire, but the 1923 British Mint Report records that in that year it reconsidered its position, confirmed that the Treasury still approved its operating as a commercial mint, and took the plunge with the Egyptian coinage. Henceforth, the Royal Mint would decide whether it or the private mints would undertake any particular foreign orders, and this change was to have a serious effect on The Birmingham Mint for many years.

Aside from this, the period 1889–1922 had been a very active and profitable one for The Mint. Almost two billion (actually 1.895 billion) coins were produced, with production averaging over a million coins per week throughout the period. The average year involved about 19 issues for seven different countries, but as the graph opposite shows, the average year was more a mathematical concept than an actual occurrence.

In addition to this coinage, an average of over 30 million blanks was produced each year for various world mints, and bronze bars in some quantity were supplied to the Royal Mint for Imperial coinage. The supply of coinage machinery also continued to be a significant item of export.

---

[3] Sir John Craig, *The Mint* (Cambridge, the University Press, 1953).
[4] BMR 1870 pp. 51–76.

Chapter V

The Nadir – 1923–35

Mr. Bromet's management of The Mint took place during a most difficult period, beginning as it did at the time when the Royal Mint decided to become a competitor for foreign coin orders, and ending during the dark years of the Great Depression. In addition to these circumstances over which he had no control, it appears that for reasons which are not entirely clear, relations with the Royal Mint became somewhat strained during the period, although this may not have affected the volume of business placed on The Mint by the Royal Mint.

In any event, the total coinage volume during the years 1924–35 averaged only 21 million pieces per year – quite a change from the 74 million yearly average of the preceding twelve years. For a facility with an output capacity of possibly over 100 million pieces per year, this low volume had to be disastrous from a profitability standpoint.

To offset the severe reduction in coinage output, Bromet decided to diversify into the manufacture of brass sheets. In 1927 he installed the most modern and efficient equipment for the purpose. Unfortunately, relatively little immediate advantage was realized from this investment, because European competition very shortly thereafter monopolized the available business. It was quite some years before The Mint was able to make full use of the new equipment – during which time profitability was of course adversely affected.

An undated advertising booklet published by The Mint early in this period (contents would suggest around 1920) states as follows:

"To the minds of many, the title of this firm may suggest that COINING is its chief activity. Whilst in the early days, from 1829 [*sic*] onwards, the production of coinage was our principal interest, its importance has been superseded by other manufactures. One purpose of this booklet is to correct that false impression, and to show that the major activities of the Mint are in the production of Rolled Non-Ferrous Metals, Tubes, and

Metal Smallwares. Our chief object is to supply semi-manufactured materials, in economic and highly efficient forms, to many and diverse manufacturing trades, working in Brass, Copper, and numerous alloys of non-ferrous metals."

The same booklet goes on to state that: "Minting machinery is also manufactured by the firm, and complete mints have been designed and installed in many foreign countries." Even this aspect of coinage-related manufacture, however, slowed to a standstill in these years. The Mint supplied four Uhlhorn-type presses to the Royal Mint in 1920; no more were made until their final manufacture of a single press for the Royal Mint in 1938.[1]

On the coinage side, there were some interesting emissions in these years, not the least of which was the Lundy Island issue of 1929. Bronze tokens of about the size of the current English penny and halfpenny were struck by The Mint on order from Mr. M. C. Harman, a wealthy Londoner who owned Lundy Island. Although procured ostensibly for advertising purposes, these tokens were actually used as coins on the island. The few inhabitants of the island, all employees of Mr. Harman, were paid in Puffins and made their local purchases of beer and groceries with them. Harman was charged in an English court with a misdemeanour (for violation of the Coinage Act of 1870), fined a nominal amount,[2] and required to desist. Mr. Bromet was subpoenaed as a witness for the prosecution, but The Mint was not held to be culpable for its part in the matter. Mint correspondence files contain a letter from Harman commenting on the first designs, to wit:

> "There is one criticism I have to make. The Puffin is a bird very tidy with his feathers. The bird in your sketch looks as if he slept in his clothes and he ought actually to appear as if he had just completed his morning toilet."

In 1929 the Depression began to make itself felt. Its effect on the coinage business is well illustrated by comments by the Deputy Master in the 1929 Royal Mint report, pages 4 and 5, regarding a potential coinage of Egypt:

> "...The prices quoted by a small continental Mint were so low as to involve a substantial contribution to Egypt from the Treasury of the country of manufacture."

Further comments related to the general situation:

---

[1] After World War II all press manufacture was subcontracted; the last Heaton presses were made in 1967 for the Nigerian Mint and for The Birmingham Mint's own use, the latter presses finally being scrapped in 1980.
[2] George Russell, "London Coin Trial Rocks Devonshire", *World Coins*, May 1974, p. 893.

Chapter V

"...The coinage business is by no means exempt from the difficulties under which manufacturers and other producers generally are now suffering the wide world over. The minting capacity of the world greatly exceeds any possible demand for coin, with the result that competition is intense, and many mints with the resources of their Treasuries behind them think it worthwhile to quote uneconomic prices.... Clearly, a competition among manufacturers on the basis of actual loss to the victors is almost as insane a business as a modern war – and in the year under review (1929), working in cooperation with my Birmingham friends (The Mint and IMI), I had already had pourparlers with some of our leading competitors in Europe with a view to arriving at some arrangement which would satisfy us all."

So with the onset of the Depression, coin orders rapidly tapered off, to the degree that only 96,000 coins were struck by The Mint in 1933. This, of course, only exacerbated a profitability situation that had been very poor for years. The extent of the deterioration is illustrated by the fact that dividends on the ordinary shares, which had averaged around 30% per year in the years 1916–21, thereafter tapered off until in 1928 no dividends were paid at all. The next several years produced only trifling profits – and no dividends.

The inevitable result of this performance was that the shareholders finally demanded action. Several bitter proxy battles were waged, eventually resulting in Bromet's retirement, the replacement of the Chairman of the Board and his later removal as a Director, and the selection by a reconstituted Board of a new Managing Director.

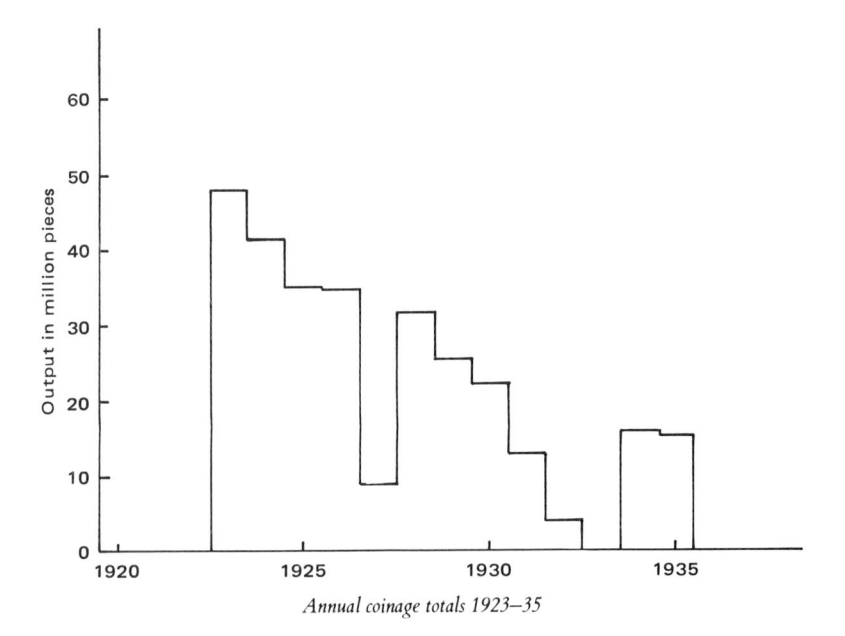

Annual coinage totals 1923–35

Chapter VI

The Modern Era – 1935 to Date

In May 1935, the operation of The Mint finally passed out of the control of a Heaton family member – and probably permanently so. In their effort to return the company to an acceptable level of profitability, the new Board brought in Mr. W. F. Brazener, formerly a metallurgist with Elliot's Metal Company, a subsidiary of Imperial Chemical Industries Ltd. Mr. Brazener was appointed General Manager, and soon thereafter became Managing Director. At the same time, the Board appointed Ralph Heaton V as Secretary to the Company, a position he held until his retirement in 1962.

The challenge given to Brazener by the Board was either to make the company profitable or to shut it down. That it became profitable is attested to by its continued existence. In fact, The Mint showed positive results by the end of Brazener's first year as Managing Director. His actions to bring the company to a sustained state of economic health were many. As a starter, he reached back into ICI Ltd and persuaded Mr. W. R. P. King, a Mechanical and Industrial Engineer with IMI, to join him in running The Mint. King was made a Department Manager in 1935, and became Mint Manager in 1937.

Early on, Brazener set up an efficient chemical and physical laboratory, and shortly thereafter introduced a change in the method of casting metals. The old coke-fired pit furnaces were replaced by low-frequency induction furnaces for lower cost and improved quality – not to mention improved pollution control.

Throughout the period of Brazener's direct management of The Mint, the coinage end of the business played a relatively minor part in total business volume. In terms of total tonnage, coinage for the years 1940–64 accounted for only 10–20% of output, the major volume being in rolled metals – especially copper and brass.[1] Nevertheless, in terms of actual mintages,

---

[1] "Birmingham Mint Introduced, Home of Famed H Mintmark", *World Coins*, January 1964, pp. 11–15.

i. W. E. Bromet, from 1920 to 1935 (courtesy Courtney Bromet);

ii. W. F. Brazener, from 1935 to 1960;

iii. W. R. P. King, from 1960 to 1973;

iv. C. H. Perry, from 1973

Plate X. *Managing Directors of The Birmingham Mint since 1920.*

coinage showed considerable improvement over the Depression years. The Royal Mint report for 1936 stated that the Royal Mint and the two private mints (The Birmingham Mint and IMI) were operating at full capacity, although in 1936 The Mint produced only 29 million coins – a far cry from the 162 million produced in 1898. A respectable volume was achieved in 1937–9, averaging almost 1.2 million coins per week (60% of which was for British West Africa).

With the advent of World War II, coinage volume dropped again to low levels, averaging only about 18 million coins per year for the years 1940–5. War materials production took precedence, especially that of brass sheet and strip for ammunition purposes, copper tube for shell driving-bands, and aluminium–brass cylinders for Rolls–Royce aeroplane engines. The works operated around the clock, six and a half days per week, fifty-two weeks per year.

During the Battle of Britain, The Mint was fortunate in receiving no direct hits from the intensive German bombing, but did suffer considerable blast damage from near misses. Extensive damage to roofs and windows took place, but of perhaps more importance was the wear and tear on equipment caused by continuous operations without opportunity for normal preventive maintenance. By the time peace returned in 1945, plant equipment was in a seriously run-down condition. The immediate post-war years witnessed a great effort to return The Mint to an efficient production basis. Not until 1952, however, was the war-damaged strip-mill roof completely repaired.

Coinage machinery no longer constituted any part of the output of The Mint. A note in the 1948 Royal Mint report states that "...It was decided to add a further six medium sized Heaton type coining presses. The makers, The Mint, Birmingham, Ltd., were unable to supply but very kindly agreed to lend us the drawings for making the presses in the Mint. The castings were ordered in Birmingham and the frames were machined at Woolwich Arsenal. The presses were well on the way by the end of the year, with three of them nearing completion." A follow-up note in the 1953 Royal Mint Report says that "Work proceeded on the manufacture of six new coining presses of the Heaton pattern.... The improvements have been well justified by most successful working and sweet running of the presses..."

At this time coins only accounted for about 5% of The Mint's output. Copper tubes and fittings for the building industry became a major product line for the company, whose trade mark, MBL, appeared on a significant portion of the total English output of such products.

In 1949 The Mint participated for the first time in the manufacture of the Maria Theresa thalers. An interesting commentary on this historic coin is provided in the Royal Mint Report for 1935–6, page 18, as follows:

> "The only 'trade dollar' which now survives is therefore the well-known Maria Theresa Thaler. This handsome coin, which bears on the obverse the effigy of the Empress Maria Theresa, on the reverse her Imperial Arms with the date 1780, and in raised letters round the rim the inscription 'IUSTITIA ET CLEMENTIA', is not legal tender by the enactment of any of the territories in which it circulates – which include the Anglo-Egyptian Sudan, the Colony of Aden and the Arab territories along the

Red Sea. Nevertheless, it persists by long custom as the principal coin of commerce in that quarter of the globe, and there has recently sprung up a strong demand for fresh supplies. Owing to political circumstances, upon the nature of which it is beyond my province to comment, these Thalers are no longer obtainable as they used to be by British firms bringing silver to be converted into coin at the Vienna Mint. In order to meet the resulting embarrassment and dislocation to British Trade, I received authority in 1936 to mint supplies in London and during that year some 150,000 of these handsome coins were struck at the Royal Mint. The supply is proceeding at a greatly accelerated rate during the current year, but owing to the extreme congestion to which I have already alluded, I have hitherto been far from able to meet all demands, and the problem of allotment to the traders who are pressing for supplies has presented some difficulty. It is not easy to understand why exactly there is such a demand for these Thalers; sooner or later the territories concerned will no doubt reach saturation point, particularly as some of the Continental Mints are now following our example. But, during the past year – though considerable quantities of the same coin are being struck at the Roman Mint to the order of the Italian Government for use in Abyssinia – the demand has greatly exceeded supplies and the coins have consequently stood at a considerable premium in the territories in which they circulate."

The "political circumstances" to which the Deputy Master referred apparently had to do with the fact that Italy "persuaded" Austria (with Germany's help) in 1935 to transfer complete production of the Maria Theresa thalers to the Rome Mint. Italy did not achieve the monopoly that she sought, since at least the London, Brussels, Paris, Bombay, and Birmingham Mints at one time or another all struck the thalers in the years between 1935 and 1961. The Birmingham Mint apparently only produced the thalers to the order of a single English bullion dealer. The Mint struck thalers in 1949, 1953, 1954, and 1955; the Royal Mint continuing to mint them until 1961. In that year the Royal Mint Report stated: "The trade [by the Royal Mint in thalers] remained quite brisk after the end of the last war, but it was natural that following the Peace Treaty with Austria her Government should feel that the time had come to try to regain a monopoly in minting; and we have readily fallen in with their wishes."

Throughout the period of the 1950s the coinage side of the business remained at relatively low levels, averaging about 1 million coins per week. This was augmented somewhat by the production of tokens, coin blanks, and a number of medallic issues. Among the latter were 1953 bronze medals commemorating the Queen's visit to New Zealand, a 1954 bronze medal for Churchill's 80th birthday, and a 1955 medal on his retirement as Prime Minister. Token issues included many for the slot machine trade, plus an order for gambling tokens for use in a new casino in Gibraltar.

On 30 April 1960 Mr. Brazener retired as Managing Director of The Mint, having established an enviable record during his quarter-century at the helm. In the tradition of the Heatons, he also devoted much time to public service. He was very active in the British Non-Ferrous Metals Federation, having served as President from 1954–7, and having led a delegation of Federation members to the United States in 1950 to study productivity in the metal trades. He was a Birmingham City Magistrate from 1947, and served as General Commissioner for Income Tax from 1951. On the humanitarian side, he was Chairman for the Visiting Service for Old People from 1952–60. These were but a few of his outside activities, to the full list of which the Heatons would have certainly said "Well done!".

On 1 May 1960 William Raymond Pearce King took over as Managing Director, coincident with the beginning of one of the more interesting decades in The Mint's history. As previously noted, King had come to The Mint in 1935, having worked at IMI for the ten previous years. He was made Assistant Works Manager in 1940, and Works Manager in 1944, the position he held until becoming Managing Director in 1960.

In 1960, coinage constituted 13% of Mint revenues, but this side of the business underwent a great resurgence during the decade following, along with a similar growth in the production of coin blanks for various overseas mints. In addition, some 1680 tons of bronze $\frac{1}{2}$ pence blanks and 466 tons of copper-nickel 10 pence blanks were furnished to the new Royal Mint at Llantrisant to aid the Government's massive production of the new decimal coinage in 1968–71.

Even more impressive was the growth in the coinage business itself. In 1965 The Mint, along with IMI, joined in a consortium set up by the Royal Mint to promote and produce export coinage. This was coincident with a huge surge in export orders, as can be seen in the graph on the next page. It should be noted that most of the data for these graphs were derived from coinage figures in the annual reports of the Royal Mint, and are subject to some inaccuracy especially in the later years when actual coinage figures were no longer broken down for each of the three participating mints (Royal Mint, The Birmingham Mint, and IMI).

The huge demands on The Mint of especially the years 1964–6 made it apparent that additional facilities were required. Accordingly, in May 1966 a new mint facility was begun on an adjacent site previously occupied by a button factory. This construction was completed in July 1967, and equipment was transferred from the old mint to the new with the loss of less than a week's production. The addition of new machinery, including three presses of the Heaton design made by a local Birmingham firm, provided the necessary increase in capacity – and The Mint was ready for continued growth.

Unfortunately, the very next year, 1968, saw the beginning of a surprising downturn in orders from the Royal Mint, only slightly relieved by their

Annual coinage totals 1936–70

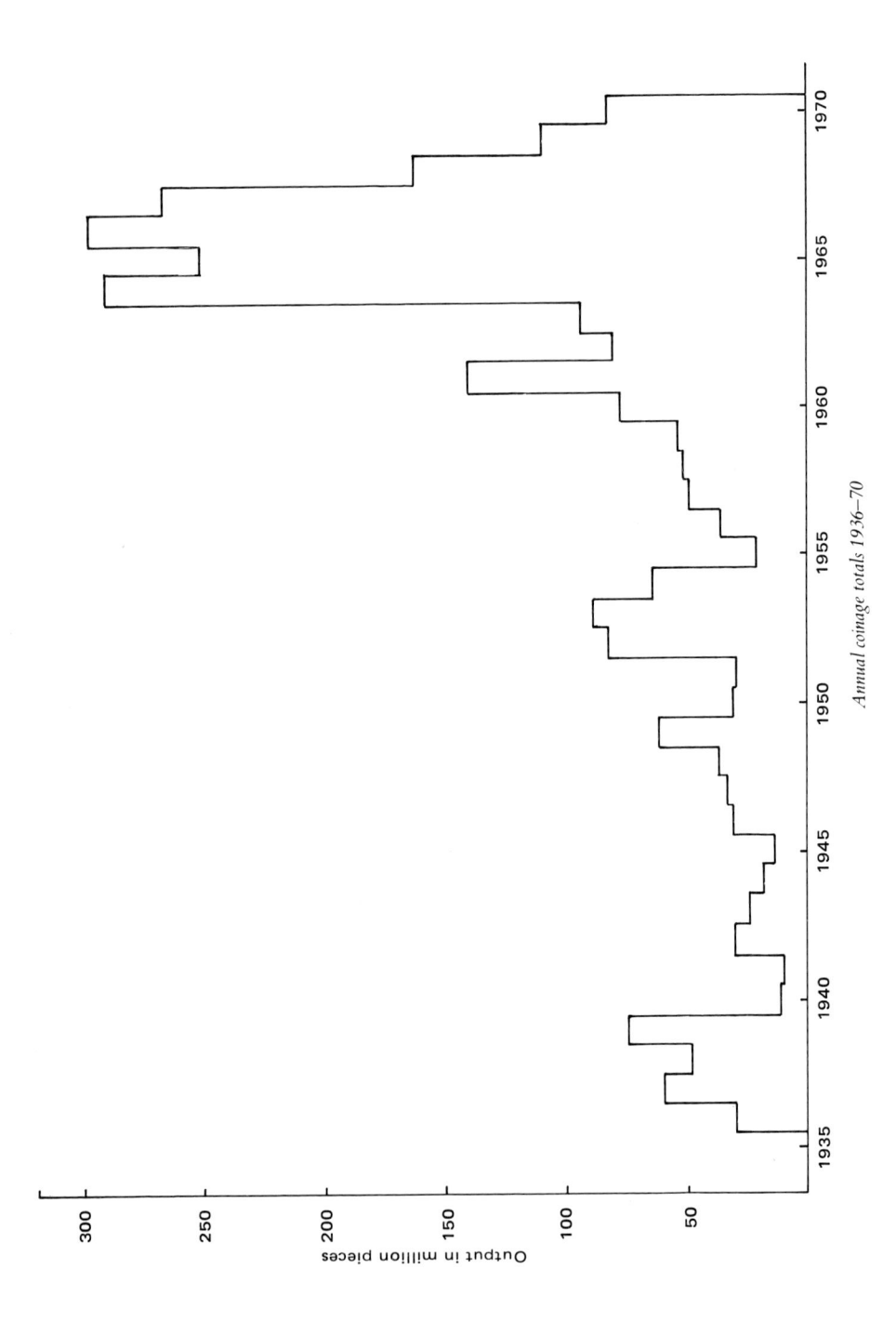

new demands for blanks for decimal coinage. The Royal Mint had generally subcontracted about a third of its overseas coinage orders to the two Birmingham mints, and it continued to do so while its own orders were dropping from 1.2 billion export coins in 1967 to only 433 million in 1969.

The decade of the 1960s was marked by a startling growth in corporate mergers and takeovers on both sides of the Atlantic, and The Mint felt some of the effects of this trend. An acquisition offer was received from a foreign private mint — or at least some overtures were made — but these were rejected. More serious, however, was an attempt made at takeover by E&HP Smith, an English company. The *Birmingham Post* followed the progress of this attempt, as in the following condensation:

- 31/5/1963 – E&HP Smith offered the Mint shareholders an exchange of stock.
- 26/6/1963 – E&HP Smith offer will expire July 5. The Mint has asked for a cash offer, which will not be made, and an explanation of the basis for Smith's projected profit increase, which will not be given.
- 26/6/1963 – The Mint Directors urge shareholders to reject offer.
- 26/7/1963 – The Mint shareholders reject Smith's offer.

This brief description fails to show the intense concern that must have been felt by the Directors and Management of The Mint at the time. Actually, it was a tight squeeze — the takeover attempt was rejected by but little more than half of the shares voted. As a consequence, Management resolved to try to shield the company from any further takeover attempts, and did take steps in this direction early in the 1970s by arranging for First National Finance Corporation Ltd. in London to subscribe for 25% of the shares. Later in the decade, this holding was sold to several financial institutions.

Earlier, in the first quarter of 1962, The Mint itself had joined the merger parade with the acquisition of Charles Eades, Ltd., a Birmingham firm which specialized in the manufacture of nameplates, a line complementary to products of The Mint.

As the 1960s drew to a close, The Mint was positioned to participate strongly in any growth in demand for coinage, having a fine management team, skilled employees, and efficient modern coining equipment. When it celebrated its 120th anniversary as a mint in 1970, it was the oldest continuously operated private mint in the world. Its output of over 1.7 billion coins in the decade just past, and its annual production capability of some 400 million coins per year, probably made it also the world's *largest* private mint. When Ralph Heaton III wrote to his father in 1855 saying: "I am convinced this is only the commencement of another SOHO", he truly described the future of this fine and durable company.

42   *Chapter VI*

Plate XI.   The Birmingham Mint in 1980.
  i. View of the frontage on Icknield Street, which includes the original 1860 façade.
  ii. The coining department.

Epilogue – The 1970s in Brief

Important managerial changes took place in the 1970s. In April 1973, Mr. King turned over responsibility for Group operations to Mr. Colin Perry, the new Managing Director. At the same time, Mr. King became Vice-Chairman of the Board of Directors, and Chairman in April 1974. He retired from that office in 1977, and from the Board in 1978. He died on 28 May 1980. Like his predecessors, Mr. King found the time and energy to make many public contributions. At the end of World War II he was a member of a British Commission sent to the Continent to advise on reparations. He was active in the Birmingham Chamber of Industry and Commerce, serving as its President in 1971–2. He also served as Chairman of Birmingham Productivity Services Ltd., and President of the British Non-Ferrous Metals Federation in 1969–71. In recognition of his contributions, the Queen made him a C.B.E. in 1973. He will be missed.

Mr. Perry, Managing Director of The Birmingham Mint Ltd. – the new company name adopted in 1974 – received his M.B.A. from the European School of Business Administration in Fontainebleau, France. Prior to joining The Mint, he had worked for International Publishing Corporation Ltd. as Executive Vice-President of one of their American subsidiaries.

Change has continued to be the norm at The Mint. Although coinage continues to be the largest single activity, there have been several changes in the company's other product lines. Early in the decade, The Mint formed a new company called Mint Security Ltd., to provide guard services and security for cash-in-transit. This activity flourished for a period, but was sold to Securicor Group Ltd. in January 1979 when it became evident that its rapid expansion would necessitate substantial additional investment which might divert needed funds from the minting business. In 1973 The Mint purchased the Birmingham firm of J. R. Gaunt & Son Ltd., manufacturers of metal badges, buttons, and accoutrements for the uniformed services. Gaunts possess the Royal Warrant as Ribbon Suppliers to Her Majesty The Queen, and through previous amalgamations can trace their history back even further than The Mint.

In 1975 the old line of copper pipe and water-fittings, which had fallen victim to the economic recession of the period, was sold to Econa Ltd. This disposal provided the means for a substantial improvement of the minting facilities at the Icknield Street factory. In the early 1970s the company had developed the technique of continuous casting applied to coinage alloys such as cupro-nickel. In a £1 million investment programme in 1976–7, additional continuous casting lines were installed, making a total of four such lines, and the older furnaces were phased out. At the same time most of the Heaton coin presses (originally introduced in the late 1850s) were replaced by modern HME Coinmasters, each capable of striking up to 300 coins per minute, and the factory layout was completely rearranged.

This modernization was interrupted in 1977 when an underground fire was discovered beneath the new casting lines. The fire had to be dug out to a depth of nearly 30 feet. The Mint was well insured, however, and in 1979 the pace of investment was resumed and orders were placed for a further £1½ million expenditure on a rolling mill, together with a new annealing, cleaning, and blanking plant. Completion of the project was scheduled for year end 1980, and will hopefully result in The Mint having one of the most modern facilities of its kind in the world for coinage manufacture.

In 1975 a new subsidiary was set up to market silver medals, plates, and other collectibles directly to the general public, this under the name of The Birmingham Mint Collection Ltd. The minting of proof-quality coins and medals, mostly in precious metals, was considerably expanded in the years following, and more recently this division has added jewellery to its product range.

In 1980 the pressings business, which had also been expanding rapidly, was formed into a separate subsidiary named Birmingham Mint Pressings Ltd. However, in the same year the manufacture of nameplates and trim was discontinued as a result of the declining fortunes of its customers in the U.K. domestic appliance industry.

While all of this was going on, The Mint's profits also grew – from £261,000 before tax in the financial year ending 31 March 1976, to £911,000 in the financial year ending 31 March 1980. In the same five-year period, coins were struck for over 50 countries, and in 1979 a record output of 13 million coins per week was attained. Clearly, The Mint can face the future with confidence.

Chapter VII

The Heaton Mintmarks

Almost since coinage began, mintmarks have been used to identify the mint of issue. This practice became especially important for several hundred years preceding 1900 when:

(a) Gold and silver were the usual metals in the coinage systems of the world.
(b) Transportation was inadequate; it made sense for even small countries to have mints located conveniently throughout the country.
(c) National standards were imposed governing the weight and metal content of the coinage output of the dispersed mints.

Under these circumstances it became necessary for the coinage to be identified by mint, so that deficient coinage could be identified back to the responsible source and the deficiency corrected (while heads rolled).

At least at the outset, none of these conditions described the operations of the Heaton Mint. It did not produce gold or silver coins. Its operations were usually under the direct and continuous scrutiny of representatives of the Royal Mint — particularly for Imperial and Colonial coinages, but not exclusively so. Transportation was not a factor in its *raison d'être* — rather only that the Royal Mint was not adequate to the coinage needs of the Empire. Under these circumstances, the Heaton Mint really did not need to use mintmarks — and so the perplexing variety of marks that it did use at one time or another over the years have not really served the basic purpose of mintmarks — which is to identify for control purposes. Thus it might be concluded — with some justification — that the use of mintmarks on Heaton issues has been more for corporate ego purposes, and likely also for commercial advertising purposes.

Whatever the reason, The Birmingham Mint has used more different marks than almost any other mint — government or private. In the main, this probably came about because they have served a wider variety of customers

— on the customer's terms, and under more different circumstances — than have most other mints. Whereas an established government mint such as the Paris Mint can insist on using its own identifying marks, a private mint such as Heatons has no real basis for enforcing such a rule, and so its marks will likely be a compromise between what the client government needs and what the private mint wants. That it actually worked this way will be evident in the following catalogue of Heaton mintmarks, which are listed here in the approximate order of their year of first appearance.

M1 – H&S

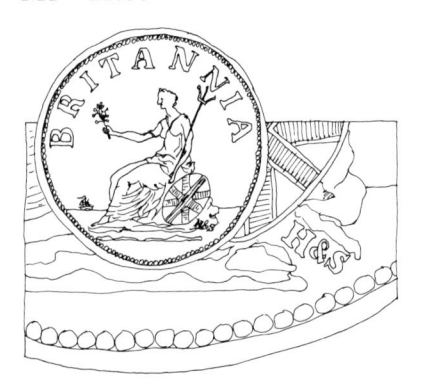

Such a compromise was probably not involved in the choice of the very first mintmark that Heatons used. The customer, the Melbourne mercantile firm of Annand Smith & Co., may very well have dictated the design of the tokens they were ordering for use in the currency-starved economy of Australia, but they probably did not care in the slightest what mintmark appeared thereon. These tokens involved a reverse die that had been used by Boulton & Watt for Imperial pence back in 1806–7,[1] a die that originally had the SOHO mark of the Boulton mint at the base of the Britannia design below the shield. It was a simple change for Heatons to make (involving an interesting coincidence of letters) to eradicate the SOHO mark and replace it with their own — an H&S for Heaton & Son. The same H&S mintmark appeared on the very similar Iredale tokens (Andrews No. 291,[2] Clarke No. T19[1]) of about the same period — but thereafter never showed up again on any Heatons' coinage.

m2 – H

The H&S mintmark, which began and ended with the Australian tokens, was soon replaced by the single letter H, which first appeared on a coinage for Chile in 1851. In that year two varieties of Medio and Un Centavo pieces appeared, differing in several important details. The Heaton issues featured a large flat star in the centre of the obverse, with the date below between two small stars. On the small star to the left of the date on the Un

---

[1] Robert L. Clarke, *The Coins and Tokens of British Oceania*, SIN, Fifth Edition, 1971.
[2] Arthur Andrews, *Australasian Tokens and Coins*, Sydney, Australia, 1921.

Centavo piece (CH2) was a tiny Roman H in intaglio in a depression in the centre of the star. This was the first of billions of H mintmarks yet to come.

It likely represented a decision by Heatons to change to a mintmark that could be more easily worked into the coin design, and which would reproduce more consistently throughout the life of the coining dies. The ampersand used in the "H&S" would become a blob in the later stages of die wear, and the relatively large amount of space required by the "H&S" mark made it more difficult to achieve inconspicuousness and readability at the same time. Thus the H – for Heaton. Interestingly, although Heaton standardized (more or less) on use of the H, he certainly did not standardize on the style of the H, as will be seen.

Probably the most frequently used type style has been the Roman H, as exemplified by the Guatemala $\frac{1}{4}$ Real of 1900, and the Chile Un Centavo of 1851. In these examples the H is characterized by a square shape, and the more or less equal width of the vertical and horizontal letter elements. A variation of the Roman H, appearing on the Italian 10 Centesimi of 1866, is the Bodoni style, characterized by the heavily exaggerated vertical letter elements. Still another variation is to be found on the Dominican Republic 2½ Centavos of the year 1888. In this variety the serifs look like bent-over extensions of the vertical letter elements. Probably the most frequently used style other than the Roman is the Sans Serif, shown here on the British West Africa One Penny of 1952. The Sans Serif style appears to have been used where the available space was quite limited, and where it was intended to diminish the prominence of the mintmark. In the example shown, it is only about 0.7 mm high, or about 1/50th of the diameter of the coin. It is hardly noticeable, even though located on an uncrowded field.

m3 – HEATON

The second national coinage that Heatons struck was a series of copper coins for Venezuela in 1852. The 1 Centavo of that series had the word HEATON as a quite explicit mintmark. Only an H appeared on the smaller ¼ and ½ Centavos of the same series, but on the large 1 Centavo pieces the available space was enough to admit the use of the larger mark. It is interesting that a sovereign nation such as Venezuela would allow a private firm this degree of prominence on their official currency. Other instances of the use of the word HEATON as a mintmark are as follows:

Venezuela: 1 Centavos of 1858, 1862, and 1863.
Haiti: 5, 10 and 20 Centimes of 1863.
Romania: 2, 5, and 10 Bani of 1867.
Ecuador: 1 and 2 Centavos of 1872.
Bulgaria: 2, 5, and 10 Stotinki of 1881.

m10 – MA

In 1853 Heatons began executing a coinage contract for the French Government. For five years Heatons operated a mint at Marseilles, producing bronze 1, 2, 5, and 10 Centimes using Heaton personnel, Heaton equipment, and Heaton methods. The mintmark on this coinage was a monogram made up of the first two letters of the word Marseilles. At the conclusion of this contract the Heaton personnel packed up and went back to Birmingham. The mint equipment was sold to a private firm. The mintmark was retired – it has not reappeared on French coins to the present time. Because these coins were in every sense Heaton products, the MA is included herein as a legitimate Heaton mintmark.

m11 – M

When at long last a unified Italy came into being in 1860, the necessity arose to create a uniform coinage system, replacing the state coinage that had existed for hundreds of years – since the Middle Ages. This required a tremendous output of a new coinage in a very short time, and so the Italian Government marshalled all available resources. One such resource was Ralph Heaton & Sons, who agreed to move into an existing Government Mint at Milan and produce a part of the new coinage. As it had done for the Napoleon Government in the 1850s, Heatons put its own people and equipment to work in the Milan Mint, and in the course of only two years produced over 360 million coins for Italy. These coins, made from bronze blanks shipped from the Heaton Mint in Birmingham, all carried an M mintmark for the Milan Mint. The M had been used for many decades before Heatons took over the operation of the Milan Mint, and it continued to be used after Heatons turned the Milan Mint back over to the Italian Ministry of Finance. Thus it is in every sense a mintmark of Milan, but since all coins produced in the years 1862–3 by Milan can be truly credited to Heatons, it is also included here as one of the many Heaton mintmarks.

m5 – HEATON BIRMINGHAM

This has to be acknowledged as the most explicit of all Heaton mintmarks. In fact, it may well be the most explicit of *all* mintmarks. Its first appearance was on the coinage executed by Heatons for Ecuador in 1884, and thereafter it regularly appeared on Ecuadorean issues until 1895. No Heaton issues for other countries carry this particular mintmark, nor do all of the Heaton strikes for Ecuador show it. Indeed, more different Heaton mintmarks appear on Ecuadorean coinage than on that of any other country. This mintmark is also the largest of the Heaton mintmarks, and must be among the largest of any mintmarks anywhere.

m2a – H H

Strictly speaking, this mintmark has to be classified as a variant of the m2 single H mark. It was used on only two issues, and somewhat differently on each of them. The 2½ Centavos of the Dominican Republic of 1888 have the two Hs on the reverse on either side of the small star beneath the denomination. The 1894 4 Reales of Guatemala have an H on both obverse and reverse. This latter is a most unusual mintmark arrangement – few coin types by any mints carry such redundant marks. One wonders if it was really intended.

m4 – HEATON BIRM^M.

As is the case with the m5 mintmark, this mark leaves little to the imagination. And also like m5, it appears on a South American coin. The Costa Rica silver issues of 1889–94 all had this mintmark, with the exception of the 5 Centavos pieces which had only a single H. Why the abbreviated BIRM^M. was used on these coins, as compared with the full BIRMINGHAM on the Ecuador issues of about the same size and available space, can only be a matter of speculation. Possibly the reason was to establish another point of difference between the two coinages.

m8 – BI

Within a period of thirty or so years Heatons produced 10 Centesimi pieces for Italy with three different mintmarks. In 1861–2 the M (m11) was used; in 1866–7 the H (m2) was used; and in 1893–4 The Mint produced a large issue of 10 Centesimis with a monogram consisting of the first two letters of BIrmingham. This mintmark was peculiar to this issue; neither before nor since has The Mint used such a mark. In design concept it has several points of similarity with the MA (m10) mark used on the Marseilles coinage of 1853–7, both involving the first two letters of the mint location arranged atop one another.

m6 – BIRMINGHAM

It has already been pointed out that a large variety of mintmarks were used on the coins of Ecuador by Heatons. There is some correlation between the coin metal and the corresponding mintmarks, although this may have been accidental rather than intentional. The bronze coins have either an H or HEATON; the silver coins have either HEATON BIRMINGHAM or BIRM^M H; and the gold coins all have the single word BIRMINGHAM as a mintmark. In the period 1850–1970 The Mint struck at least five different gold issues, the others being for South Africa (1874) and Newfoundland (1882). However, the only time that the BIRMINGHAM mintmark has been used was on the Ecuadorean gold issues of 1899, 1900, and 1928.

m9 – ڪليڇ
m9a – ڪليڇ

At least to the Western observer, some of the more intriguing of The Mint's marks are those appearing on a series of coins produced for Morocco in the years 1903–6. The translation is simply "in England". Four bronze and five silver denominations were struck, and slightly different versions of the same Arabic characters appear on the bronze (m9) and on the silver (m9a) coins. Other mints which contributed to this same series of coins were the Paris, Fez, and Berlin mints, and the mintmarks on their issues were all equally specific in identifying the source.

m7 – BIRM^M H

In 1915 the final version of the HEATON BIRMINGHAM group of mintmarks appeared on the Medio and Un Decimo coins of Ecuador, bringing to a conclusion the long period of creativity Heatons had exercised in the design of mintmarks. The abbreviation BIRM^M H on these coins was very nearly the last appearance of any mintmark other than the traditional H on The Mint's strikings; the only exception was the

The Heaton Mintmarks

one-time use of the m6 BIRMINGHAM mark on the Ecuador gold Un Condor of 1928. Thereafter, The Mint was either to use an H or no mintmark at all, this latter case now being the rule rather than the exception. Since the Hong Kong 1972 5 cents issue, there have been no official coinage issues by The Mint with a mintmark, a fact that will be regretted by collectors everywhere. At least through 1979, only The Mint's modern medallic issues continue to bear the venerable H mintmark.

The Quasi-Mintmarks

qm1 – RK&Co

A few years after producing the Australian tokens for Annand Smith and Iredale, Heatons received an order for tokens for the Bank of Upper Canada. The circumstances that generated the need for these tokens were identical to the Australian circumstances previously described; i.e., the lack of an official currency. These Canadian tokens, however, did have an official character, having been authorized by the Provincial Government and issued under the name of a chartered bank. The order was placed with Heatons through an agent acting for the bank, and the tokens bear permanent witness to this fact in the form of a quasi-mintmark. Some sources have opined that the initials are RH&Co for Ralph Heaton & Co., and although the K on the coin could be read as an H, this theory is faulty on two counts. First, the mint's name was Ralph Heaton and Sons, and second – and conclusively – the 1850 issue of these tokens was entirely produced by the Royal Mint. The agent was the London firm of Rowe, Kentish & Co., located at 16, Change Alley. It is truly their initials which appear below the dragon on the obverse of the token, replacing the

Pistrucci signature on the original St. George design. In strict reality they are on the tokens to identify the London agent for this coinage – and nothing more. They are therefore called quasi-mintmarks here – to recognize their existence, but to distinguish them from true mintmarks.

qm2 – SHAW

In 1870 Heatons struck a series of coins for Paraguay. These included the 1, 2, and 4 Centesimos of bronze, and all have the word SHAW to the right of the date on the reverse. As was the case with the Canadian tokens twenty years earlier, the word SHAW on these coins pertains to the Birmingham agent for the Government of Paraguay, the firm of Charles J. Shaw & Co. As far as is known, this was the only occasion when the coinage of a sovereign nation bore the name of a commercial firm other than the minter. Since this was not intended as a mintmark, even though it is peculiar to an issue by Heatons, it is designated here as a quasi-mintmark. One other order was placed on Heatons by the Shaw firm, that being for an 1869 issue for Uruguay. These latter coins, however, do not contain the Shaw name, but do have an H mintmark. The dies were prepared by the Paris Mint, and have the Bee privy mark used by the Paris Mint in those years, which has been the cause of some confusion in the attribution of the Uruguay coins.

qm3 – PL

Just as the first true Heaton mintmark appeared on an Australian token in about 1850, their last quasi-mintmark was on the Australian Half Penny of 1951 – just about one hundred years later. In 1951 the Royal Mint struck pennies and half pennies for Australia with a PL mintmark, a Latin abbreviation indicating a London genesis (for a full explanation, see the Australia section of the Catalogue), and one of the very few mintmarks used by the Royal Mint in modern times. Using the same dies, The Birmingham Mint struck Half Pennies in 1952 bearing a 1951 date and the PL mark, as did also the Royal Mint. Thus at least as far as the 1951 Half Penny is concerned, the PL can only be considered a quasi-mintmark.

Summary

For quick reference purposes, the following list includes all of the Heaton mintmarks that are known to the author, as well as the quasi-mintmarks that have graced their issues. Each has been given an identifying code, consisting of an "m" or "qm" (for "mintmark" or "quasi-mark") and a number. These have been used in the preceding text.

m1	– H&S	qm1 – RK&Co
m2	– H	qm2 – SHAW
m2a	– HH	qm3 – PL
m3	– HEATON	
m4	– HEATON BIRMM	
m5	– HEATON BIRMINGHAM	
m6	– BIRMINGHAM	
m7	– BIRMM H	
m8	– B (BI)	
m9	– ىلىۋ	
m9a	– ىلىۋ	
m10	– M (MA)	
m11	– M	

It is doubtful that any other mint in modern times has struck coins with such a wide variety of mintmarks, and it is certain that no other commercial establishment has been so widely advertised on the circulating coins of so many of the sovereign nations of the world.

Since the Royal Mint began accepting foreign coinage orders in 1923, the use of mintmarks by The Birmingham Mint has gradually declined to vanishing point. Of all the coins struck by The Mint in the 1960–70 period, only those issues for Malaya and British Borneo, East Africa, and Hong Kong have carried the H mintmark, and of these only the Hong Kong issues have appeared in the 1970s with the Heaton signature, the last such being the 1972 5 cents issue. Apparently, in the future only non-circulating issues by The Mint will carry forward the mintmark tradition started by Ralph Heaton II in 1850. During the 120 years ending in 1970, however, billions of coins were produced with the well-known H imprinted thereon, and the coinages of several countries bore either the Heaton mintmark, or no mintmark at all. These included British Honduras, Cyprus, Guernsey,

Nicaragua, Jersey, Sarawak, British North Borneo, and Yugoslavia. Except for the KN mintmark on the 1918–19 pence, the English coinage of the period would also be included in the above list, since the Royal Mint used no mintmarks on its English coinages.

Note: The author is indebted to Robert M. Sweeny of South Lawrence, Mass. for the line drawings used in this chapter.

Chapter VIII

The Manufacture of Blanks

The process of manufacturing coins is a long and intricate one, involving many discrete steps. As practised in the mid and late 1800s, the process started with raw materials such as virgin metal ingots, old coins, or metal scrap. Whichever, the materials went into a melting furnace where they were alloyed by the addition of other metals to achieve the correct formulation. This done, the molten metal was poured into moulds, yielding bars $\frac{1}{2}$ to 1 inch thick and as wide as several (often 3) of the coins to be produced. These bars were then rolled into fillets, which were strips of metal of essentially the same width as the bars, but only as thick as the ultimate coins. Depending on several factors, the fillets may have required an anneal between the stages of rolling. The next step, which was called "cutting-out", involved producing the coining blanks by running the fillets through presses which punched out the blanks – as many as three or more at a time across the width of the fillet. The unused portion of the fillet, called scissel, usually amounting to between 40% and 50% of the original weight of the fillet, was recycled back through the whole process. The blanks were then annealed to soften them for coining, and blanched by immersion in dilute sulphuric acid to remove the oxidation formed in the heat anneal. The next step was called "marking", a process involving rolling the blank in a special machine to upset the edge so as to provide the relief necessary to protect the design – and allow the coins to stack. At this point the blank was finally ready to receive the design impression in the coining press – only the last of many involved and time-consuming operations.

Any well-appointed mint was set up to carry out all of these operations, as indeed were both the Royal Mint in London and the Heaton Mint in Birmingham. But despite having an adequate capacity for performing all of the usual minting processes, the Heatons decided very early that it was simply good business to contract for any part of the operation offered them.

The first opportunity came very soon after mint operations were begun. In 1851 the Royal Mint, busy with the production of gold and silver coins,

58   *Chapter VIII*

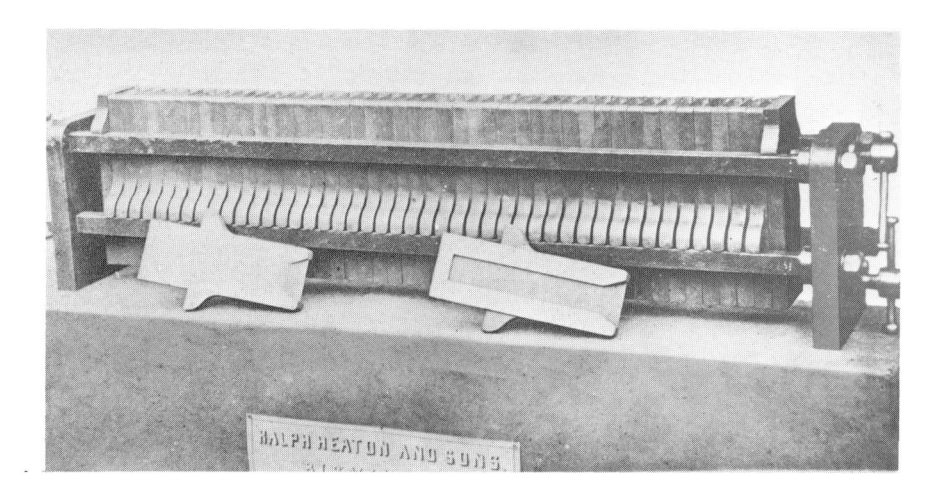

Plate XII.   Heaton casting and rolling plant of the 1880s.
  i. Set of pack moulds for casting metal ingots.
  ii. Twin rolling mill.

ordered blanks from Heatons for a copper coinage of pence, halfpence, farthings, half- and quarter-farthings. The extent of the order is not known for certain, but existing records in the Public Record Office in London suggest that most, if not all, of the English copper coinage of 1851 and 1852 was produced in the Royal Mint on Heaton blanks. This order for some 30 to 35 tons of copper blanks was the first of many to come from the Royal Mint.

The Manufacture of Blanks

The reason was that the Royal Mint was simply not equipped to carry out the total coinages required by the country – much less by the remainder of the Empire. At first the limitation was in the rolling and cutting operations. Only one metal could be handled at a time, and so when the demand for gold and silver was heavy, the production of copper or bronze coins could only be handled by purchase of the blanks. Later, as the demand for bronze coinages continued to increase, melting capacity became a limitation, so that outside purchase of bars or fillets occasionally had to be made. Here, too, Heatons were ready – and willing.

The records of those early years are far from complete, but it would appear that the next order for blanks involved a coinage by the Royal Mint of 10 million one cent pieces for Canada in 1858 and 1859. By then, Heatons had accumulated considerable experience in working with bronze, having produced the bronze coinage for France in the Marseilles Mint. The Royal Mint, on the other hand, had little experience with bronze, so it was expedient that they obtain the bronze blanks for the Canadian coins from Heatons.

Only shortly thereafter, beginning in 1860, the English subsidiary coinage was changed from copper to bronze, requiring a massive effort for the conversion. Most of the contract coinage was placed with James Watt & Co., but it is probable that Heatons made a major contribution in the form of bronze blanks to both Watt and the Royal Mint. The basis for this supposition lies in the fact that Ralph Heaton III reported in 1866[1] that Heatons had sold 2500 tons of copper and bronze blanks since mintage operations began in 1850. It is speculated that this quantity was made up as follows:

British Imperial copper coinage of 1851–2	34 tons
Milan Mint bronze coinage of 1861–2	1600 tons
Canadian 1858 bronze cents by the Royal Mint	100 tons
Indian $\frac{1}{4}$ anna copper coinage by Watt in 1860	400 tons
54 lakhs of blanks for India lost at sea in 1857	35 tons

leaving 330 tons unaccounted for, which could have been supplied to Watt as part of Watt's 1720 tons of Imperial bronze coinage in 1861–3. Some part of the 330 tons may have also gone to the Royal Mint in the same period, or possibly to India.

From this time on, manufacture of blanks and bars became a continuous and important item of commerce for Heatons, not only in supplying the Royal Mint, but also other mints around the world. Some of the interesting orders that Heatons received in the next few decades are as follows:

---

[1] Ralph Heaton, "Birmingham Coinage", *Industrial History of the Birmingham and Midland Hardware District*, Timmons, London, 1866, p. 556.

Plate XIII. Heaton coining machinery.
 i. *Cutting-out or blanking press of the 1890s.*
 ii. *Upsetting or rimming machine – this one was shipped to the Bogota Mint, Colombia in 1883.*
 iii. *Coining press – the nameplate is dated 1899 and shows its destination to be China.*

The Manufacture of Blanks

1869 – Bronze blanks for 10 and 20 reis were provided to the Rio Mint for its 1870 production. A portion of this same coinage was also produced in Brussels, although probably not on Heaton blanks.

1871 – Heatons' only contributions to the coinage of Jersey consisted of furnishing the Royal Mint with the bronze blanks for the last issues of the old 1/13 and 1/26 shilling denominations struck in 1871, and of producing the actual coinage of the first issues of the new 1/12, 1/24, and 1/48 shillings struck in 1877.

1870–1900 – Major portions of the bronze coinages of Denmark, Norway, and Sweden were produced in those mints on Heaton blanks. For instance, Heatons provided the blanks for all of Norway's production of 1, 2, and 5 öre coins from at least 1876–1902.

1875–6 – Over 300 tons of bronze 1 and 2 pfennig blanks were shipped to the German mints at Berlin, Hanover, Frankfurt, and Hamburg.

1881 – In addition to striking 4 million copper-nickel $2\frac{1}{2}$ centavos for Colombia, Heatons furnished 4 million blanks to the Paris Mint for an identical coinage.

1886–97 – All of Mexico's 8 gram copper 1 Centavos were produced in Mexico on Heaton blanks. Also, in the 1905–14 period, what few of the nickel 5 centavos that were not struck in Birmingham were struck in Mexico on blanks from Birmingham.

1891–2 – Over 37 million bronze and silver blanks were shipped to Lisbon, where they were used for all of Portugal's 1892 coinage.

1893 – About 100 tons of 4.7, 9.25, and 9.4 gram copper blanks were ordered by the Persian Gulf Trading Co. (London) for shipment to Bushire, Persia for mule-back delivery 1000 miles overland to an unidentified destination.

1904 – Having obtained an entrée through sale of minting equipment, The Mint shipped out to China 117 million bronze 10 cash blanks, amounting to some 880 tons.

During all this time, sales of blanks and bars were being made to the Royal Mint, mostly in bronze, but occasionally in copper-nickel (especially for the Jamaican coinage), and several times in silver.

In the years since the turn of the century, this product line of The Birmingham Mint has continued to be an important part of total mint operations. It has had its ups and downs, just as has the coining side. Both

World Wars affected these sales unfavourably, as did the Depression of the 1930s. After World War II, however, the sales of blanks again attained considerable volume, as witness these typical orders of the 1960s:

- 1962–70 – Most, if not all, of the 414 million copper-nickel 1 baht coins (Y84) were struck in Thailand on blanks produced in Birmingham.
- 1963–6 – The Bogota Mint used Heaton blanks for the 1964 and 1965 coinage of copper-nickel 50 centavos, as well as for large portions of the 1964–6 issues of 10 and 20 centavos.
- 1965–8 – Most of the Iranian copper-nickel 5 rials of SH1347–49, and a large portion of the 10 rials of SH1346, were struck in the Tehran Mint on Birmingham planchets.
- 1967–70 – The 27 million bronze and copper-nickel blanks furnished to Singapore were probably used to strike the 1968 and 1969 one cent and five cents, and the 1969–71 twenty cents.
- 1968 – In this year Switzerland changed from silver to copper-nickel for the half, one, and two francs, and the blanks for all three issues were produced by The Birmingham Mint.
- 1969–70 – Even the Vienna Mint found it necessary to obtain blanks from The Birmingham Mint; most of the 1969 and 1970 five schillings were probably minted on the 31 million planchets sent out from Birmingham.

Again during this period the Royal Mint was finding it convenient to obtain blanks from The Mint. When Britain changed over to decimal coinage in 1968–71, The Mint was called on for some 1680 tons of New Penny bronze blanks and 466 tons of Ten New Pence copper-nickel blanks, reminiscent of the time a hundred years earlier when Britain changed to bronze from copper for the subsidiary coins, and then found it necessary or desirable to involve the Heaton factory.

It can be seen that the commercial policies that were established by the second Ralph Heaton have stood the test of time. Even today The Mint is willing to contribute to the world's coinage needs in any way that allows it to be remunerated for its contribution.

Chapter IX

Advertising Pieces

Coin-forms have been used in great number to advertise all kinds of commercial activities, but their use for advertising commercial coinage and minting equipment has been relatively infrequent. From the very beginning, however, the Heaton Mint employed this means of showing potential customers real examples of their skill in coin and die work. Existing records provide little information concerning the specific purpose of individual Heaton pieces, but the wide variety to be found certainly makes for interesting speculation.

The first such pieces may well be the medals that Heatons struck on the occasion of the Crystal Palace Exhibition in London in 1851. It is probable that Heatons exhibited their wares at this show – they certainly did at the 1862 International Exhibition in London – and so these pieces may well have been used as handouts to advertise the quality of their manufacture. The only specimen in metallic form that has been observed by the author is here designated Adv 1, and is a copper piece of 9.75 grams and 30.3 mm

Adv 1

diameter. Other similar pieces, but of different sizes and inscriptions, are preserved as cardboard die impressions in the Birmingham City Museum. All have a nicely executed image of the Crystal Palace on the obverse, along with the words CRYSTAL PALACE LONDON 1851. Most, if not all, have the word HEATON in small but easily seen letters in the exergue at left immediately below the Palace, and BIRM at right opposite HEATON.

64   Chapter IX

The larger pieces carry additional descriptive words on the obverse. The reverses vary; some are blank, others carry varying descriptions of the Crystal Palace.

	Diameter mm	Reverse
Adv 1	30.3	Blank
Adv 2	23	?
Adv 3	26	?
Adv 4	30	Description
Adv 5	34	?
Adv 6	38	Description

Another interesting piece (Adv 10), and probably their first carrying a specific advertising message, is referred to by Batty,[1] and a cardboard die impression of the reverse is among those in the Birmingham City Museum. The obverse reads RALPH HEATON & SON GENERAL COINERS BIRMINGHAM. Use of the singular SON identifies this piece as having been produced in 1853 or earlier; thereafter the plural SONS was used. The reverse is very similar to the reverse of the English shilling of the period, with the words A COUNTER replacing ONE SHILLING within the wreath below the crown.

In 1872 Heatons struck an issue of 2 centavos for Ecuador (EC2) in copper. They apparently liked the design of the coin, because they used the reverse die of the Ecuador issue, mated with an obverse die of their own design, to produce an advertising piece in 75/25 copper-nickel. The obverse

Adv 12

reads RALPH HEATON & SONS BIRMINGHAM in the outer circle, and THE MINT in the centre. The diameter is 30.7 mm and the weight 10.05 grams. There is no date, but the piece must have been struck between 1872 and 1889.

Another piece of the same period was struck with an identical obverse die, but with a reverse design consisting of a large radiate star, much like the

---

[1]Batty, *Copper Coinage of Great Britain, Ireland, British Isles and Colonies*, p. 591.

Advertising Pieces 65

Adv 13

coins struck by Heatons for Paraguay in 1870 (PA1–3). One wonders if these may have been used to persuade Paraguayan officials of Heatons' competence. The piece is 25.2 mm diameter, 4.7 grams, and made of 80/20 copper-nickel, a material otherwise used by Heatons only for Jamaican coins. Indeed, it is likely that blanks for the Jamaican halfpenny were used for these pieces, since Heatons furnished blanks to the Royal Mint on several occasions, specifically including in 1869.

Sometime before 1889 Heatons struck an imaginative advertising piece apparently to promote their wares in the Latin American area. The obverse

Adv 15

shows a well-executed female bust, with the fictional inscription REPUBLICA DE PILOSI, and the Heaton mintmark below the bust. On the reverse is the fictional denomination 2 CUARTOS. The piece is bronze, has no date, and is 30 mm diameter and 10.4 grams. A specimen is in the cabinet of The Mint in Birmingham.

These next three pieces were obviously intended for general advertising purposes; both obverse and reverse identify them as products of the Heaton Mint. They are undated, but must have been produced before 1889, since the company was no longer known as Ralph Heaton & Sons after its change from a privately owned to a publicly owned enterprise. The larger piece is copper, 31.3 mm and 9.85 grams. One smaller piece is also copper, 25.2 mm and 5.05 grams. The other is nickel, 25.3 mm and 4.7 grams. Their designs are identical with the larger piece, except that the reverse field of the nickel piece is blank. The shield, which appears in different form on later pieces, is quartered. The first and fourth quarters are blue (horizontal lines), the second and third quarters are indented, with yellow (dots) and red (vertical lines). Over all is a diagonal of nine white lozenges or diamonds. The motto FORWARD is on a scroll below the shield.

66   *Chapter IX*

Adv 18   Adv 19

Adv 20

An interesting variant of Adv 18 is Adv 21, a bronze piece 37 mm. in diameter and struck with mismatched dies. The obverse die was the same as was used to produce the 31 mm. Adv 18. The reverse die was full size. The reverse design shows the word CENT within a wreath, and the curved inscription SPECIMEN PIECE above the wreath.

A variant of Adv 21 has also been observed (Adv 22). It is a uniface piece, 37 mm. diameter, struck with the reverse die used for Adv 21. Its composition, determined by X-Ray spectrometer analysis, appears to contain about 70% copper, 15% nickel, and 15% zinc (nickel silver).

Adv 22

One additional pre-1889 piece was made of 70/30 brass in the style of a Chinese cash coin, with a 6 × 6 mm square hole in the centre and a wide flat border. The English inscription on the obverse reads RALPH HEATON & SONS BIRMINGHAM ENGLAND. The reverse appears to be a highly stylized inscription suggestive of Chinese characters. The weight is 4.1 grams, and the diameter 22.3 mm.

Advertising Pieces 67

Adv 23

Probably during 1889, The Mint produced a series of advertising pieces which employed modifications of the design used for Adv 19. Identical pieces were produced in nickel, pure aluminium, and copper (Adv 24, 25, and 26 respectively) weighing 5.5, 1.0, and 5.6 grams. All were about 25.6 mm in diameter. The aluminium piece has a reeded edge, the others are plain. The obverse carries the new company name THE MINT, BIRMINGHAM, LIMITED around a design featuring the old Birmingham City

Adv 24

coat of arms, with figures of a male worker and a female artist standing on either side of a shield as used on Adv 19, differing only in shape. Above the shield is an arm and hammer; below is the motto FORWARD on a scroll. The reverse carries the explanation FORMERLY RALPH HEATON & SONS, surrounded by the claim COINERS TO THE ENGLISH AND FOREIGN GOVERNMENTS. Although these, like most of the other advertising pieces, are undated, the obverse design was certainly used in 1889, for it appears on a medal struck to commemorate the visit to The Mint by the Shah of Persia in 1889.

Later, when the need was no longer felt to relate The Mint, Birmingham, Ltd. to Heatons' former company name, the same obverse design was again used for advertising purposes, but this time the reverse message was changed

Adv 29

Chapter IX

to catalogue the products of the company. The circular inscription reads MANUFACTURERS OF NON-FERROUS ALLOYS, and in the centre is the further explanation IN SHEETS STRIP WIRE BLANKS TUBES STAMPINGS, ETC AND COINAGE. This piece was struck in various metals and in a variety of planchet thicknesses; observed specimens are listed in the following table. It is certainly possible that additional variations will surface.

	Metal	Weight grams	Diameter mm	Edge
Adv 28	Nickel	5.2	25.5	Plain
Adv 29	75/25 Copper–Nickel	5.3	25.5	Plain
Adv 30	75/25 Copper–Nickel	5.6	25.5	Plain
Adv 31	75/25 Copper–Nickel	8.7	25.6	Plain
Adv 32	Aluminium ($3\frac{1}{2}$% Magnesium)	1.8	25.5	Reeded

Probably shortly after the turn of the century, the preceding obverse design was repeated on a new piece, this time with the reverse product listing replaced by the simple statement 20TH CENTURY COINS. One observed variety (Adv 35) is of nickel, weighs 6.9 grams, and is 26.1 mm

Adv 35

diameter. It has a reeded edge. Another variety (Adv 36) is of 70/30 brass, weighs 6.4 grams, is also 26.1 mm diameter, and has a plain edge. It is considered possible that other similar pieces in different metals were struck, and so the following speculative numbers are assigned: Adv 37 – Copper-nickel; Adv 38 – Bronze; Adv 39 – Aluminium.

In 1905 The Mint made an unaccepted tender in China for nickel blanks of 6, 4, and $2\frac{1}{2}$ grams. It was probably in connection with this tender that some advertising pieces were made in the style of modern struck Chinese silver coinage. The obverse bears a dragon of the same size and style used by THE MINT for the Shensi 20c (CN28) struck in 1898.[2] The reverse shows a large numeral within a beaded circle surrounded by the inscription THE MINT BIRMINGHAM LIMITED ENGLAND. The obverse has

---

[2] Mr. Jess Peters, Decatur, Illinois, kindly provided the illustrations of Adv 42 and 44.

Advertising Pieces 69

Adv 42   Adv 44

SPECIMEN NICKEL COIN above the dragon with the weight in GRAMMES below. Adv 42 is the piece referenced by Kann on page 285 of his masterpiece *Illustrated Catalog of Chinese Coins*. An example was sold as Lot No. 870 in the 5 March 1977 Chicago International Coin Fair auction. A specimen of Adv 44, the 2½ GRAMMES piece, was sold as Lot No. 268 in the Jess Peters Mail Auction Sale of 14 November 1978. It is assumed that a companion 4 GRAMMES piece, with the numeral 5 denoting 5 cents, will eventually come to light, in which case it will be numbered Adv 43.

In recent years The Mint has continued to use coin-forms for advertising purposes. Two novelty pieces were designed to be used as spinners, to

Adv 52

Adv 53

facilitate decision-making in pubs. One advertises THE MINT; the other MINT SECURITY. This latter was until 1979 an affiliated company which, as the inscription on the reverse states, provided GUARDS, C.I.T., INVESTIGATIONS, GENERAL SECURITY SERVICES. This piece is made of brass and weighs 10.9 grams. The piece advertising THE MINT is of bronze and weighs 10.7 grams. Both are 30.9 mm in diameter.

Certainly the most highly personalized advertising piece is the one which Mr. King, past Chairman of The Mint Group, used as a business card. It

Adv 60

carries a bust of Mr. King on the obverse, and his name and title on the reverse. The specimen shown above is of silver, 29.6 mm in diameter, and 9.45 grams weight.

The author is indebted to Mr. W. L. S. Barrett of Montreal for much of the information in this chapter. Mr. Barrett has put together a specialized collection of Heaton advertising pieces, which he very kindly loaned to the author for use here.

Chapter X

Minting Equipment

When Heatons started coinage operations in 1850, they had four steam-powered screw presses of Boulton's design – very similar to those in use by the Royal Mint at the time. There were better presses available – although Heatons either was unaware of this fact, or chose to disregard it. In 1817, a German named Diedrich Uhlhorn patented a lever press using a knuckle-joint to transfer power from a fly-wheel to the dies. It was better in almost every respect than the old screw presses, being quiet, fast, and not requiring a massive foundation. He set up to manufacture his press, and by 1847 his company had delivered some 57 presses in three sizes to nine European mints. Uhlhorn died in 1837, but the business was carried on by his sons. By 1876 they had sold 200 presses,[1] but by 1882 the company had gone out of business. Some of these presses were purchased by the Paris Mint, probably in the early 1840s, and these became the basis for further improvements conceived by the Frenchman Thonnelier. The Thonnelier presses, made in France by J. F. Cail et Cie, were adopted for use in the Paris Mint in 1845.

When, in 1852, Heatons accepted a contract to equip and operate a mint at Marseilles, Ralph III went to Paris and there purchased four Thonnelier presses. Shortly afterwards he sent back to Birmingham scale drawings of the presses. Although Ralph III was enthusiastic about their capabilities, his father was not so impressed, writing his son that "...you will see the multiplicity of the pieces (making up the press) and all only to obtain the same results we have by our screw presses." In the same letter, he agreed that they were "...beautifully made and I have little doubt we shall make them work ditto."

He soon got a chance to see how well they worked. In 1853 Joseph Taylor, a Birmingham machinery manufacturer and founder of the firm that

---

[1] This information, and much background material, was provided by Ing. J. G. Sligte VDI of Amsterdam, who has made an extensive study of the development of coining presses, and especially those by Uhlhorn.

72 Chapter X

Plate XIV. Architect's drawing of the Canton Mint reproduced in the London Graphic, May 19th, 1888.

1. New Brass Coin (obverse).
2. New Brass Coin (reverse).
3. Old Brass Coin of the time of the Fifth Emperor of the present Dynasty.
4. New Silver Coinage—Half-Dollar (obverse).
5. New Silver Coinage—Half-Dollar (reverse).

later became Taylor & Challen, accepted a contract to outfit the new Sydney, Australia, Mint. Heaton was one of the sureties for this contract, and it is probable that Taylor used the press designs that had been sent over from Marseilles. It is certain that he used other Heaton designs, because the contract specified that cutting-out and marking machines "...similar to those used by [and probably made by] Messrs. Heaton & Son..." would be furnished. The Sydney Mint representative who visited the Paris Mint reported back that "I have twice been over to the French Mint. ... The lever presses are certainly the only part of machinery worthy of imitation." His observation was partially confirmed by the fact that the French Government, in connection with Heatons' equipping the Marseilles Mint, offered to forgive any import duties if Heatons would make available for the Paris Mint's use their designs for rolling equipment. Heatons refused.

Two lever presses were made by Taylor for the Sydney Mint.[2] Heaton assisted by suggesting modifications to the design of the presses, and the final acceptance tests, witnessed by Sydney Mint representatives, were actually made in Heatons' shops.

Despite his scepticism, Heaton did make one of the lever presses for use in his own shops. In 1855 he wrote to the Dutch Ministry of the Colonies, in response to a request for tenders on a large coinage for the East Indies, saying: "We have lately constructed and set to work a new press for striking coins. It is on a very simple plan and we find it very effective. It is a wheel and eccentric and costs about £250, and will strike without alteration except dies any size coin from 1 to 4 centimetres diam., on which we would be happy to strike at any time whatever part of your coinage may be less forward than you could wish, or use any or all our 4 screw presses we are now using for the British Coin."

When Ralph III returned from Marseilles, he and his brother George began experimenting with the lever press – probably the one made in their shop from the drawings which he had sent over earlier. They developed several improvements for which an English patent was assigned to the two of them in 1859. Their improved press was installed in the new Icknield Street Mint in 1859–60, along with eleven screw presses made by Joseph Taylor.

In 1862 both Heaton and Uhlhorn were exhibitors at the International Exhibition in London. Although existing records neither confirm nor deny this, it is not unlikely that discussions at the Exhibition led to the agreement, formally documented in 1883, whereby Heatons would enjoy exclusive

---

[2] One of these presses, which had been used to strike the first Australian sovereign in 1855 in the Sydney Mint, was sold to Sir William Dixson when the Sydney Mint was closed in 1926. It is now in the Dixson Library in Sydney. Much of the above information regarding the Sydney Mint presses was supplied through the courtesy of the Dixson Library.

rights in England to build and sell Uhlhorn-type presses, modified by improvements of their own invention. It is a fact, however, that only shortly thereafter the Heatons began building the Uhlhorn press — first for their own use, but soon for sale to other mints. By 1865 there were twelve lever presses in their own mint, and in 1864 they accepted their first contract for minting equipment using the lever press.

The Mandalay Mint[3] This was a turnkey contract — complete including building, equipment, training, and start-up. The order was probably dated 1863 — delivery was in early 1865. Initial operation took place on 11 November 1865, and the mint continued in operation until about 1885, turning out some 36 million silver peacock coins in four denominations ($\frac{1}{8}$, $\frac{1}{4}$, $\frac{1}{2}$ and 1 kyats). It is possible that the whole output was achieved using the 600 pairs of dies originally shipped out from Birmingham. The mint building was about 60 by 80 feet, and was located in a corner of the Palace grounds in Mandalay. It apparently included only one press, but could produce about 15,000 kyats per day.

The Royal Mint — London From 1810 to 1872, the only presses used in the London Mint were the screw presses obtained from Boulton's Soho Foundry. However, in preparation for a new mint, the Royal Mint borrowed a lever press from Heatons in 1871, and were so pleased with its operation that they rented four lever presses from Heatons in 1872 to help meet a peak demand for coinage. These were returned in 1873, and their first purchase of a lever press from Heatons took place in 1875. Extensive tests were run to compare screw and lever presses, and the 1875 British Mint Report showed the results to be that the lever press yielded nearly twice the number of coins per die, and about a seventh the number of rejects as the screw presses. Charles Fremantle, Deputy Master of the Royal Mint, summed up the results by saying: "The superiority of the lever press, as regards economy and accuracy in working and freedom from noise, has now been abundantly proved...".

Thereafter the Royal Mint gradually acquired additional lever presses and other machinery from Heatons, as shown in the following résumé:

	Lever presses	Punch presses
1875–9	4	5
1880–9	12	3
1890–9	4	—
1920	4	—

[3] M. Robinson, "The Mandalay Mint", *Coins and Medals*, February 1979, pp. 19–21.

Minting Equipment

These, less one retired earlier, constituted the entire press capacity of the Royal Mint from 1882 until 1920, when 22 new Taylor & Challen presses were added. In 1938 The Mint provided one last medium lever press, this being their last press manufacture. In 1941 an emergency mint was set up by the Royal Mint at Iver Heath, Bucks, which contained 8 medium Heaton presses and 4 Heaton punch presses, leaving 14 Heaton coin presses, 4 Heaton punch presses, and 22 Taylor & Challen coin presses in London. All the equipment at Iver was returned to London in 1945.

In 1948 six additional presses were ordered from The Mint, who could not comply but who agreed to loan the drawings to the Royal Mint for manufacture there. In 1955 another six were completed, giving the Royal Mint 54 presses, of which about 34 were of the Heaton design. These presses continued in use, but starting in about 1962 more modern high-speed presses were added. Finally, in 1970 the British Mint Report reported: "...we shall soon see the demise of the Heaton coining press at the Royal Mint. These presses ... were the mainstay of our production for the following 40 years (from 1882).... Among the most recent coins struck on these versatile presses were the Churchill crowns and the new 50p coins.... Three of these old presses are still at work in the Numismatic Coin Unit where their double striking facility on large proof coins and medallions has made their retention worthwhile."

Osaka Mint In 1868 the Hong Kong Mint, which had been established in 1864, was closed down due to its poor economic performance, and the equipment was sold to Japan. The antiquated Boulton-type screw presses were soon concluded to be inadequate, so new lever presses were ordered from Heatons; two in 1872 and eight in 1873. The 1872 Japanese Mint Report states: "Two Uhlorn [*sic*] presses have been recently erected in this department, resulting in greatly improved gold coins." The 1874 Report states that "In the coining department there are now ten 'Uhlorn' and two 'Thonnelier' presses, with six 'Watt's' presses (screw type) in the copper coining room...". No further equipment was supplied to Osaka by The Birmingham Mint. In July 1974 Mr. Hideo Miwa, Superintendent of the Osaka Mint Operative Control Department, wrote to the author, saying that "Now our mint has only one Uhlhorn type press which has been possible to be used until 1964." This is undoubtedly one of the Heaton presses sent out in the 1870s. A 1:5 scale model of this press is now displayed in the Osaka Mint Museum.

Romania In 1867 Heatons produced, with Watt's help, the first distinctive coinage for this country which was not to gain its full independence from Turkey until 1878. Records in The Mint show that Heatons next furnished a complete package of minting equipment at a price of £164,024 (including two lever presses obtained from Uhlhorn) to Romania in 1868. As was often the case, this order included dies for a new issue of 50 bani, 1 leu and 3 lei silver coins. Specimen strikes from these dies, dated 1869, are in the cabinet of The Mint. The dies were apparently never used by the Bucharest Mint. It is to be noted that Bucharest's first coinage emissions were dated 1870, a factor consistent with the foregoing.

Colombia Colombia already had three silver mints in operation (Medellin, Popayan, and Bogota) when it ordered a complete modern mint from Heatons in 1882. This new mint included a large and a small coining press, plus a full complement of all other required equipment. Edward Wyon went out from Birmingham to supervise erection and to teach the Colombians to use the new equipment. Thereafter, at least until 1922, The Mint continued to supply dies and spare parts to Bogota, in addition to having produced several coinage issues for Colombia.

Germany? Heatons' Orderbook records an order received in 1886 from Knape Heim of Magdeburg (now East Germany) for two lever presses and one milling machine. This is the same firm that supplied the first modern minting equipment to Wuchang (Hupeh, China) in 1893. It is speculated that these Heaton presses also found their way to China under Knape Heim's guidance – possibly to the Tientsin Arsenal Mint which apparently started up in 1888.

The Indian Mints Existing records of minting equipment shipments to India are, to say the least, confusing. Some are quite explicit; others show only material ordered and port of entry, and some omit even the port destination. Work still remains to be done in sorting out these records, but the following tentative conclusions appear to have some validity.

Baroda An 1888 order through the Walsh Lovett Co. of London specifies: "A plant of minting machinery as per specifications of 21 February 1888 with the addition of one pair of dies for rupees as per sample left with us and tools for same as well as for $\frac{1}{2}$, $\frac{1}{4}$ and $\frac{1}{8}$ rupees." No destination is shown in the Orderbook. Possibilities would include both Baroda and Hyderabad, but based on later orders, this one is presumed to be for Baroda.

Hyderabad The first order that can be positively attributed to Hyderabad was entered on 14 April 1891, and covered a steam engine and associated equipment for "rolling mills as already ordered". This entry goes on to report that "the mint building is now nearly ready to receive the machinery." The order was placed by D. Gauntlett, Superintending

Engineer for His Highness the Nizam. Additional orders in 1893 and 1894, specifically for Hyderabad, covered the four lever presses and other equipment needed for a complete mint. Finally, an order of 11 September 1900, by J. Spencer of Glasgow, but without destination indicated, covered matrices, punches, dies and collars for 1, $\frac{1}{2}$, $\frac{1}{4}$ and $\frac{1}{8}$ rupees.

Other In addition, The Mint supplied on several orders during the period 1893–1900 at least two lever presses, two rolling mills, punches and dies to as yet unidentified Indian mints. Possibilities, in addition to the above, would include Indore, Gwalior, and Travancore.

Sweden The Mint's only equipment sale to Sweden was a punch press, suitable for 1, 2 and 5 öre blanks, shipped in 1890. This machine was last used in 1974, in which year it was retired when the Swedish Mint moved to its new location in Eskilstuna.

Portugal In 1891 the Lisbon Mint, through the offices of Baron de Costa Ricci in London, purchased a large lever press, capable of hand operation in case of power failure.

Chile The Santiago Mint ordered in 1894 two rolling mills – one for gold and one silver – and one edge-marking machine.

Australia The Perth Mint was established in 1896, and was outfitted principally with machinery from The Birmingham Mint. This included a boiler and steam engine, 3 rolling mills, 2 cutting-out presses, 2 coining presses, and 1 edge-marking machine. In 1899 a third cutting-out machine was ordered, and in 1901 a third lever press was acquired.

Siam In 1900 Siam ordered a complete minting plant suitable for production of 100,000 ticals per day of ten hours. This plant included four coining presses; twelve more were added at some later date. In 1974 Mr. Chakrabandh, then Director of the Mint Division, confirmed that all sixteen coining presses were still in use, as well as one of the original edge-marking machines.

The difficulties of a foreigner in that part of the world in 1901 are rather plaintively stated in a letter to Mr. Hugh Middleton in Birmingham (a Mint Manager) from Captain F. M. Martin in Bangkok. Capt. Martin, who had been sent out to oversee the installation of the minting equipment, wrote on 26 June 1901: "...Well, I have received nearly all the plant and some [is] in a dreadful rusty condition. ... They have laid 3 weeks upon Singapore wharf in the weather ... Things are dreadful here. The heat and fever and cholera and smallpox are dreadful. 2000 dying per week. Singapore has put all our ships in quarantine. With God's help I have struggled through but have gone through more than I can describe."

Nepal The author has so far not located an order from Nepal for minting equipment. However, orders for dies, punches, and collars in the period 1905–20 clearly imply that The Mint supplied two coining presses to Nepal, sometime before 1904, and probably in the 1890s.

Afghanistan The British Mint Report for 1891, page 54, states that "Under Mr. Pyne's directions [Chief Engineer to the Emir of Afghanistan] a mint has been established at Kabul for the coinage of rupees and subsidiary silver pieces, specimens of which he has been so good as to present to the Museum of this Department. Notwithstanding the difficulties under which they have been produced, they are satisfactorily struck, and form a marked contrast to the native pieces formerly in circulation." The first machine-struck coinage of Afghanistan was dated AH1308, the year before Mr. Pyne's visit to the Royal Mint. However, the cabinet of The Mint contains a machine-struck rupee dated AH1304 (specimens are also in the cabinet of the American Numismatic Society, and in private collections in the U.S.A.). It is presumed that this copper-nickel specimen was produced in connection with an effort to obtain an order for the Kabul mint machinery. Whether The Mint actually obtained the order has not been definitely determined, but clearly suggesting the possibility is a 1933 order for parts for rolling mills and three sizes of coining presses. On this very speculative basis, it is concluded that the Kabul Mint was outfitted from Birmingham.

Finland In 1929 Finland ordered one lever press, plus an edge-marking machine and a milling machine, from The Mint. In 1974 Mr. Soiniemi, then Mint Director, advised that the Birmingham press was still in use, but was scheduled for retirement in 1975. In his words, "...That coining press has earned its price many times over."

The Chinese Mints Chang Chih-tung, undoubtedly one of the most progressive leaders in China at the turn of the century, can be truly considered the father of modern coinage in China. More than anyone else, it was he who brought about the transition from the ancient cast coinage to the new struck silver coinage. This process only started after Chang became Viceroy of the Kwangtung and Kwangsi provinces in 1884. In 1887 he authorized China's first modern silver mint, to be built in Canton as a provincial mint. Thereafter, the development of the provincial mints spread at a rapid pace throughout China, and The Birmingham Mint played a leading role in outfitting them. Much of the record is clear and definite – but much still remains to be sorted out. The following chronicle will

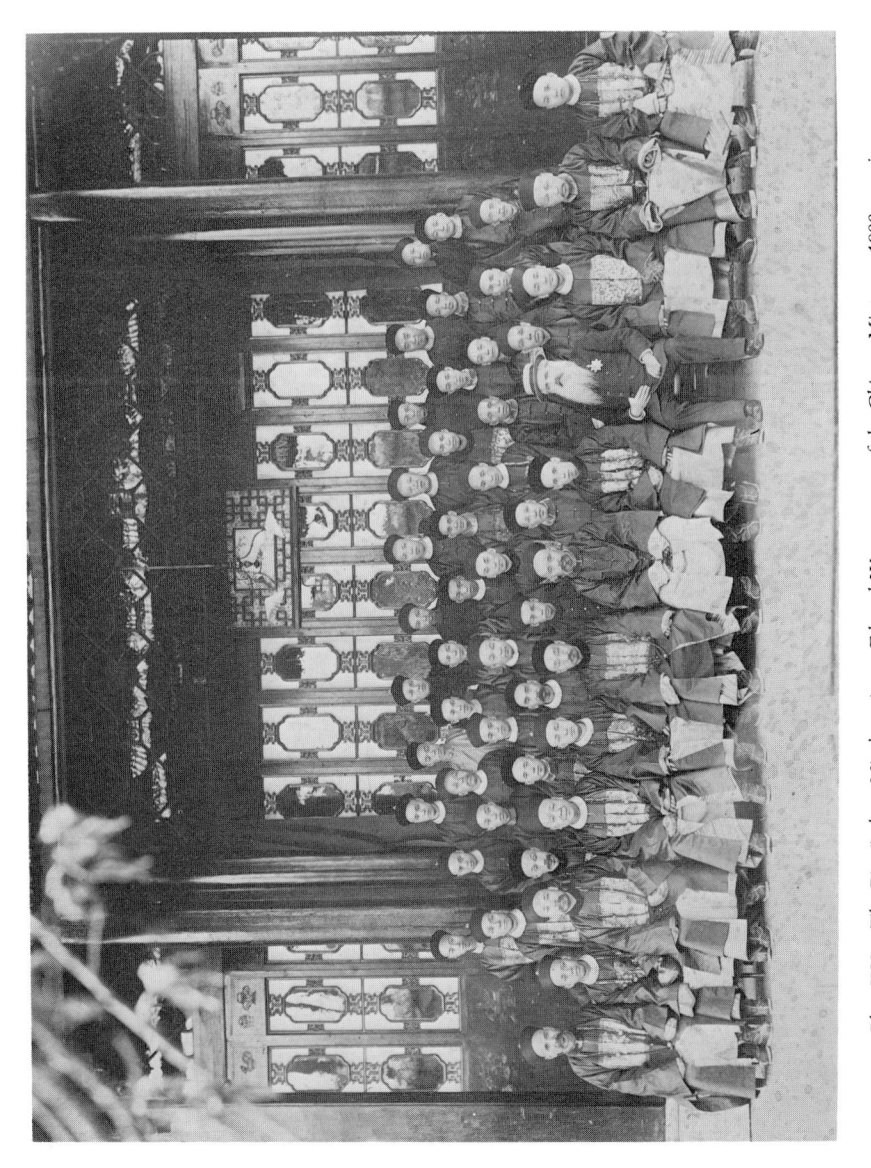

Plate XV. *The Birmingham Mint's engineer, Edward Wyon, at one of the Chinese Mints, ca. 1900, wearing the Order of the Double Dragon and Blue Button awarded to him by the Chinese Government.*

include both known facts and speculation, with the latter always being identified as such.

Kwangtung Province   In April 1887 Heatons received an order for a complete mint to be erected at Canton. The size of the mint was enormous. It had a capacity of 2.6 million cash coins per day, simultaneous with 100,000 silver coins per day. It required 90 coining presses to achieve this output, plus thousands of tons of peripheral equipment. It was unquestionably the largest mint – government or private – in the world, both then and for a long time to come. Heatons' contract was for the entire project, including buildings, equipment, start-up, and training. The buildings were designed by Mr. Edwin C. Middleton of Birmingham, and had an overall size of 657 feet by 424 feet. Completion of the plant was required in 18 months, and, in spite of some delays in the construction of the buildings, actual minting operations began in early 1889. Some 60 million cash coins were produced in that year.

Follow-on orders continued for many years afterwards. Another 12 coining presses were ordered in 1904, along with a new rolling mill. There were even orders for such diverse items as lawn mowers and a two-wheel hand-drawn fire engine. The original order was probably the largest single order ever placed on a manufacturer of minting equipment; it was certainly Heatons' largest undertaking.

Hupeh Province   In 1889 Chang Chih-tung moved on to become Viceroy of the Hunan and Hupeh provinces, and in 1893 a silver mint was authorized for Hupeh. This first mint – at Wuchang – was furnished by Knape Heim of Magdeburg. A copper mint was next furnished to Wuchang in 1898 by the Ferracute Machine Co. of the U.S.A. Thereafter, these two mints drew heavily on Birmingham for both equipment and dies. In 1897 a complete rolling mill was supplied to the Wuchang Silver Mint, and in early 1898 various support equipment, plus steel dies for $1, 50c, 20c, and 10c were shipped to China. During the next seven years The Mint supplied nineteen coining presses for copper, and two coining presses for silver, plus a variety of other equipment to the two Wuchang mints.

At the point where the Han River joins the Yangtse, there are three large cities: Wuchang, Hanyang, and Hankow. All three cities boasted minting plants, the latter two having been furnished by The Mint. In all for Hankow, Birmingham sent out six coining presses and various other equipment between 1903 and 1913. A complete copper mint with twelve coining presses was shipped to the Hanyang Arsenal in early 1905.

Kiangsu Province   In 1894, Chang Chih-tung became Viceroy of Liang Kiang, an administrative entity made up of the provinces of Kiangsi, Kiangsu, and Anhwei (the latter two having previously been known as Kiangnan). As he had in Kwangtung, so Chang also authorized the establishment of a mint in Kiangsu – to be located in the capital city of Nanking. Kann notes the existence of four mints in the province, located in Nanking, Soochow, Chingkiang, and Shanghai (which only started operations in 1933).

The first was in Nanking, to which The Mint supplied in 1896 a complete plant suitable for an output of 1 million copper and 100,000 silver coins per day. This order was a very large one, involving an estimated 37 coining presses and all the complementary equipment. A major extension of the Nanking Mint took place in 1903, with Birmingham furnishing the full equipment requirements, including six additional coining presses. Then in 1905 a second major addition took place; a copper mint was set up in the Kiangnan Arsenal – fully equipped by Birmingham, including 45 coining presses. Taken together, these two mints – both operating in Nanking – made up a facility of about the same size as the Canton Mint, making it the second largest mint in the world.

In 1903 The Mint received an order for a minting plant for Soochow, consisting of two coining presses and the usual rolling mills, cutting-out presses, etc. The equipment order suggests that this plant was only used for copper coins.

In 1905 the third Kiangsu mint was set up at Chingkiang to produce copper coins. The equipment was all supplied by The Mint. At the outset it included only six coining presses, but the intention must have been for this to become a major copper facility, because in 1904 The Mint received an order for all the necessary gearing, shafting, belting, etc. sufficient for 54 coining presses. The records do not indicate, however, that orders for the additional 48 presses were ever placed on The Birmingham Mint.

Hunan Province An arsenal mint was already operating in Changsha in 1898 when The Mint received an order for a cutting-out press, an edge-marking machine, a hand press for dies, a sizing press, and matrices and punches for $1 and 50c coins. All of this equipment could be functional in any mint, regardless of who supplied the associated equipment. However, the Chinese Bulletin of 1925 indicates that the Changsha machinery all came from Great Britain, and so it is possible that The Mint also supplied the presses on some unrecorded previous order.

Shensi Province On 17 March 1899, an order was booked for a complete silver mint, including one coining press and matrices and punches for 5 denominations of silver coins. The plant left England marked for Sian, but it never went into operation there. What happened to the equipment is not known. Wright[4] thinks it possible that it was diverted to Wuchang.

---

[4] R. N. J. Wright, "Some Further Information on the Origins of the Milled Coinage of Imperial China", *Numismatic Chronicle*, 7th Series, Vol. XIV, 1974.

Another reasonable possibility is that the machinery actually arrived in Shensi as ordered, but was destroyed by the Boxers, whose destructive drive to eliminate the hated foreigners really began in the Shensi Province in 1899.

The Imperial City Perhaps the whole story of the Peking Mint will never be known. Certainly the fact of The Birmingham Mint's involvement only adds to, rather than lessens, the mystery.

The sequence of events appears to have been as follows. In 1899 the Government at Peking ordered the new Hangchow Mint, which had only recently been activated with German machinery, dismantled and shipped to Peking. It was reassembled as the Imperial Mint in Peking, but before any business coinage could take place the mint was destroyed as a result of the Boxer uprising. All of this action took place between late 1899 and August 1900, with the actual destruction occurring between June and mid-August.

Records in The Birmingham Mint reveal that on 6 March 1900 Sir Chihchen Lofengluh (the Chinese Minister to the Court of St. James) signed a contract with The Mint for the supply of minting equipment to the Imperial Mint at Peking. The contract price of £3502, of which half was paid when the contract was signed, covered a steam engine and six rolling mills, ten lathes (altered on 6 June 1900 to sixteen lathes), one No. 4 coining press, and miscellaneous supplies. Shipment was required by 6 August 1900, and the contract provided penalties for late delivery. Although this material would not have arrived in Peking until after the Imperial Mint was destroyed, the known circumstances strongly support the conclusion that shipment did take place on time. Where the machinery actually went can only be guessed. One possibility is that it was placed in storage in Tientsin, and used when an Imperial Mint was reestablished there in 1902.

Chehkiang Province Kann notes that Chehkiang produced silver 10 and 20 cent pieces in 1896–7, probably from an arsenal mint in Hangchow. Their first regular mint, however, was constructed in Hangchow with German equipment (see above) in 1898, but was shipped to Peking in 1899. In 1902 an order was placed with The Birmingham Mint for complete mint machinery for an output of 50,000 silver or copper coins per day, for shipment to Hangchow. This would have required two coining presses, in addition to all the ancillary equipment. A second mint was erected in Hangchow in 1905, but the machinery did not come from Birmingham.

Anhwei Province A mint started up in Anking in 1897, only to be dismantled and shipped to Wuchang in 1899. A new mint for copper coins was installed in 1902, to which The Mint furnished two rolling mills in 1903. An addition, involving complete mint equipment, was ordered from

Minting Equipment

Plate XVI. *Heaton presses newly installed at the Royal Mint, Bangkok, 1903.*

Birmingham in June 1904 and shipped out the same year. The Orderbook record fails to indicate how many coining presses were involved, but considering the subsequent spare parts orders, it was probably in the order of six to ten presses.

Other China In addition to all the foregoing rather clearly defined orders, there were a number of other orders for which the existing records do not identify the destinations, but which in total add up to an impressive amount of machinery. The major ones are as follows:

14 May 1903   5 coining presses and 2 cutting-out presses for 10 cash.
22 June 1904   12 coining presses for 28 mm 10 cash.
21 December 1904   5 coining presses for 28 mm plain-edge 10 cash.
17 January 1905   3 coining presses, tooled for 10 cash.

The Mint's very extensive participation in the modernization of Chinese minting was probably due primarily to two factors. First, the successful operation of the Canton Mint, China's first and largest modern mint, provided ample evidence of the quality of the Birmingham equipment. Second, The Mint was fortunate in having an aggressive and energetic representative on the scene in China. On 2 January 1893, and again on 22 April 1905, The Mint signed an agency agreement with the firm of Buchheister & Co. of Shanghai making them their agent for all equipment sales in China – with the exception of sales to the Canton Mint. These agreements included having John Palmer Junior & Co. of London as sub-agent. Thus all orders went from Buchheister to John Palmer to Birmingham. All equipment carried nameplates with the name of Buchheister & Co. in Chinese characters, presumably in place of the manufacturer's name. It turned out to be a very profitable arrangement for both.

Note: For additional information on the Chinese mints in this period, see the excellent articles by Commander Wright referenced in the China section of the Catalogue.

Summary As is now evident, The Birmingham Mint was a major source of minting equipment in the period between 1864 – when it accepted its first commercial contract from the Government of Burma – and about 1910 – by which time the huge orders from China had dwindled down to a trickle. Throughout this period The Mint actually manufactured in its own shops the coining presses, cutting-out machines, die presses, and edge-marking machines which it used and sold to other mints. Most of the other equipment, such as boilers, steam engines, and rolling mills, was subcontracted out to various other Birmingham firms.

In total, The Mint manufactured over 355 coining presses (more than 270 for China alone). This compares with the slightly more than 200 machines made by the Uhlhorn company, and the 108 presses made by both Boulton and Watt & Co. One wonders why The Mint, with the dominance it achieved towards the turn of the century, elected to quit this line of products. The answer probably lies in the fact that the technology was neglected; better presses were designed and built by other firms such as Taylor & Challen, while The Mint made little effort to advance the art themselves. Possibly they considered this only a passing sideline to the traditional minting business. From an outsider's viewpoint, however, it does appear that an opportunity was lost.

Catalogue

Coinage Issues of The Birmingham Mint

As evidenced by the following compilation, the official coinage produced by Ralph Heaton & Sons and its successor company The Mint, Birmingham, Ltd. (now The Birmingham Mint Ltd.) covers an amazing range of coin types, metals, and countries of the world. In its one hundred and thirty-odd years of coinage history, this private mint has struck coins for most of the countries of the British Empire, and for other nations in all continents. Its product has flowed through all the world's channels of trade, in quantity and geographical extent second to the output of no other private mint, and exceeding that of many governments.

This listing does not attempt to cover the whole range of Heaton numismatic issues. Specifically omitted, except for a very few issues of broad interest, are tokens, medals, and counters. Specifically included is the whole of their coinage output through 1970; that is, all money issues struck for provisional or fully constituted governments, including those issues that may have been recalled and melted down. Also included are patterns, die trials, specimen strikes, mules, and off-metal strikes of regular issues, so far as these are known to the author.

Some explanation of the elements of the listing is in order:

TYPE NUMBER – Each distinct type is identified by an assigned number which is unique to that particular type. If a specimen cannot be categorically attributed to THE MINT (as, for instance, where identical pieces were also struck by other mints), the assigned type number is followed by an "x". Thus number BZ1x (Brazil 100 Reis 1901) is so designated because identical pieces were also struck in the Paris and Vienna Mints, making it impossible to attribute an individual specimen to THE MINT. Other characters used with the type number are "m" for mule, "p" for pattern, "s" for specimen strike, and "a", "b", or "c" for various off-metal strikes.

DATE – The *italicized* date in the listing is the date which actually appears on the coin. In many cases, an issue was struck in several different years with the same date. Where this has occurred, the year of striking is identified by a date preceded by the letter "m", signifying "*m*inted in". In those many cases where the coin date is in other than the Christian Era system, the actual date is shown, preceded by letters indicating the dating system, and followed by the nearest Christian Era date in parentheses. A typical case is the IR3 entry in the Iran listing:

	AH*1337*(1919)
IR3	m1919
IR3	m1920

Thus "AH" indicates the Mohammedan Calendar, "*1337*" the date on the coin (١٣٣٧), "1919" that the equivalent Christian Era date is AD1919, and "m1919" and "m1920" that the coin was struck in both years with the same date "*1337*" on the coin. Where the Christian Era date is not in parentheses (see Egypt EG31: AH*1338/1920*), both dates appear on the coin.

DENOMINATION – The name of the denomination is intended to be consistent with that which appears on the coin, or is the most widely accepted English transliteration thereof. The quantity is usually shown in Arabic numerals, even though the coin may bear words instead of numbers. Thus CH1 (Chile) is listed as a "$\frac{1}{2}$ Centavo", although the denomination on the coin actually reads "Medio Centavo".

MINTMARK – The intent is to show accurately in the Catalogue the mintmark in essentially the same form as it appears on the coin.

METAL – As with the mintmark listing, the intent is to show the metal content of the coin as accurately as possible. In doing so, the following convention has been employed except in those few cases where the exact metal content is not known.

METAL LISTING	ACTUAL METAL CONTENT
Copper	Unalloyed copper
Bronze	95% copper, 4% tin, 1% zinc
Bronze$_1$	95$\frac{1}{2}$% copper, 3% tin, 1$\frac{1}{2}$% zinc
Bronze$_2$	96% copper, 0% tin, 4% zinc
Bronze$_3$	96% copper, 2% tin, 2% zinc
Bronze$_4$	97% copper, $\frac{1}{2}$% tin, 2$\frac{1}{2}$% zinc
Bronze$_5$	95% copper, $\frac{1}{2}$% tin, 4$\frac{1}{2}$% zinc
Bronze$_6$	95% copper, 0% tin, 5% zinc (Gilding metal)
Brass	70% copper, 0% tin, 30% zinc
Tin–Brass	79% copper, 1% tin, 20% zinc
Nickel–Brass	79% copper, 0% tin, 20% zinc, 1% nickel
Nickel	Unalloyed nickel
Copper–Nickel	75% copper, 25% nickel (Cupro-nickel)
Copper–Nickel$_1$	80% copper, 20% nickel (Cupro-nickel)
0.XXX Silver	XXX parts silver, 1000 – XXX parts copper
0.250 Silver$_1$	25% silver, 70% copper, 5% manganese
0.500 Silver$_1$	50% silver, 40% copper, 5% nickel, 5% zinc
0.XXX Gold	XXX parts gold, 1000 – XXX parts copper
Aluminium	96$\frac{1}{2}$% aluminium, 3$\frac{1}{2}$% magnesium

MINTAGE – The basic mintage data have been derived from the British Mint Reports (BMRs), which have been double-checked against existing records at The

Birmingham Mint. In many cases the BMR's year of mintage does not correspond to the coin dates, and so the BMR data require interpretation. Since the main purpose of this book is to record the history of The Birmingham Mint, it is thought appropriate to show more mintage details than if the focus were mainly on coin types. Accordingly, where a single coin date was struck in two or more years, the individual year mintages are shown, rather than the more usual consolidated figures.

REFERENCE – Here are shown the type numbers as assigned in several widely-used English language references. Specifically, Friedberg[1] numbers are shown for gold coins, and Yeoman[2] numbers (as modified by Krause[3]) for most others. All of these are by the kind permission of the publishers.

ILLUSTRATIONS – The intent here is to illustrate every different obverse and reverse design struck by THE MINT. Where two or more denominations bear identical designs, only one photograph is shown. Except where otherwise indicated, the photographs are of coins in THE MINT collection. A few photographs are regrettably missing.

The list which follows is probably neither complete nor entirely accurate, even though both have been sought-after objectives. Where the data are known to be in question, it is so indicated. This occurs particularly where estimates are made in the absence of source data, or where the available source data are internally inconsistent or otherwise doubtful. The author will welcome having any needed corrections brought to his attention.

[1] Robert Friedberg, *Gold Coins of the World*, 3rd Edition (New York, The Coin and Currency Institute, Inc., 1971).
[2] R. S. Yeoman, *A Catalog of Modern World Coins*, 12th Edition (Racine, Wisc., Western Publishing Co., Inc.).
[3] Krause and Mishler, *Standard Catalog of World Coins*, 7th (1981) Edition (Iola, Wisconsin, Krause Publications, 1980).

Coinage Issues of The Birmingham Mint

No.   Date   Denomination   Mintmark   Metal   Mintage   Ref.

ABYSSINIA – *see* Ethiopia

AFGHANISTAN When the Amir of Afghanistan decided in the 1890s to establish a modern minting facility at Kabul, The Birmingham Mint apparently made a bid for the equipment order, and in the process produced a sample to demonstrate their capabilities. It is a machine-struck near-duplicate of the hand-made rupees of the period (Craig No. 977).

AF1

AH*1304*(1886)
AF1s   m1886?   1 Rupee   None   Silver   Unknown   YA10

ALGERIA This was the first coinage of the Republic of Algeria, a North African country which gained its independence from France in 1962.

AL4

AH*1383/1964*

AL1	m1964	1 Centime	None	Aluminium	35,000,000	Y4
AL2	m1964	2 Centimes	None	Aluminium	50,000,000	Y5
AL3	m1964	5 Centimes	None	Aluminium	40,000,000	Y6
AL4	m1964	1 Dinar	None	Copper–Nickel	15,000,000	Y10

ANGOLA The following issues are the only pure nickel coinages of either Portugal or its possessions. This coinage order was probably placed with THE MINT because the Lisbon Mint was unprepared to strike nickel coins.

AN1

No.	Date	Denomination	Mintmark	Metal	Mintage	Ref.
AN1	*1922*	50 Centavos	None	Nickel	6,000,000	Y17
AN1	*1923*	50 Centavos	None	Nickel	4,780,000	Y17
AN1	m1924	50 Centavos	None	Nickel	1,220,000	Y17

At 10.5 grams, these were the largest nickel coins so far struck by any mint. They were struck "... under the direction of the Mond Nickel Company Limited." of Birmingham, per the 1922 BMR.

ARABIA – *see* SAUDI ARABIA

ARGENTINA (Buenos Aires)   The evidence for crediting this Provincial issue to Heatons is to be found in a letter in THE MINT files. It is dated 1 January 1861, is addressed to Messrs Ralph Heaton & Sons, and reads as follows:

"We have received your favor of yesterday, enclosing a specimen of the coin which you have recently been executing for us, and which will doubtless be satisfactory to the Buenos Ayres Government. We would thank you to have them carefully packed and addressed 'Banco y Casa de Moneda' Buenos Ayres and forwarded to Messr Dunlop Schoales & Co of Southampton."

It was signed by a London representative of the Provincial Government. No records have been located to disclose the size of the order.

AR1	*1860*	2 Reales	None	Copper	Unknown	C53
AR1	*1861*	2 Reales	None	Copper	Unknown	C53

AUSTRALIA   Like Canada and many other countries, Australia's economy initially subsisted on a diet of tokens and non-indigenous coins. The Heaton mint produced a large – but as yet not completely defined – variety of tokens at the instigation of the Australian mercantile establishment. A trial listing of these tokens will be found in Appendix VI. Not until 1912, however, did THE MINT participate in the authorized coinage of the country.

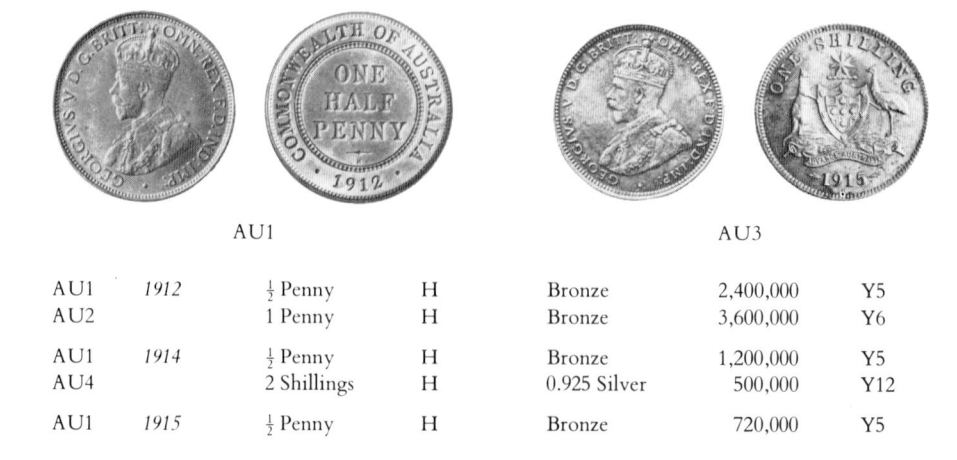

AU1   AU3

AU1	*1912*	½ Penny	H	Bronze	2,400,000	Y5
AU2		1 Penny	H	Bronze	3,600,000	Y6
AU1	*1914*	½ Penny	H	Bronze	1,200,000	Y5
AU4		2 Shillings	H	0.925 Silver	500,000	Y12
AU1	*1915*	½ Penny	H	Bronze	720,000	Y5

No.	Date	Denomination	Mintmark	Metal	Mintage	Ref.
AU2	1915	1 Penny	H	Bronze	1,320,000	Y6
AU3		1 Shilling	H	0.925 Silver	326,000	Y11
AU3	m1916	1 Shilling	H	0.925 Silver	174,000	Y11
AU4		2 Shillings	H	0.925 Silver	750,000	Y12

AU5

No.	Date	Denomination	Mintmark	Metal	Mintage	Ref.
AU5	1951 m1952	½ Penny	PL	Bronze$_1$	5,040,000	Y21

In the 1951 BMR the Deputy Master wrote of the PL mark: "This is a mintmark. The same letters were used ... for the same purpose on coins struck at London during the Roman Occupation. No contemporary expanded version has yet been found and I will not venture to judge between the various suggestions as to the full form. Prima (officina) Londinii, Londiniensis or Londinio – the first workshop of London, the first London workshop or the first workshop at London – all have well-qualified champions. Some suggest that P is an abbreviation of pecunia; others favor percussa. Whatever be the extended form, however, the significance was the same in 1951 as in Roman times, that the coins were struck in a mint in London." That may have been true in 1951, but when coins of the same design and date, indistinguishable from the London coins, were struck in Birmingham in 1952, the PL lost its claim to being a mintmark – at least on the halfpenny issue.

AUSTRIA – *see* Maria Theresa Thaler

BAHAMAS Aside from an 1806 penny, the first distinctive issue for the Bahamas was struck in the British Royal Mint in 1966. The Birmingham Mint assisted the Royal Mint in the production of the 1969 issue.

BA1

No.	Date	Denomination	Mintmark	Metal	Mintage	Ref.
BA1x	1969 m1970	1 Cent	None	Nickel–Brass	1,000,000	Y1

The cent was reduced in diameter in 1970. The larger version was struck by

92 *Catalogue*

No.	Date	Denomination	Mintmark	Metal	Mintage	Ref.

THE MINT, and the smaller by The Franklin Mint. Arnold Machin was the designer of this series.

Belgian Congo (Now ZAIRE)   During World War I the Belgian Government functioned from a base at Le Havre, and while there ordered coins from THE MINT for use in the Belgian Congo. At that time the Brussels Mint was in German hands. The great scarcity of these issues suggests that many were never placed in circulation.

BC2

No.	Date	Denomination	Mintmark	Metal	Mintage	Ref.
BC1	1917 m1918	5 Centimes	None	Copper–Nickel	1,000,000	Y17
BC2	m1918	10 Centimes	None	Copper–Nickel	500,000	Y18
BC1x	1919	5 Centimes	None	Copper–Nickel	2,000,000	Y17
BC1x	m1920	5 Centimes	None	Copper–Nickel	1,000,000	Y17
BC2x		10 Centimes	None	Copper–Nickel	1,000,000	Y18
BC2x	m1920	10 Centimes	None	Copper–Nickel	500,000	Y18
BC1x	1921	5 Centimes	None	Copper–Nickel	3,000,000	Y17
BC2x		10 Centimes	None	Copper–Nickel	3,000,000	Y18

BELGIUM

BG1

No.	Date	Denomination	Mintmark	Metal	Mintage	Ref.
BG1	1914	1 Franc	None	0.835 Silver	10,563,162	Y34
BG1	1917	1 Franc	None	0.835 Silver	8,540,000	Y34
BG1	1918	1 Franc	None	0.835 Silver	1,469,220	Y34

The 1917 and 1918 BMRs record the above war-time issues, and the Royal Mint of Belgium, by letter dated 28 June 1973, states:

> "I have the honour of informing you that the pieces of Belgium money of 1 franc in silver 83.5%, coined by THE MINT of Birmingham during the 1914–1918 war, were ordered by the Belgium Government installed in Le Havre. These pieces were coined for use by the Belgians residing in territory not

Coinage Issues of The Birmingham Mint 93

No.	Date	Denomination	Mintmark	Metal	Mintage	Ref.

occupied by German troops. The pieces made at Birmingham were identical to those made by the Brussels Mint before 17 August 1914, they bore no distinctive marks. . . . ten million pieces dated 1917 were coined during the years 1917 and 1918, but it is doubtful that they entered circulation. The proportion of 50% of the coins in the French legend and 50% in the Flemish legend was respected for these coinings. Three million of these Belgium coins were sent to the Congo for local needs. . . ."

The author concludes that the 1917 and 1918 francs never entered circulation, including any that may have been sent to the Congo. Both dates exist in the cabinet of THE MINT, but officials at Birmingham are also under the impression that almost all of the total coinage was melted down. For additional information, see "Royal Mint [*sic*] Strikes Belgium Franc," *World Coins*, XI (June 1974), p. 1214.

BELIZE – *see* British Honduras

BOLIVIA The Potosi Mint struck almost all of Bolivia's silver and gold coins, but the requirements for other metals were farmed out, usually to the Paris Mint but occasionally to others such as THE MINT.

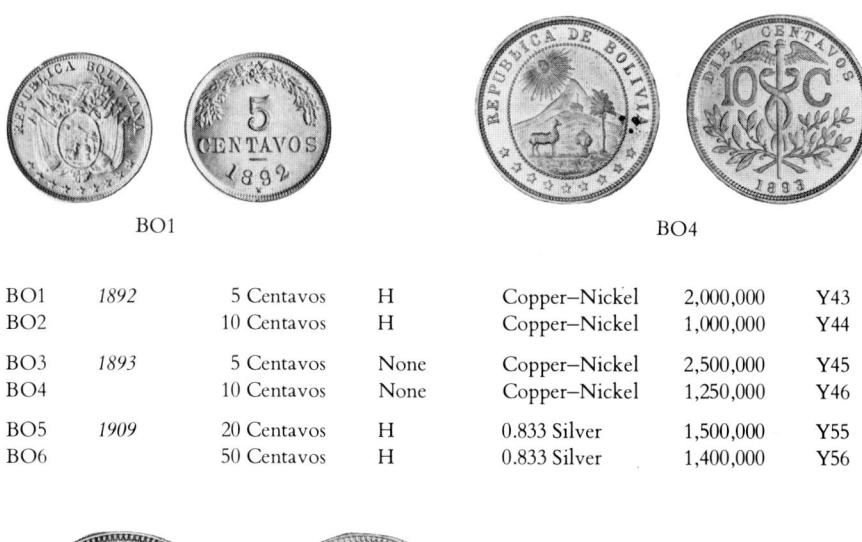

BO1

BO4

BO1	*1892*	5 Centavos	H	Copper–Nickel	2,000,000	Y43
BO2		10 Centavos	H	Copper–Nickel	1,000,000	Y44
BO3	*1893*	5 Centavos	None	Copper–Nickel	2,500,000	Y45
BO4		10 Centavos	None	Copper–Nickel	1,250,000	Y46
BO5	*1909*	20 Centavos	H	0.833 Silver	1,500,000	Y55
BO6		50 Centavos	H	0.833 Silver	1,400,000	Y56

BO6

BO8

No.	Date	Denomination	Mintmark	Metal	Mintage	Ref.

Interestingly, these were the only Bolivia silver issues minted by other than the Potosi Mint, as well as Bolivia's last silver coinage. This country thus became the first independent American nation permanently to desert precious metal coinage.

No.	Date	Denomination	Mintmark	Metal	Mintage	Ref.
BO3	1918	5 Centavos	None	Copper–Nickel	530,000	Y45
BO4		10 Centavos	None	Copper–Nickel	1,335,000	Y46
BO3	1919	5 Centavos	None	Copper–Nickel	4,370,000	Y45
BO4		10 Centavos	None	Copper–Nickel	6,165,000	Y46
	1951					
BO7	m1952	1 Boliviano	H	Bronze$_1$	14,540,000	Y62
BO7	m1953	1 Boliviano	H	Bronze$_1$	460,000	Y62
BO8	m1952	5 Bolivianos	H	Bronze$_1$	8,962,500	Y63
BO8	m1953	5 Bolivianos	H	Bronze$_1$	6,037,500	Y63

The issues of 1892, 1909, and 1951 were all one-year types, but the type of 1893 was also struck by the Paris Mint from 1895 to 1909, and finally again by THE MINT in 1918 and 1919. The Birmingham and Paris issues are differentiated by the presence of the Paris Mint privy marks on all of their issues. The obverse designs of the 1951 coinage were produced by Mr. T. H. Paget.

BRAZIL A new coinage was commenced in 1901, a large issue of copper–nickel pieces designed by the French artist M. Tasset. The design has a female head on the obverse, representing the Brazilian Republic, and the arms of Brazil with laurel branch on the reverse. In addition to the Birmingham coinage listed below, other mints participated as follows: Paris Mint – 27 million pieces; Vienna Mint – 20 million pieces; Brussels Mint – 40 million pieces; all over a two-year span (1901–2).

BZ3

No.	Date	Denomination	Mintmark	Metal	Mintage	Ref.
	MCMI					
BZ1x	m1901	100 Reis	None	Copper–Nickel	15,764,000	Y12
BZ1x	m1902	100 Reis	None	Copper–Nickel	11,000	Y12
BZ2x	m1901	200 Reis	None	Copper–Nickel	8,910,000	Y13
BZ2x	m1902	200 Reis	None	Copper–Nickel	3,715,000	Y13
BZ3x	m1901	400 Reis	None	Copper–Nickel	4,260,000	Y14
BZ3x	m1902	400 Reis	None	Copper–Nickel	1,271,250	Y14

British Honduras (Now BELIZE) These coins would have been struck in the Royal Mint but for the extremely heavy demands in those years which made it necessary to contract the job out to THE MINT.

Coinage Issues of The Birmingham Mint 95

| No. | Date | Denomination | Mintmark | Metal | Mintage | Ref. |

BH1 rev.   BH2

BH1	1912	1 Cent	H	Bronze	50,000	Y10
BH2		5 Cents	H	Copper–Nickel	20,000	Y12
BH3	1916	1 Cent	H	Bronze	125,000	Y11
BH2		5 Cents	H	Copper–Nickel	20,000	Y12

BH3

The one cent was reduced in diameter slightly between the 1912 and 1916 issues, it being felt in the Colony that the old bronze cents were inconveniently large.

British North Borneo (Now SABAH state of MALAYSIA)   In January 1878 an Austrian, Baron von Overbeck, and an Englishman, Alfred Dent, acquired by grant from the Sultan of Sulu rights to a large area of northeast Borneo. According to an analysis and tentative conclusions by Major Pridmore,[4] a first step in planning for the administration of the territory was to approach Heatons regarding a distinctive coinage. These pieces, specimens of which are in THE MINT collection (two also in Major Pridmore's collection), were apparently the first patterns prepared in response to their request.

BN1   BN2

[4]F. Pridmore, "Are They Pattern Coins for British North Borneo?", *The Numismatic Circular*, September 1979, pp. 178–80.

No.	Date	Denomination	Mintmark	Metal	Mintage	Ref.
	AH1295Yr2 (1879?)					
BN1p	m1879?	¼ Cent	None	Bronze	Unknown	–
BN2p	m1879?	½ Cent	None	Bronze	Unknown	–
BN3p	m1879?	1 Cent	None	Bronze	Unknown	–

BN3

These pieces are 28.9 mm 9.3 grams, 23.2 mm 4.6 grams, and 18.1 mm 2.3 grams respectively. They correspond to similar denominations then current in Sarawak and Straits Settlements, and relate to the Mexican Dollar then circulating in the same general area.

Early in 1879 Baron von Overbeck withdrew from the enterprise, and Dent and other London associates then sought support from the British Government. Great Britain formally recognized their rights in 1880, as well as the consequent formation of the British North Borneo Provisional Association Ltd., in March 1881. A Royal Charter was granted this company on 7 November 1881, and in May 1882 it became the British North Borneo Company. In anticipation of this, the company apparently placed another order on Heatons for a new pattern.

	No Date					
BN5p	m1882?	1 Cent	H	Copper	Unknown	–

A proof specimen of this uniface pattern appeared in the NASCA Wayte Raymond auction of 14 August 1978 as Lot No. 766. It was described as follows: "Obverse of regular issue (arms with native supporters), except no date. H mintmark in normal position. The reverse is blank, with a thin raised edge. Double thickness."

This administrative arrangement continued until Borneo was made a Crown Colony in July 1946, it being at that time the last British territory administered by a chartered company. While so administered, the territory obtained all its coinage from THE MINT. The early issues bore the name BRITISH NORTH BORNEO CO.

| BN5 | 1882 | 1 Cent | H | Copper | 2,000,000 | Y2 |

A 5 July 1883 letter to Heatons from the Chairman of the North Borneo Co. states: "I have much pleasure in attesting to the excellence of your workmanship in executing the details of the design supplied you by this Company for a Copper Coinage...."

| BN5 | 1884 | 1 Cent | H | Copper | 2,000,000 | Y2 |

Coinage Issues of The Birmingham Mint

No.	Date	Denomination	Mintmark	Metal	Mintage	Ref.

BN5

No.	Date	Denomination	Mintmark	Metal	Mintage	Ref.
BN4	1885	½ Cent	H	Copper	500,000	Y1
BN5		1 Cent	H	Copper	1,750,000	Y2

The above mintage figures disagree with those in the 1885 BRM, but are in accord with THE MINT's Orderbook record for that year.

BN4	1886	½ Cent	H	Copper	1,000,000	Y1
BN5		1 Cent	H	Copper	5,000,000	Y2
BN4	1887	½ Cent	H	Copper	500,000	Y1
BN5		1 Cent	H	Copper	6,000,000	Y2
BN5	1888	1 Cent	H	Copper	6,000,000	Y2
BN5	1889	1 Cent	H	Copper	9,000,000	Y2
BN5	1890	1 Cent	H	Copper	8,002,700	Y2
BN4	1891	½ Cent	H	Copper	2,000,000	Y1
BN5		1 Cent	H	Copper	3,000,000	Y2
BN5	1894	1 Cent	H	Copper	1,000,000	Y2
BN5	1896	1 Cent	H	Copper	1,000,000	Y2

Starting in 1903 a change in the coinage occurred, involving new denominations in new metals, and a new legend reading STATE OF NORTH BORNEO.

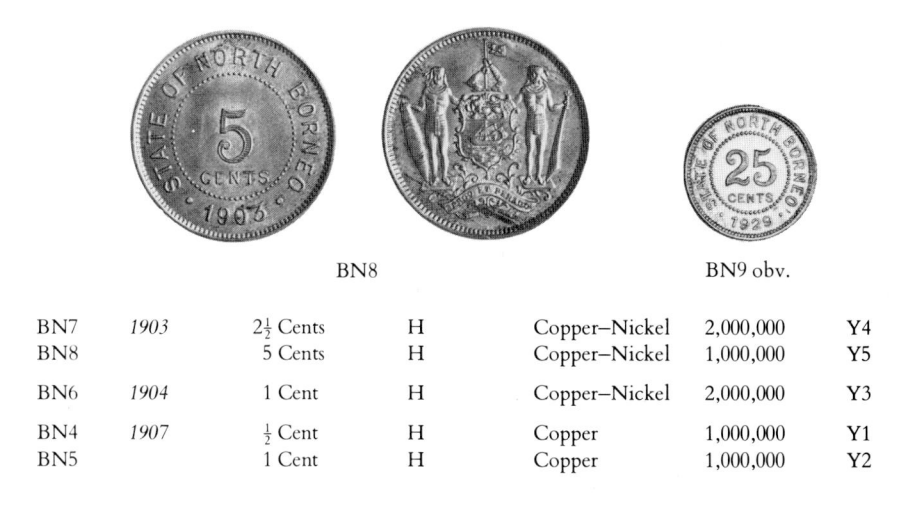

BN8   BN9 obv.

BN7	1903	2½ Cents	H	Copper–Nickel	2,000,000	Y4
BN8		5 Cents	H	Copper–Nickel	1,000,000	Y5
BN6	1904	1 Cent	H	Copper–Nickel	2,000,000	Y3
BN4	1907	½ Cent	H	Copper	1,000,000	Y1
BN5		1 Cent	H	Copper	1,000,000	Y2

No.	Date	Denomination	Mintmark	Metal	Mintage	Ref.

The author could not learn why the above obsolete design was used in 1907.

No.	Date	Denomination	Mintmark	Metal	Mintage	Ref.
BN7	1920	2½ Cents	H	Copper–Nickel	280,000	Y4
BN8		5 Cents	H	Copper–Nickel	100,000	Y5
BN6	1921	1 Cent	H	Copper–Nickel	1,000,000	Y3
BN8		5 Cents	H	Copper–Nickel	500,000	Y5
BN8	1927 m1926	5 Cents	H	Copper–Nickel	150,000	Y5
BN8	1928	5 Cents	H	Copper–Nickel	150,000	Y5
BN9	1929	25 Cents	H	0.500 Silver	400,000	Y6

This was the only silver issue ever struck for British North Borneo. The larger denomination — another first — may have resulted from the euphoria which preceded the economic Depression of the 1930s.

No.	Date	Denomination	Mintmark	Metal	Mintage	Ref.
BN6	1935	1 Cent	H	Copper–Nickel	1,000,000	Y3
BN6	1938	1 Cent	H	Copper–Nickel	1,000,000	Y3
BN8		5 Cents	H	Copper–Nickel	500,000	Y5
BN8	1940	5 Cents	H	Copper–Nickel	500,000	Y5
BN6	1941	1 Cent	H	Copper–Nickel	1,000,000	Y3
BN8		5 Cents	H	Copper–Nickel	1,000,000	Y5

The 5 Cents type of 1941 had been struck by THE MINT since 1903, making it the second longest run of a single type struck by THE MINT. Only the Guernsey types were struck over a longer period.

North Borneo became a Crown Colony in 1946. No distinctive coinage was issued for this administrative entity until 1956 when a common coinage for Malaya and British Borneo (q.v.) was struck. In 1963 North Borneo joined with thirteen other states to form Malaysia (q.v.), for whom THE MINT continued to produce coins.

British West Africa The West African Currency Board provided a single coinage for the Colonies of Nigeria, Gold Coast, Gambia, and Sierra Leone beginning in 1907. For several years the coinage bore the legend NIGERIA BRITISH WEST AFRICA. The last such issue was the one-year type of 1911, the whole of which was produced by THE MINT.

No.	Date	Denomination	Mintmark	Metal	Mintage	Ref.
BW1	1911	1/10 Penny	H	Copper–Nickel	7,200,000	Y4
BW2		½ Penny	H	Copper–Nickel	3,360,000	Y5
BW3		1 Penny	H	Copper–Nickel	1,920,000	Y6

The Gold Coast and Dependencies Coinage Order of 1912 established a common subsidiary coinage for the West African colonies, implemented by the omission of NIGERIA in the new coin legends. Although the 1912 coinage was entirely by THE MINT, later various other mints were also used, including the Royal Mint, J. R. Gaunt & Sons of Birmingham, King's Norton Metal Company of Birmingham, and the Pretoria S.A. Mint.

Coinage Issues of The Birmingham Mint

No.	Date	Denomination	Mintmark	Metal	Mintage	Ref.

BW6

BW8

No.	Date	Denomination	Mintmark	Metal	Mintage	Ref.
BW4	1912	1/10 Penny	H	Copper–Nickel	10,800,000	Y7
BW5		½ Penny	H	Copper–Nickel	3,120,000	Y8
BW6		1 Penny	H	Copper–Nickel	1,560,000	Y9

Late in 1912 the West Africa Currency Board approved designs for a distinctive silver coinage to replace Imperial silver previously circulating. The tree on the reverse of the florin and shilling is the Oil Palm (*Elaeis quineensis*) (see next page).

No.	Date	Denomination	Mintmark	Metal	Mintage	Ref.
BW4	1913	1/10 Penny	H	Copper–Nickel	1,080,000	Y7
BW5		½ Penny	H	Copper–Nickel	216,000	Y8
BW6		1 Penny	H	Copper–Nickel	144,000	Y9
BW7		3 Pence	H	0.925 Silver	496,000	Y14
BW8		6 Pence	H	0.925 Silver	400,000	Y15
BW9		1 Shilling	H	0.925 Silver	3,540,000	Y16
BW10		2 Shillings	H	0.925 Silver	1,176,000	Y17
BW4	1914	1/10 Penny	H	Copper–Nickel	20,088,000	Y7
BW5		½ Penny	H	Copper–Nickel	585,600	Y8
BW6		1 Penny	H	Copper–Nickel	72,000	Y9
BW7		3 Pence	H	0.925 Silver	1,560,000	Y14
BW8		6 Pence	H	0.925 Silver	952,000	Y15
BW9		1 Shilling	H	0.925 Silver	11,292,000	Y16
BW10		2 Shillings	H	0.925 Silver	635,000	Y17
BW10	m1915	2 Shillings	H	0.925 Silver	2,000	Y17

In addition, 3,360,000 halfpennies with a K mintmark were struck by King's Norton (see note under the 1914 issue for the East Africa & Uganda Protectorates). Also, the Royal Mint struck a large quantity of pence, plus smaller issues of florins, shillings, halfpence, and tenth pence in 1914.

No.	Date	Denomination	Mintmark	Metal	Mintage	Ref.
BW4	1915	1/10 Penny	H	Copper–Nickel	10,032,000	Y7
BW5		½ Penny	H	Copper–Nickel	3,576,720	Y8
BW6		1 Penny	H	Copper–Nickel	3,295,200	Y9
BW7		3 Pence	H	0.925 Silver	270,000	Y14
BW9		1 Shilling	H	0.925 Silver	254,000	Y16
BW10	m1916	2 Shillings	H	0.925 Silver	65,654	Y17
BW4	1916	1/10 Penny	H	Copper–Nickel	480,000	Y7
BW5		½ Penny	H	Copper–Nickel	4,045,680	Y8
BW6		1 Penny	H	Copper–Nickel	3,460,800	Y9
BW7		3 Pence	H	0.925 Silver	820,000	Y14
BW8		6 Pence	H	0.925 Silver	400,000	Y15
BW9		1 Shilling	H	0.925 Silver	11,837,732	Y16

100   *Catalogue*

No.	Date	Denomination	Mintmark	Metal	Mintage	Ref.

BW9   BW16 obv.

No.	Date	Denomination	Mintmark	Metal	Mintage	Ref.
BW10	1916	2 Shillings	H	0.925 Silver	9,824,480	Y17
BW4	1917	1/10 Penny	H	Copper–Nickel	9,384,000	Y7
BW5		½ Penny	H	Copper–Nickel	213,600	Y8
BW6		1 Penny	H	Copper–Nickel	444,000	Y9
BW7		3 Pence	H	0.925 Silver	3,600,000	Y14
BW8		6 Pence	H	0.925 Silver	2,400,000	Y15
BW9		1 Shilling	H	0.925 Silver	15,018,000	Y16
BW10		2 Shillings	H	0.925 Silver	1,059,000	Y17
BW5	1918	½ Penny	H	Copper–Nickel	489,600	Y8
BW6		1 Penny	H	Copper–Nickel	993,600	Y9
BW7		3 Pence	H	0.925 Silver	1,722,000	Y14
BW8		6 Pence	H	0.925 Silver	1,160,000	Y15
BW9		1 Shilling	H	0.925 Silver	9,486,000	Y16
BW10		2 Shillings	H	0.925 Silver	7,294,000	Y17

With the single exception of the 1914 issue, all West African coinage through 1918 was produced by THE MINT. Thereafter, other mints also participated.

No.	Date	Denomination	Mintmark	Metal	Mintage	Ref.
BW4	1919	1/10 Penny	H	Copper–Nickel	912,000	Y7
BW5		½ Penny	H	Copper–Nickel	4,950,480	Y8
BW6		1 Penny	H	Copper–Nickel	21,864,000	Y9
BW7		3 Pence	H	0.925 Silver	16,780,000	Y14
BW7	m1920	3 Pence	H	0.925 Silver	3,046,000	Y14
BW8		6 Pence	H	0.925 Silver	7,240,000	Y15
BW8	m1920	6 Pence	H	0.925 Silver	1,436,000	Y15
BW9		1 Shilling	H	0.925 Silver	992,045	Y16
BW10		2 Shillings	H	0.925 Silver	8,155,000	Y17
BW10	m1920	2 Shillings	H	0.925 Silver	2,711,000	Y17

On 9 February 1920 Orders in Council legalized new alloy metal coins of 79% copper, 20% zinc, and 1% tin, which could be called tin–brass. Large quantities of alloy florins, shillings, sixpence, and threepence were struck in 1920 by King's Norton. In addition, J. R. Gaunt & Sons, using old-fashioned drop stamps (stamping machines operated by ropes and pulleys, and using gravity for applying the stamping pressure), produced 16,000 1920 alloy shillings before returning the order to the Royal Mint. This was their only coinage venture.

On 25 March 1920 Orders in Council authorized the issue of silver coins of 500 millesimal fineness; all were produced by THE MINT, as follows.

Coinage Issues of The Birmingham Mint

No.	Date	Denomination	Mintmark	Metal	Mintage	Ref.
BW4	1920	1/10 Penny	H	Copper–Nickel	1,560,000	Y7
BW5		½ Penny	H	Copper–Nickel	26,019,360	Y8
BW5	m1921	½ Penny	H	Copper–Nickel	265,200	Y8
BW6		1 Penny	H	Copper–Nickel	37,533,600	Y9
BW6	m1921	1 Penny	H	Copper–Nickel	336,000	Y9
BW11		3 Pence	H	0.500 Silver	3,616,029	Y14b
BW12		6 Pence	H	0.500 Silver	2,948,000	Y15b
BW13		2 Shillings	H	0.500 Silver	1,925,960	Y17b

After 1920 THE MINT played a relatively less important part in the coinage of British West Africa. During the Depression years through 1935 most of their coinage was produced by the Royal Mint. Thereafter, King's Norton and THE MINT struck nearly equal quantities, each producing over 400 million coins for BWA. The major production was from the Royal Mint, however, which struck over a billion coins for BWA in the whole period from 1920 through 1958.

Also after 1920, silver was no longer used in the coinage of this country, being replaced initially by the tin–brass alloy, and later by nickel–brass.

No.	Date	Denomination	Mintmark	Metal	Mintage	Ref.
BW18	1923	6 Pence	H	Tin–Brass	2,000,000	Y15a
BW19		1 Shilling	H	Tin–Brass	24,384,000	Y16a
BW20		2 Shillings	H	Tin–Brass	8,832,000	Y17a
BW20	m1924	2 Shillings	H	Tin–Brass	3,864,233	Y17a
BW18	1924	6 Pence	H	Tin–Brass	1,000,000	Y15a
BW19		1 Shilling	H	Tin–Brass	9,566,800	Y16a
BW4	1925	1/10 Penny	H	Copper–Nickel	12,000,000	Y7
BW4	1928 m1929	1/10 Penny	H	Copper–Nickel	2,964,000	Y7
BW14	1936 m1937	1/10 Penny	H	Copper–Nickel	768,000	Y18
BW14	m1938	1/10 Penny	H	Copper–Nickel	636,000	Y18
BW15		½ Penny	H	Copper–Nickel	624,240	Y19
BW15	m1937	½ Penny	H	Copper–Nickel	1,775,760	Y19
BW16		1 Penny	H	Copper–Nickel	5,467,200	Y20
BW16	m1937	1 Penny	H	Copper–Nickel	7,132,800	Y20
BW16m (Y21)						

All these copper–nickel pieces bear the name of Edward VIII, who became King in January and abdicated in December 1936. The 1/10 penny is considered by Remick[5] to be one of the rarest of British Empire coins, with only 15–35 extant. Its rarity, however, may well be approached by the muled BWA penny dated 1936 with an East Africa 10 cents of the same period. According to officials of THE MINT, only very few of the 1936H mules (perhaps no more than 500) could have escaped their careful quality control.

No.	Date	Denomination	Mintmark	Metal	Mintage	Ref.
BW17	1936 m1937	3 Pence	H	Tin–Brass	1,000,000	Y14a
BW18	m1937	6 Pence	H	Tin–Brass	480,000	Y15a
BW19	m1937	1 Shilling	H	Tin–Brass	10,920,000	Y16a
BW20	m1937	2 Shillings	H	Tin–Brass	8,703,000	Y17a

[5]Jerome H. Remick, "Rarest Coins in the British Commonwealth", *COINS*, Nov. 1968, pp. 22–4.

No.	Date	Denomination	Mintmark	Metal	Mintage	Ref.
BW19s						

These tin–brass pieces bear the effigy of George V, who died in January 1936. A proof 1936H 1 Shilling, identical to BW19 but with the word SPECIMEN inscribed on the reverse above the date, was offered as Lot No. 777 in the NASCA Aug. 16, 1978 Wayte Raymond sale.

George V's likeness is on these coins because BWA's urgent need for coins in 1937 did not admit of awaiting the preparation of dies with George VI's image.

No.	Date	Denomination	Mintmark	Metal	Mintage	Ref.
BW22	1937	½ Penny	H	Copper–Nickel	1,011,840	Y23
BW22	m1938	½ Penny	H	Copper–Nickel	3,011,040	Y23
Bw22	m1940	½ Penny	H	Copper–Nickel	777,120	Y23
BW23		1 Penny	H	Copper–Nickel	5,887,200	Y24
BW23	m1938	1 Penny	H	Copper–Nickel	3,432,000	Y24
BW23	m1939	1 Penny	H	Copper–Nickel	2,680,000	Y24
BW23a		1 Penny	H	Bronze	Unknown	Y24a

According to Garry Charman (see Format 6, page 4), only about six of these off-metal pieces (struck on a 1937 East Africa 10 cents blank) are known.

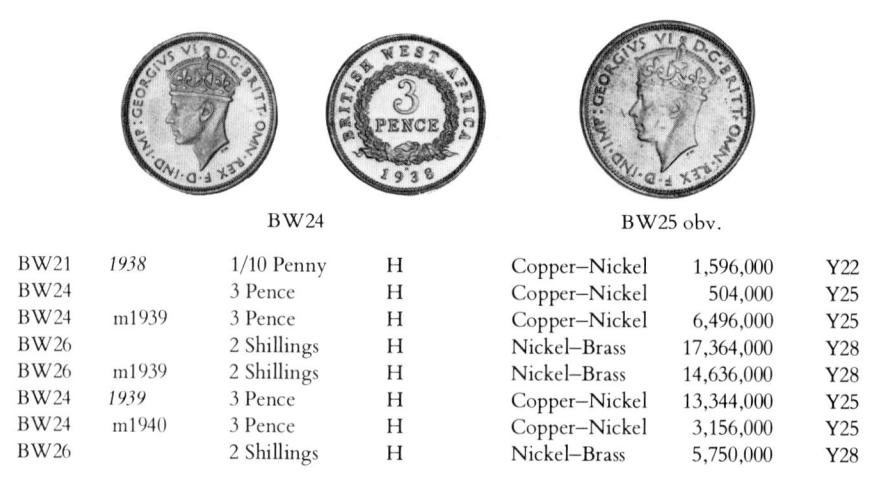

BW24

BW25 obv.

No.	Date	Denomination	Mintmark	Metal	Mintage	Ref.
BW21	1938	1/10 Penny	H	Copper–Nickel	1,596,000	Y22
BW24		3 Pence	H	Copper–Nickel	504,000	Y25
BW24	m1939	3 Pence	H	Copper–Nickel	6,496,000	Y25
BW26		2 Shillings	H	Nickel–Brass	17,364,000	Y28
BW26	m1939	2 Shillings	H	Nickel–Brass	14,636,000	Y28
BW24	1939	3 Pence	H	Copper–Nickel	13,344,000	Y25
BW24	m1940	3 Pence	H	Copper–Nickel	3,156,000	Y25
BW26		2 Shillings	H	Nickel–Brass	5,750,000	Y28

Shillings of both 1939 and 1940 exist with faint impressions of the H mintmark. According to Remick[6] these were produced at the Royal Mint from punches from which the H had not been completely obliterated. Royal Mint practice was to apply KHN on all BWA matrices; then the producing mint would remove the unwanted mintmarks from the punches.

No.	Date	Denomination	Mintmark	Metal	Mintage	Ref.
BW23	1940	1 Penny	H	Copper–Nickel	52,800	Y24
BW23	m1941	1 Penny	H	Copper–Nickel	2,347,200	Y24
BW24	m1941	3 Pence	H	Copper–Nickel	1,184,000	Y25
BW24	m1942	3 Pence	H	Copper–Nickel	1,496,000	Y25
BW24	m1943	3 Pence	H	Copper–Nickel	368,000	Y25
BW24	m1943 1941	3 Pence	H	Copper–Nickel$_1$	814,000	Y25
BW22	m1942	½ Penny	H	Copper–Nickel	2,400,000	Y23
BW24	m1943	3 Pence	H	Copper–Nickel$_1$	4,602,000	Y25

[6]Remick *et al.*, *British Commonwealth Coins*, 3d Ed., (Winnipeg: Regency Stamp & Coin Co. Ltd., 1971), p. 88.

Coinage Issues of The Birmingham Mint

No.	Date	Denomination	Mintmark	Metal	Mintage	Ref.
	1941					
BW24	m1944	3 Pence	H	Copper–Nickel$_1$	430,000	Y25
BW23	1943	1 Penny	H	Copper–Nickel$_1$	3,787,200	Y24
BW23	m1944	1 Penny	H	Copper–Nickel$_1$	3,352,800	Y24
BW24	m1944	3 Pence	H	Copper–Nickel$_1$	5,106,000	Y25
BW23	1945	1 Penny	H	Copper–Nickel$_1$	9,000,000	Y24
BW24	m1946	3 Pence	H	Copper–Nickel$_1$	998,000	Y25
BW25		1 Shilling	H	Nickel–Brass	3,808,000	Y27
BW25	m1946	1 Shilling	H	Nickel–Brass	9,056,000	Y27
BW21	1946	1/10 Penny	H	Copper–Nickel	4,788,000	Y22
BW21	m1947	1/10 Penny	H	Copper–Nickel	216,000	Y22
BW23		1 Penny	H	Copper–Nickel	7,334,000	Y24
BW23	m1947	1 Penny	H	Copper–Nickel	3,111,600	Y24
BW25		1 Shilling	H	Nickel–Brass	Unknown	Y27

Although THE MINT did not produce any shillings dated 1946 for circulation, three specimens exist in THE MINT collection.

No.	Date	Denomination	Mintmark	Metal	Mintage	Ref.
BW26	1946	2 Shillings	H	Nickel–Brass	8,604,000	Y28
BW26	m1947	2 Shillings	H	Nickel–Brass	1,896,000	Y28
BW22	1947	½ Penny	H	Copper–Nickel	4,626,720	Y23
BW22	m1948	½ Penny	H	Copper–Nickel	10,591,680	Y23
BW23		1 Penny	H	Copper–Nickel	4,542,040	Y24
BW23	m1948	1 Penny	H	Copper–Nickel	7,871,880	Y24
BW23	m1949	1 Penny	H	Copper–Nickel	28,800	Y24
BW24		3 Pence	H	Copper–Nickel	7,256,000	Y25
BW24	m1948	3 Pence	H	Copper–Nickel	2,744,000	Y25
BW25		1 Shilling	H	Nickel–Brass	10,000,000	Y27
BW26		2 Shillings	H	Nickel–Brass	975,000	Y28
BW26	m1948	2 Shillings	H	Nickel–Brass	3,976,000	Y28
BW26	m1949	2 Shillings	H	Nickel–Brass	104,000	Y28
BW27	1949	1/10 Penny	H	Copper–Nickel	3,700,320	Y29
BW28		½ Penny	H	Copper–Nickel	3,190,560	Y30
BW28	m1950	½ Penny	H	Copper–Nickel	2,718,720	Y30
BW29		1 Shilling	H	Nickel–Brass	9,816,000	Y33
BW29	m1950	1 Shilling	H	Nickel–Brass	184,000	Y33
BW30		2 Shillings	H	Nickel–Brass	5,720,000	Y34
BW30	m1950	2 Shillings	H	Nickel–Brass	1,780,000	Y34
BW29	1951	1 Shilling	H	Nickel–Brass	7,952,000	Y33
BW29	m1952	1 Shilling	H	Nickel–Brass	2,048,000	Y33
BW30		2 Shillings	H	Nickel–Brass	4,772,000	Y34
BW30	m1952	2 Shillings	H	Nickel–Brass	1,794,000	Y34
	1952					
BW31	m1953	½ Penny	H	Bronze$_1$	27,603,360	Y30a
BW32		1 Penny	H	Bronze$_1$	3,096,000	Y31a
BW32	m1953	1 Penny	H	Bronze$_1$	13,699,200	Y31a
BW32	m1954	1 Penny	H	Bronze$_1$	9,338,400	Y31a
BW32	m1955	1 Penny	H	Bronze$_1$	4,660,800	Y31a
BW29		1 Shilling	H	Nickel–Brass	33,928,000	Y33
BW29	m1953	1 Shilling	H	Nickel–Brass	10,168,000	Y33
BW30		2 Shillings	H	Nickel–Brass	2,490,000	Y34

No.	Date	Denomination	Mintmark	Metal	Mintage	Ref.
BW30	*1952* m1953	2 Shillings	H	Nickel–Brass	1,920,000	Y34
BW33	*1956*	1 Penny	H	Bronze$_1$	13,503,200	Y39
BW33	*1957*	1 Penny	H	Bronze$_1$	5,340,000	Y39
BW34	m1958	3 Pence	H	Copper–Nickel	800,080	Y40

The scarcity of these 1957H three pence pieces suggests that they may have been returned to the melting pot.[7]

In addition to the 1936H penny mule, two others with an H mintmark have been observed. They are as follows:

BW23m	Obverse of the BW16 penny; reverse of the 1945H BW23 penny.	YA24
BW33m	Obverse of the BW32 penny; reverse of the 1956H BW33 penny.	YA39

Officials of THE MINT have no knowledge of these muled coins.

The coinage of British West Africa ended with the one penny issues of 1958 by Imperial Chemical Industries (formerly the King's Norton Mint). Independence came to each of the member countries as follows: Ghana – 6 March 1957; Nigeria – 1 October 1960; Sierra Leone – 27 April 1961; The Gambia – 18 February 1965. For all except The Gambia, THE MINT has since produced coinage issues.

BRUNEI The first coinage for the British-protected independent Sultanate of Brunei was produced by Heatons in 1887. Not until 1967, when the British Royal Mint struck a series of Sen pieces, did another issue take place.

BR1

No.	Date	Denomination	Mintmark	Metal	Mintage	Ref.
BR1	AH*1304*(1887) m1887	1 Cent	None	Copper	1,000,000	Y1

BULGARIA Bulgaria achieved independence from the Ottoman Empire in 1878, and in 1881 contracted with Heatons for its first national coinage in modern times, authorized by Bulgarian Law dated 9 June 1880. See 1880 BMR, p. 29.

BU3

[7] Remick, "Collectors Spot New BWA Dates", *World Coins*, March 1969, p. 294.

Coinage Issues of The Birmingham Mint

No.	Date	Denomination	Mintmark	Metal	Mintage	Ref.
BU1	1881	2 Stotinki	HEATON	Bronze	5,000,000	Y1
BU2		5 Stotinki	HEATON	Bronze	10,000,000	Y2
BU3		10 Stotinki	HEATON	Bronze	15,000,000	Y3

In 1922 THE MINT quoted on two occasions, the first being for 1 and 2 Lev coins of an alloy of 91% copper and 9% aluminium, and the second requiring an alloy of 90% aluminium, 8% zinc, and 2% copper. It would appear from records in THE MINT that the order went to Arthur Krupp for the second alloy coinage, and the 1923 BMR shows a production by the Austrian Mint at Vienna of aluminium–bronze pieces for Bulgaria. THE MINT did not produce any coins in either alloy for circulation, although they did produce a few samples, their cabinet presently containing the following pieces in the second alloy.

BU5

BU4s	1923	1 Lev	H	Aluminium alloy	Unknown	KM1
BU5s		2 Leva	H	Aluminium alloy	Unknown	KM2

BURMA Sometime in the years 1863–4 the Government of Burma placed an order on Heatons for a complete mint to be erected in Mandalay, plus dies for four denominations of coins intended to become the national currency. Six hundred pairs of dies were ordered: 300 pairs of 1 kyat dies, and 100 each of the other three denominations. Specimen sets of the four coins were prepared in Birmingham – presumably for approval prior to completion of the die order. THE MINT collection contains a set in perfect mint state condition. This is the famed Peacock coinage – considered by many to be among the world's most beautiful coins. The listing below refers to the rare specimen sets struck in Birmingham.

BM4

CS*1214*(1853)

BM1s	m1864	1 Mu	None	Silver	Unknown	Y4

No.	Date	Denomination	Mintmark	Metal	Mintage	Ref.
	CS*1214*(1853)					
BM2s	m1864	1 Mat	None,	Silver	Unknown	Y5
BM3s	m1864	5 Mu	None	Silver	Unknown	Y6
BM4s	m1864	1 Kyat	None	Silver	Unknown	Y7

A set of these proof coins appeared in the Paramount auction of Heaton issues in August 1975.

Just one hundred years after providing a complete mint to Burma, THE MINT received an order for an issue of circulating coins.

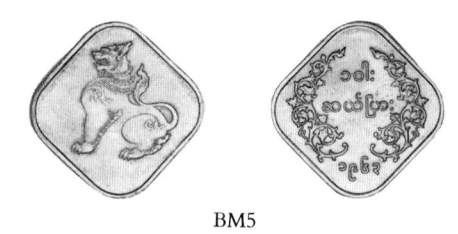

BM5

	1963					
BM5x	m1964	10 Pyas	None	Copper–Nickel	2,880,000	Y20
BM5x	m1965	10 Pyas	None	Copper–Nickel	2,870,000	Y20

In addition to the above, another 5,000,000 pieces without mintmark were struck by ICI/IMI at the same time.

CAMBODIA – *see* French Indo-China.

CANADA Prior to the Confederation in 1867, the only official coinage of Canada was an issue of decimal cents in 1858–9, for which Heatons furnished the blanks to the Royal Mint. A variety of tokens was issued by several Canadian banks and Provinces, and these were officially declared coins of the realm by proclamation dated 1 October 1870. They remained legal tender until 1876 when they were finally withdrawn from circulation.[8] Heatons' participation in this token coinage follows.

Province of Canada – Bank of Upper Canada The following account, essentially derived from incomplete records in the Public Record Office in London, is believed to be correct in all details, even though it conflicts with other published accounts.

In 1850 the Bank of Upper Canada, a private bank in Toronto, received permission from Provincial authorities to issue a token coinage, hopefully to displace the many spurious tokens then in use. The financial agent for the Province of Canada, the respected London firm of Glyn Mills & Co., acted as agent for the bank in this matter, and they in turn commissioned the London firm of Rowe, Kentish & Co.

---

[8]Fred Bowman, "The Decimal Coinage of Canada and Newfoundland", *The Numismatist*, Vol. 60, pp. 197, 354.

Coinage Issues of The Birmingham Mint 107

No.	Date	Denomination	Mintmark	Metal	Mintage	Ref.

of 16 Change Alley to handle the actual procurement. Rowe, Kentish & Co. had dies prepared featuring an excellent reproduction of Pistrucci's Saint George, and these were delivered to the Royal Mint in late 1850. The Royal Mint struck £2500 sterling value each of pennies and halfpennies dated 1850, these being about equal in weight and value to five-sixths (actually 0.822) of the English penny and halfpenny then current. The total coinage weighed just ten tons of each denomination. In 1851 a duplicate order for £5000 was placed on the Royal Mint. Production was delayed, and on 30 April 1852 the Royal Mint rather testily replied to Glyn Mills' complaint, saying: "... the copper tokens required by the Bank of Upper Canada will be executed as soon as the more important demands upon the Mint will permit." Only a portion had been completed by the time the ocean shipping season ended in August 1852, and so Glyn Mills arranged to have the dies and remaining blanks shipped (via the Grand Junction Canal Co.) to the Heaton Mint for completion of the order. This was done by Heatons in 1853, using the 1852 dated dies which were then returned to the Royal Mint and destroyed.

CA2

1852

CA1x	m1853	½ Penny	None	Copper	1,000,000	B720[9]
CA2x	m1853	1 Penny	None	Copper	500,000	B719[9]

The quantities shown above, equal to about 70% of the total order, are based on the assumption that all of the blanks originally furnished by Glyn Mills and *not* shipped to Heatons were used in the Royal Mint to produce acceptable tokens. This allows for no rejects, which is unlikely, and so Heatons' production is probably understated.

Twice more the Bank of Upper Canada placed orders for tokens, and twice more Heatons executed the order, first in 1854 for £5000 sterling value, and again in 1857 for about £10,000 sterling value. The quantities shown herein are from records in THE MINT, but are consistent with information in a 29 December 1851 letter from Rowe, Kentish & Co. to the Royal Mint, which stated in part: "... 730,000 Penny Pieces and 1,460,000 halfpenny pieces being the equivalent of £5000 Sterling...".

---

[9] Breton numbers are used here.

No.	Date	Denomination	Mintmark	Metal	Mintage	Ref.
CA1	1854	½ Penny	None	Copper	1,500,000	B720
CA2		1 Penny	None	Copper	690,000	B719

Specimens of this date, and of the 1857 issue, are to be found in the coin cabinet of The Birmingham Mint.

No.	Date	Denomination	Mintmark	Metal	Mintage	Ref.
CA1	1857	½ Penny	None	Copper	1,840,000	B720
CA2		1 Penny	None	Copper	2,000,000	B719

It is interesting to note that Rowe, Kentish & Co. had their own initials placed on the dies for these coinages, in the same location where Pistrucci's were normally found on that English coinage containing his rendition of St. George and the Dragon. A 5 January 1857 letter from Rowe, Kentish & Co. to Heatons stated: "We wish also that you would have the letters in the ground RK&Co. made more clear and distinct, although to be very small." (A somewhat similar occurrence is to be found on the Paraguay 1870 coinage). When the Bank of Upper Canada failed in 1868, its vaults were found to contain some 11 tons of these copper tokens – which were ultimately melted.[10]

Province of Canada – Bank of Quebec

CA4

No.	Date	Denomination	Mintmark	Metal	Mintage	Ref.
CA3	1852	½ Penny/1 Sou	None	Copper	480,000[11]	B529[12]
CA4		1 Penny/2 Sous	None	Copper	240,000[11]	B528

The firm of Charles Clifford acted as agent for the Bank of Quebec in placing the order for this coinage with Heatons.

Province of New Brunswick Not to be outdone by the other Provinces, New Brunswick received the approval of the Queen on 30 June 1852 to procure from Birmingham a coinage valued at £3000, half in pennies and half in halfpennies. Records in THE MINT show a coinage of 7 tons 4 cwt. and 3 tons 14 cwt.

---

[10] P. N. Breton, *Coins and Tokens Relating to Canada*, Montreal, 1894.
[11] J. A. Haxby & R. C. Willey, *Coins of Canada*, 2nd Edition (Racine, Wisc., Whitman Publishing Co., 1973), p. 151.
[12] Breton numbers are used here.

Coinage Issues of The Birmingham Mint

No.	Date	Denomination	Mintmark	Metal	Mintage	Ref.

respectively. The Royal Mint ledger for 1854 shows a billing by Heatons to the agent Baring Bros. of £1318.11.1 for copper and £309.6.2 for work.

CA6

| CA5 | 1854 | ½ Penny | None | Copper | 720,000 | B912 |
| CA6 | | 1 Penny | None | Copper | 360,000 | B911 |

These coinage quantities assume the value of the NB penny equal to the English penny, as appears to have been the case for Nova Scotia.

Province of Nova Scotia These were the last of a long series of Nova Scotia tokens, beginning in 1823 and ending with the advent of official currency in 1858.

CA8

| CA7 | 1856 | ½ Penny | None | Copper | 600,000 | B876 |
| CA8 | | 1 Penny | None | Copper | 300,000 | B875 |

A Royal Mint letter dated 16 February 1856 asked Heatons for prices for the above quantities of tokens. The 1891 BMR indicates the value of these mintages to be £1250 each. Thus the token was valued equal to the English penny. Baring Bros. was the agent, and Heatons were paid £1220.4.11 for copper and work.

Prince Edward Island

| CA9 | 1871 | 1 Cent | None | Bronze | 2,000,000 | Y1 |

After years on an unhealthy diet of tokens, PEI ordered these decimal cents from Heatons in 1871. They are the only Canadian decimals struck by Heatons without

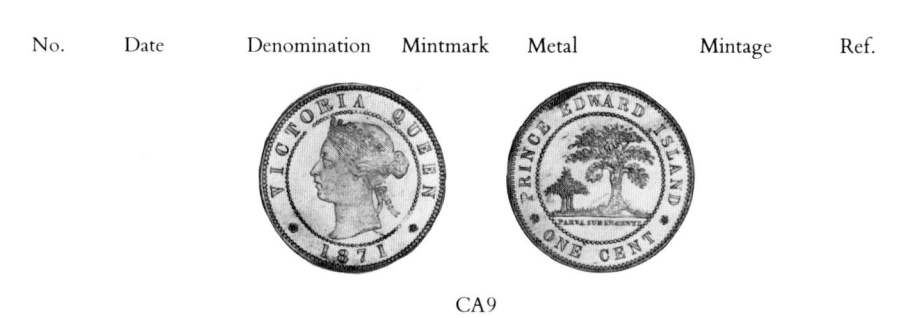

| No. | Date | Denomination | Mintmark | Metal | Mintage | Ref. |

CA9

the H mintmark. The dies were by L. C. Wyon based on designs specified by the Bank of PEI. The Royal Mint was unable to produce the coins before winter halted shipping, and so it was decided to place the order on a private mint. Tenders were invited from James Watt and Heatons, who won out with a slightly lower bid. The dies were dispatched to Birmingham on 16 October, and the entire coinage was delivered to the Birmingham & Midland Bank for shipping on 21 November 1871. An interesting sidelight is found in a letter of 30 September 1871 from Balmoral to the Royal Mint, in which it was reported that the designs for the coinage had received Royal approval, but that the Queen had commented that the effigy was ugly. No comment was proffered on the reverse design which, according to the Royal Museum Catalogue, shows a "... large oak tree sheltering three small maple trees." This is generally taken to suggest the benevolent protection of the Provincial Government over the three counties of Prince Edward Island.

Dominion of Canada

CA14

CA12	1871	10 Cents	H	0.925 Silver	1,870,000	Y3
CA13		25 Cents	H	0.925 Silver	748,000	Y8
CA14		50 Cents	H	0.925 Silver	45,000	Y9

The above issue by Heatons was stated to be valued at £81,500 in the 1871 BMR (although it is not included in the 1891 BMR summary of Colonial Coinages, nor in the 1908 summary). The above mintages are taken from Krause (*Standard Catalog of World Coins*), and are consistent with the value of £81,500.

This was Heatons' first silver coinage. One thousand 50 Cent pieces were struck on 18 December 1871 under close supervision by Royal Mint personnel. The special security measures included two night watchmen who fired a muzzle-loaded rifle at intervals during each night to let the Birmingham police know that all was well.

Coinage Issues of The Birmingham Mint 111

No.	Date	Denomination	Mintmark	Metal	Mintage	Ref.
CA11	1872	5 Cents	H	0.925 Silver	2,000,000	Y2
CA12		10 Cents	H	0.925 Silver	1,000,000	Y3
CA13		25 Cents	H	0.925 Silver	2,240,000	Y8
CA14		50 Cents	H	0.925 Silver	80,000	Y9

Here again a discrepancy exists in the records. The 1872 BMR values this coinage at £270,833. The above mintages are in accord with those in the 1908 BMR Summary on page 150. They are confirmed by a 12 July 1872 letter by Sir John Rose, which shows the total value of the issue to be $800,000.

CA11	1874	5 Cents	H	0.925 Silver	800,000	Y2
CA12		10 Cents	H	0.925 Silver	600,000	Y3
CA13		25 Cents	H	0.925 Silver	1,600,000	Y8
CA11	1875	5 Cents	H	0.925 Silver	1,000,000	Y2
CA12		10 Cents	H	0.925 Silver	1,000,000	Y3
CA13		25 Cents	H	0.925 Silver	1,000,000	Y8

CA10

CA10	1876	1 Cent	H	Bronze	4,000,000	Y5
CA10a		1 Cent	H	Copper–Nickel	Unknown	KM11
CA10p		1 Cent	H	Bronze	Unknown	KM12

According to Krause's *Standard Catalog of World Coins*, this pattern (CA10p) has the young head of Victoria as was on the 1858 penny.

CA11	1880	5 Cents	H	0.925 Silver	3,000,000	Y2
CA12		10 Cents	H	0.925 Silver	1,500,000	Y3
CA13		25 Cents	H	0.925 Silver	400,000	Y8
CA10	1881	1 Cent	H	Bronze	2,000,000	Y5
CA11		5 Cents	H	0.925 Silver	1,500,000	Y2
CA12		10 Cents	H	0.925 Silver	950,000	Y3
CA13		25 Cents	H	0.925 Silver	820,000	Y8
CA14		50 Cents	H	0.925 Silver	150,000	Y9
CA10	1882	1 Cent	H	Bronze	4,000,000	Y5
CA11		5 Cents	H	0.925 Silver	1,000,000	Y2
CA12		10 Cents	H	0.925 Silver	1,000,000	Y3
CA13		25 Cents	H	0.925 Silver	600,000	Y8

The 1882 BMR shows $350,000 in silver 20 cents [*sic*], 10 cents, and 5 cents struck by Heatons. The 1891 and 1908 BMRs show the above mintages. Heatons' Orderbook for 1882 agrees with the above values, so it is assumed that the 1882 BMR is in error.

112   *Catalogue*

No.	Date	Denomination	Mintmark	Metal	Mintage	Ref.
CA11	1883	5 Cents	H	0.925 Silver	600,000	Y2
CA12		10 Cents	H	0.925 Silver	300,000	Y3
CA13		25 Cents	H	0.925 Silver	960,000	Y8

From 1882 through 1883 all Canadian coinage was produced in the Heaton Mint. During this period the Royal Mint was subject to capacity limitations, and thus unable to undertake all the coinage for the colonies in addition to the needs of the Empire. The general renovation of the Royal Mint in 1882 corrected the capacity shortcomings, whereupon the Deputy Master of the Royal Mint made it clearly known to the High Commissioner for Canada in London that hereafter Canada's requirements would be handled by the Royal Mint. Less than ten years later, however, capacity limitations again made it necessary to use the services of THE MINT.

No.	Date	Denomination	Mintmark	Metal	Mintage	Ref.
CA10	1890	1 Cent	H	Bronze	1,000,000	Y5
CA11		5 Cents	H	0.925 Silver	1,000,000	Y2
CA12		10 Cents	H	0.925 Silver	450,000	Y3
CA13		25 Cents	H	0.925 Silver	200,000	Y9
CA14		50 Cents	H	0.925 Silver	20,000	Y9

The 1890H 50 cents is not only the scarcest of all the Canadian 50 cent issues, but is also the only 50 cent piece showing two different portraits of the ruling monarch.[13]

No.	Date	Denomination	Mintmark	Metal	Mintage	Ref.
CA10	1898	1 Cent	H	Bronze	1,000,000	Y5
CA10	1900	1 Cent	H	Bronze	2,600,000	Y5

CA16

CA17 rev.
(courtesy Western Publishing)

No.	Date	Denomination	Mintmark	Metal	Mintage	Ref.
CA16	1902	5 Cents	H	0.925 Silver	2,200,000	Y11a
CA18		10 Cents	H	0.925 Silver	1,100,000	Y12
CA19		25 Cents	H	0.925 Silver	800,000	Y13

The 1902 issues followed the death of Victoria, and so required all new dies. The Royal Mint found itself unable to complete the die work for the new coinage, and so the 1902H 5 cent piece was struck with an old reverse die still carrying the Royal Crown. New dies were prepared in 1903 with the correct Imperial Crown reverse.[14]

No.	Date	Denomination	Mintmark	Metal	Mintage	Ref.
CA17	1903	5 Cents	H	0.925 Silver	2,640,000	Y11
CA18		10 Cents	H	0.925 Silver	1,320,000	Y12

[13] Robert Willey, "Canadian Numismatics: A Challenge to Collectors," *COINS*, February, 1973.
[14] Fred Bowman, "The Decimal Coinage of Canada and Newfoundland," *The Numismatist*, Vol. 60 (March, 1947), pp. 197, 354.

Coinage Issues of The Birmingham Mint

No.	Date	Denomination	Mintmark	Metal	Mintage	Ref.
CA20	1903	50 Cents	H	0.925 Silver	140,000	Y14
CA15	1907	1 Cent	H	Bronze	800,000	Y10

This ended THE MINT's involvement with Canadian coinage. Beginning with the 1908 issues, practically all coinage has been struck at the Royal Canadian Mint in Ottawa.

Newfoundland

CA23m	1871	10 Cents	H	0.925 Silver	Unknown	B949[15]

The above piece is described by Breton[15] as follows: "The only specimen known of this coin was found in circulation by Mr. R. W. McLachlan. It is either a trial piece or a mule." Breton's illustration shows the H mintmark on both obverse and reverse. The obverse is like a CA23 ten cents, and the reverse like a CA12 10c dated 1871. It is most probably a mule, since a trial piece would be unlikely to have the mintmark on both sides. Also, Heatons struck both issues, thus making muling an easy possibility.

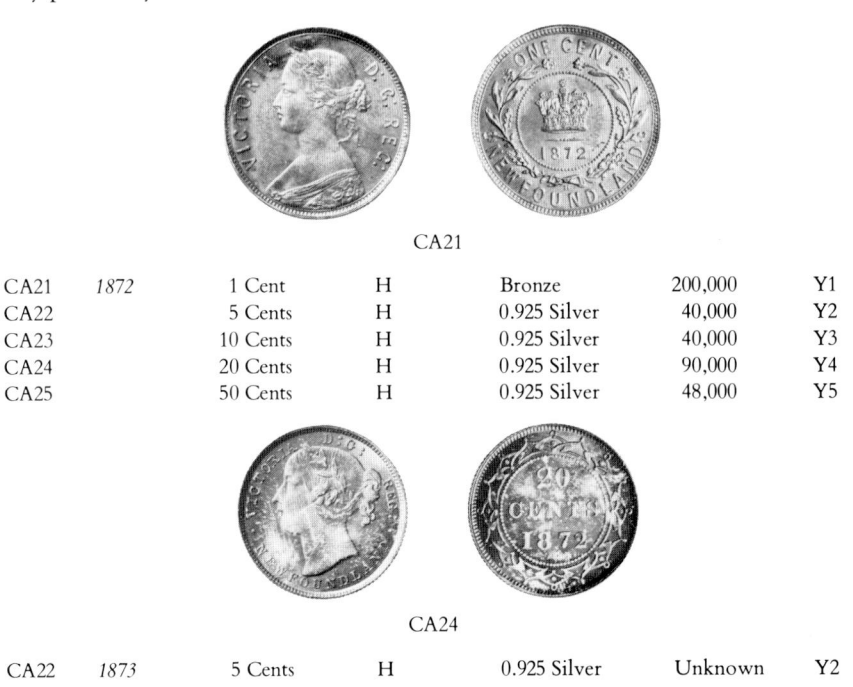

CA21

CA21	1872	1 Cent	H	Bronze	200,000	Y1
CA22		5 Cents	H	0.925 Silver	40,000	Y2
CA23		10 Cents	H	0.925 Silver	40,000	Y3
CA24		20 Cents	H	0.925 Silver	90,000	Y4
CA25		50 Cents	H	0.925 Silver	48,000	Y5

CA24

CA22	1873	5 Cents	H	0.925 Silver	Unknown	Y2

This coin does not appear as a Heaton issue in the summary of Colonial Coinages in the 1891 BMR, nor is it in THE MINT's cabinet (but then, neither is the 1904 1 cent). Remick[16] estimates that only 50 to 75 specimens are extant.

---
[15] P. N. Breton, *Coins and Tokens Relating to Canada.*
[16] Jerome H. Remick, "Rarest Coins in the British Commonwealth."

No.	Date	Denomination	Mintmark	Metal	Mintage	Ref.
CA21	1876	1 Cent	H	Bronze	200,000	Y1
CA22		5 Cents	H	0.925 Silver	20,000	Y2
CA23		10 Cents	H	0.925 Silver	10,000	Y3
CA24		20 Cents	H	0.925 Silver	50,000	Y4
CA25		50 Cents	H	0.925 Silver	28,000	Y5
CA21	1882	5 Cents	H	0.925 Silver	60,000	Y2
CA22		10 Cents	H	0.925 Silver	20,000	Y3
CA23		20 Cents	H	0.925 Silver	100,000	Y4
CA24		50 Cents	H	0.925 Silver	100,000	Y5
CA25		2 Dollars	H	0.91667 Gold	25,000	Fr1

This was only the second time that Heatons had been commissioned to strike gold coins, the one previous occasion having been a very small issue for President Burgers of South Africa (q.v.).

CA29

CA26	1904	1 Cent	H	Bronze	100,000	Y7
CA27		5 Cents	H	0.925 Silver	100,000	Y8
CA28		10 Cents	H	0.925 Silver	100,000	Y9
CA29		20 Cents	H	0.925 Silver	75,000	Y10
CA30		50 Cents	H	0.925 Silver	140,000	Y11

Ceylon (Now SRI LANKA)

CE2   CE3

CE3	1912	5 Cents	H	Copper–Nickel	1,708,000	Y20
CE3	m1913	5 Cents	H	Copper–Nickel	2,292,000	Y20
CE1x	1926	½ Cent	None	Copper	5,000,000	Y18
CE2x		1 Cent	None	Copper	3,750,000	Y19

Equal quantities of the 1926 and 1928 copper coinage were struck by the King's Norton Metal Company, also without mintmarks.

| CE2x | 1928 | 1 Cent | None | Copper | 2,500,000 | Y19 |

Coinage Issues of The Birmingham Mint   115

No.	Date	Denomination	Mintmark	Metal	Mintage	Ref.

CE4   CE5

No.	Date	Denomination	Mintmark	Metal	Mintage	Ref.
CE2x	1929	1 Cent	None	Copper	5,000,000	Y19
CE4	1968	1 Cent	None	Aluminium	22,505,000	Y43
CE4x	1969	1 Cent	None	Aluminium	10,000,000	Y43
CE5x		5 Cents	None	Nickel–Brass	2,500,000	Y45
CE6x		10 Cents	None	Nickel–Brass	6,000,000	Y46

CE6

In addition to the above, British quarter- and half-farthings for circulation in Ceylon were struck by Heatons in 1853. These are included in the listing for Great Britain. The obverse designs of the CE4–6 types were produced in 1963 by Cecil Thomas.

CHILE The first truly national coinage executed by Heatons was in all likelihood the 1851 copper coins for Chile, the order for which was placed by the firm of Henry Van Wart as Agents for the Government of Chile.

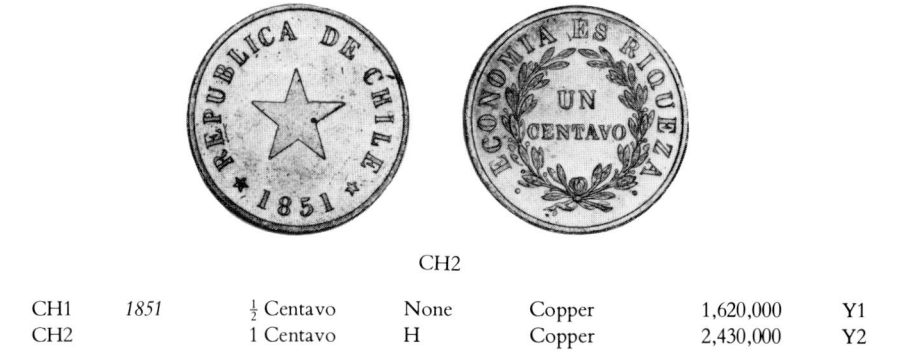

CH2

No.	Date	Denomination	Mintmark	Metal	Mintage	Ref.
CH1	1851	½ Centavo	None	Copper	1,620,000	Y1
CH2		1 Centavo	H	Copper	2,430,000	Y2

The above issues, with the obverse showing a large flat star in bas relief and the date below between small stars, are attributed by Harris[17] to a U.S.A. source.

---

[17] Robert P. Harris, *Modern Latin American Coins*, 1st Edition, Racine, Wisc., Whitman Publishing Company, 1966.

116   Catalogue

No.	Date	Denomination	Mintmark	Metal	Mintage	Ref.

However, in a book of testimonials[18] published by Heatons in about 1879, this type is illustrated as a Heaton issue, as well as the 1853 issue shown below. Most importantly, the 1851 Un Centavo has the H mintmark embossed on the small star to the left of the date. It is clearly visible in the illustration in the book of testimonials, and on the Chile specimens in THE MINT cabinet. The mintages given above are those shown by Krause for the corresponding types.[19]

CH4

CH3	1853	½ Centavo	None	Copper	2,666,666	Y3a
CH4		1 Centavo	None	Copper	2,666,667	Y4a
CH4s		1 Centavo	None	Copper	Unknown	—

The specimen CH4s is identical with CH4 but struck on a thick planchet. Hereafter, all Chilean coins were struck in the Santiago Mint.

CHINA   During the years 1888–1905, the development of Chinese provincial mints for struck silver coinage was proceeding apace, and THE MINT played a lead role in China's transition from cast to struck coinage. Indeed, THE MINT was probably responsible for the design of the dragon that became the hallmark of early Chinese silver coinage. So far as is known, THE MINT produced no coins for circulation in China, but it did produce dies for use in the provincial mints it was equipping, and also struck a variety of specimen and pattern coins for approval by the Chinese authorities. All pieces known or believed to have been actually struck by THE MINT are recorded below. Note that except for the Kwantung pieces, all of this silver coinage was based on a tael weight of 37.1806 grams, with the dollars being 0.72 of a tael (7 mace 2 candareens), as was standard on circulating issues of the Chinese provincial mints.

Chehkiang Province   Mint machinery was supplied to the Hangchow Mint in 1902 from Birmingham, along with dies for a silver coinage that was never placed in circulation. However, circulating 10 cash pieces (1 Cent or 1 Fen) did appear which were identical with the specimen coin below. Note that the circulating Hangchow issues bore the spelling CHEHKIANG, in contrast with the Birmingham patterns on which the spelling CHE-KIANG appears.

---

[18] Ralph Heaton & Sons, *Testimonials*, 1st Edition, Ca. 1879.
[19] Krause and Mishler, *Standard Catalog of World Coins*, 1976 Edition, Krause Publications, Iola, Wisc.

Coinage Issues of The Birmingham Mint   117

No.	Date	Denomination	Mintmark	Metal	Mintage	Ref.

CN1

	No date					
CN1s	m1902	1 Cent	None	Copper	Unknown	KM10
CN2p	m1902	5 Cents	None	0.820 Silver	Unknown	KM5
CN3p	m1902	10 Cents	None	0.820 Silver	Unknown	KM6
CN4p	m1902	20 Cents	None	0.860 Silver	Unknown	KM7
CN6p	m1902	1 Dollar	None	0.900 Silver	Unknown	KM9

CN6

All of the above, plus dies for the CN3–6p pieces, are in the cabinet of THE MINT. A proof specimen of the 1 cent appeared in the NASCA Wayte Raymond sale of 5 December 1977, and a specimen of the 1 dollar was in the Paramount Long Beach sale of August 1975.

Hunan Province Mint machinery, plus matrices and punches for the two denominations shown below, were shipped to China in 1898 for the Changsha Mint. The machinery was undoubtedly put into use, but the dies were never utilized for business strikes. The only specimen patterns were apparently made in THE MINT. Wright[20] concludes that THE MINT must also have produced the

---

[20] R. N. J. Wright, "The Birmingham Mint and the Imperial Chinese Dragon Coinage", *The Numismatic Circular*, April 1979 and May 1979. For additional articles by Commander Wright on this same general subject, see also the following articles:

"Some Further Information on the Origins of the Milled Coinage of Imperial China", *The Numismatic Chronicle*, Seventh Series, Vol. XIV, 1974.

"The Silver Dragon Coinage of the Chinese Provinces 1888–1949", *The Numismatic Chronicle*, Seventh Series, Vol. XVI, 1976.

| No. | Date | Denomination | Mintmark | Metal | Mintage | Ref. |

CN11

complementary Hunan 20, 10, and 5 cents, but none of these are in THE MINT collection.

	No date					
CN10p	m1898	50 Cents	None	0.860 Silver	Unknown	KM1
CN11p	m1898	1 Dollar	None	0.900 Silver	Unknown	KM2

THE MINT collection contains both of the above, as well as the corresponding dies. Proof specimens of both coins were in the NASCA Wayte Raymond sale, and the Paramount Long Beach sale included a 1 dollar specimen.

Hupeh Province Records in THE MINT show an order of 1898 for various mint machines for the Wuchang Mint, plus "steel dies for the $1, 50c, 20c, and 10c". Subsequent order entries imply that this material was actually shipped to and received by the Wuchang Mint. It was THE MINT's normal practice to produce specimen coins from any dies made for their customers, and so it is reasonable to conclude that they did so in this case. The cabinet of THE MINT has proof-like 50 cents and one dollar specimens, but no 20 or 10 cent specimens. It is not certain that the Hupeh specimens in THE MINT collection were actually produced in Birmingham; the possibility exists that they were sent back from China. Nevertheless, the weight of evidence suggests otherwise, and that the other specimen pieces could eventually show up. On that somewhat speculative basis, they are included here.

CN16

Coinage Issues of The Birmingham Mint

No.	Date	Denomination	Mintmark	Metal	Mintage	Ref.
	No date					
CN13s	m1895?	10 Cents	None	0.820 Silver	Unknown	–
CN14s	m1895?	20 Cents	None	0.860 Silver	Unknown	–
CN15s	m1895?	50 Cents	None	0.860 Silver	Unknown	–
CN16s	m1895?	1 Dollar	None	0.900 Silver	Unknown	–

Kiangnan Province One of the more notable orders that THE MINT received from China was for a mint that it provided and placed in operation in Nanking in 1897. Dies for a full set of silver coinage, as well as for a 1 cash coin, were executed in Birmingham and sent out with the mint equipment. A set of these silver dies still exists in THE MINT.

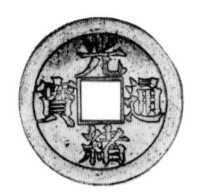

CN17

No.	Date	Denomination	Mintmark	Metal	Mintage	Ref.
	No date					
CN17s	m1896	1 Cash	None	Brass[21]	Unknown	–
CN18s	m1896	5 Cents	None	0.820 Silver	Unknown	Y141
CN19s	m1896	10 Cents	None	0.820 Silver	Unknown	Y142
CN20s	m1896	20 Cents	None	0.860 Silver	Unknown	Y143
CN21s	m1896	50 Cents	None	0.860 Silver	Unknown	Y144
CN22s	m1896	1 Dollar	None	0.900 Silver	Unknown	Y145.2
CN22a	m1896	1 Dollar	None	Bronze	Unknown	–

THE MINT cabinet contains all of the above pieces, the 1 dollars being of the plain edge variety, but otherwise identical with the circulation strikes from Nanking. The NASCA Wayte Raymond sale included a silver proof set (5 pieces) with a plain edge dollar. The Paramount Long Beach sale had four silver proofs, lacking only the 20 cent piece.

CN22

[21] The brass of this and the Kwantung CN25s are a 60% copper, 40% zinc alloy. See the BMR of 1888, page 39.

| No. | Date | Denomination | Mintmark | Metal | Mintage | Ref. |

Kwangtung Province In 1888 Heatons delivered to Canton all the equipment for the then world's largest mint. Dies[22] for the initial coinage were also sent out from Birmingham, as well as the people to train the Chinese in mint operations. Sets of specimen coins, including 100 cash pieces and five each of the 10, 20, and 50 cent pieces, as well as ten of the 1 dollar pieces, were prepared by Heatons and delivered to the Chinese ambassador in London. In October, 1888, R. H. Heaton III wrote to the editor of *The Times* of London, saying, among other things, that: "The Chinese have ordered dies and appliances for the manufacture of Taels – cent/50, cent/20, & cent/10 of the Tael, the dies are already sent out to Canton." It was these dies that were used to produce the first of the modern silver coinage of China, which coinage in turn became the prototype for the coinage of all the other provincial silver mints of China. Why the 5 cent dies were not also ordered from Heatons at the same time is unknown. It is possible that they were ordered later, but also possible that they were produced in the Canton Mint, it then being under the supervision of Edward Wyon. Dies for Kwangtung coinage in Birmingham today include neither the 5 cents nor the 10 cents die.

CN25   CN26

	No date					
CN25s	m1888	1 Cash	None	Brass (3.736 gms.)	Unknown	Y189
CN26s	m1899?	1 Cent	None	Bronze	Unknown	Y192
CN27s	m1888	10 Cents	None	0.820 Silver	Unknown	K19
CN28s	m1888	20 Cents	None	0.820 Silver	Unknown	K18
CN28a	m1888	20 Cents	None	Bronze	Unknown	–
CN29s	m1888	50 Cents	None	0.820 Silver	Unknown	K17
CN30s	m1888	1 Dollar	None	0.900 Silver	Unknown	K16

CN30

[22]These dies were engraved by Mr. Alan Wyon.

Coinage Issues of The Birmingham Mint 121

No.   Date   Denomination   Mintmark   Metal   Mintage   Ref.

Note that these first specimens were based on the standard treasury tael of 37.36 grams, whereas all subsequent issues involved a tael of 37.1806 grams. Also, these 1 dollar pieces were 0.73 of a tael (7 mace 3 candareens) with the smaller pieces showing corresponding fractions of the tael. Subsequent issues were 0.72 of the tael.

The NASCA 5 December 1977 sale contained a cased (by THE MINT) double proof set of CN25s and CN27–30s. The Paramount Long Beach sale contained the four silver specimens.

Shensi Province An order for complete coinage machinery and matrices and punches for five silver denominations was received by THE MINT in 1898, and the material was shipped in March 1899. The machinery was apparently diverted to another mint, and so no Shensi coinage was struck in China during the Ch'ing Dynasty. No dies remain in THE MINT collection, but it does include all of the following pattern coins.

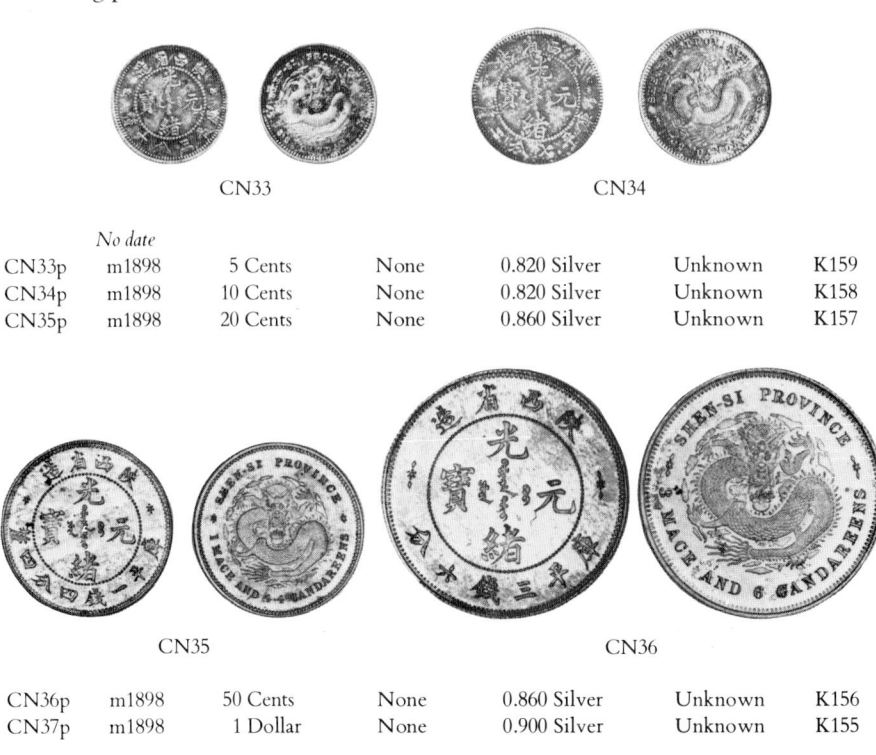

CN33   CN34

	No date					
CN33p	m1898	5 Cents	None	0.820 Silver	Unknown	K159
CN34p	m1898	10 Cents	None	0.820 Silver	Unknown	K158
CN35p	m1898	20 Cents	None	0.860 Silver	Unknown	K157

CN35   CN36

| CN36p | m1898 | 50 Cents | None | 0.860 Silver | Unknown | K156 |
| CN37p | m1898 | 1 Dollar | None | 0.900 Silver | Unknown | K155 |

The NASCA sale contained all except the 10 cents piece (CN34p). The Paramount sale lacked both the 5 and 10 cent pieces. The Kann collection contained only the 5 cents and 50 cents, both obtained in the East. Whether they were struck from the missing Shensi dies in China, or came out from THE MINT, can only be guessed. Both the Paramount and NASCA sale pieces definitely came from Birmingham.

| No. | Date | Denomination | Mintmark | Metal | Mintage | Ref. |

CN37

Szechuan Province THE MINT collection contains an FDC specimen of the piece listed below. There is no additional evidence to support its attribution to THE MINT, so it is listed here only as a possibility, albeit remote.

CN40

| CN40s | *No date* | 20 Cents | None | 0.860 Silver | Unknown | K142 |

Republic Period Much later, THE MINT was apparently approached (documentation has so far not been found) to produce an issue of the Yuan Shih-Kai dollar of the type originally produced in China in 1914 and again struck in 1919. Dies were produced for this piece and specimens struck in Birmingham (both dies and specimen coins are in THE MINT collection), but it is not definitely known that business strikes were produced.

CN50

| CN50s | *1919* m1949? | 1 Yuan | None | 0.833 Silver | Unknown | Y329 |

Coinage Issues of The Birmingham Mint 123

No.	Date	Denomination	Mintmark	Metal	Mintage	Ref.

Records in THE MINT contain references which may be taken to imply the possibility of yet additional Chinese pieces for this catalogue. Until more substantial evidence comes to light, however, they will be disregarded as being too ill-defined.

COLOMBIA   With but one exception, all of the Heaton issues for Colombia are the decimal denominations which were introduced in 1872 and thereafter circulated alongside the equivalent Real denominations (2½ Centavos = ¼ Decimo) until 1888.

CO2

CO2p
(courtesy NASCA)

CO1	1874	1¼ Centavos	None	Copper–Nickel	2,400,000	Y18
CO2	1881	2½ Centavos	None	Copper–Nickel	4,000,000	Y20

CO2p   The Wayte Raymond sale of 14 August 1978 contained a silver proof 2½ centavos of 1881 (Lot 981) described as follows: "Similar to the regular issue of 1881 (Y20) but vertical lines and no LIBERTAD on cap, other minor differences." It is not known that this was a Heaton product, but the clear likelihood exists.

THE MINT records show the 1881 order from Oeschger, Mesdach & Co. of Paris, while the 1886 order was from Eschger, Ghesquière & Co., a successor firm.

	1886					
CO3	m1885/6	2½ Centavos	None	Copper–Nickel	12,000,000	Y21
CO4p	*1891*	50 Centavos	None	0.835 Silver	25–30	Y29

CO4p

A specimen of the above pattern of the 1892 Colombian Commemorative is in THE MINT cabinet. The dies were made by THE MINT per an order from Schloss Bros., London, for approval by the appropriate authorities.

CO4	*1892*	50 Centavos	None	0.835 Silver	4,756,544	Y29

124   *Catalogue*

No.	Date	Denomination	Mintmark	Metal	Mintage	Ref.
	1892					
CO4	m1893	50 Centavos	None	0.835 Silver	69,061	Y29
CO4	m1894	50 Centavos	None	0.835 Silver	16,503	Y29

These 1892 coins were struck to commemorate the 400th Anniversary of Discovery. They were a recoinage of depreciated monies supplied by Colombia.

CO7

CO5p	*1900*	10 Centavos	None	0.666 Silver	Unknown	–
CO6p		20 Centavos	None	0.666 Silver	Unknown	–
CO7p		50 Centavos	None	0.835 Silver	Unknown	–

These patterns, like the Belgian-struck counterparts, have no design equivalent among circulation strikes. Specimens exist in the cabinet of THE MINT, but the author has seen no reference to them elsewhere. Dies dated 1899 and 1900 were delivered to Colombia, so patterns dated 1899 may also exist.

CO9   CO11

CO10	*1911*	10 Centavos	None	0.900 Silver	5,064,946	Y47
CO11		20 Centavos	None	0.900 Silver	1,205,530	Y48
CO8	*1912*	1 Peso (p/m)	H	Copper–Nickel	2,000,000	Y42
CO9		5 Pesos (p/m)	H	Copper–Nickel	2,000,000	Y44
CO12		50 Centavos	None	0.900 Silver	1,207,006	Y49

By Article 7 of Law 85 of 1910, English sovereigns were made legal tender at the rate of ten thousand per cent in relation to Colombian paper money (papel/moneda). This inflation currency had a value of 1 peso equalling 1 centavo of the silver currency. The p/m coins corresponded in size and value to the one and five centavos coins issued starting in 1917.

CO10	*1913*	10 Centavos	None	0.900 Silver	5,880,000	Y47
CO10	m1912	10 Centavos	None	0.900 Silver	2,425,000	Y47
CO11		20 Centavos	None	0.900 Silver	1,230,000	Y48
CO11	m1912	20 Centavos	None	0.900 Silver	400,000	Y48
CO12		50 Centavos	None	0.900 Silver	416,770	Y49

Coinage Issues of The Birmingham Mint 125

No.	Date	Denomination	Mintmark	Metal	Mintage	Ref.

CO12

No.	Date	Denomination	Mintmark	Metal	Mintage	Ref.
CO10	1914	10 Centavos	None	0.900 Silver	3,840,000	Y47
CO11		20 Centavos	None	0.900 Silver	2,560,000	Y48
CO12		50 Centavos	None	0.900 Silver	768,618	Y49
CO12x	1915	50 Centavos	None	0.900 Silver	945,750	Y49
CO12x	1916	50 Centavos	None	0.900 Silver	1,060,000	Y49
CO12x	1917	50 Centavos	None	0.900 Silver	98,606	Y49

The above issue is reported in the 1917 BMR. Harris[23] notes that the date has not been observed. A specimen is in the collection of the author.

After 1917 the output of the Bogota and Medellin Mints continued to have to be supplemented by outside contracts, but all such were carried out by other American mints.

Congo (Now ZAIRE) The Democratic Republic of the Congo, so-called until 1971 when it became known as Zaire, issued its coinage in the name of the Banque Nationale du Congo. A major part of its coinage was produced in British mints, including the following produced by THE MINT.

CG1

No.	Date	Denomination	Mintmark	Metal	Mintage	Ref.
CG1	1967	10 Sengi	None	Aluminium	84,996,000	Y2
CG1	m1966	10 Sengi	None	Aluminium	6,000,000	Y2

The design for these pieces was modelled by Michael Rizzello.

COSTA RICA Prior to 1947, most of Costa Rica's coins were minted in the San José Mint, but during the four year period 1889–93 all of Costa Rica's coinage was produced by THE MINT, these orders having been contracted through the London firm of C. de Murrieta & Co. In addition, all of the output of the San José Mint during the years 1885–8 was produced on blanks made in The Birmingham Mint.

[23] Robert P. Harris, *Modern Latin American Coins*.

126   Catalogue

No.	Date	Denomination	Mintmark	Metal	Mintage	Ref.

CR4

CR1	1889	5 Centavos	HBM[24]	0.750 Silver	520,000	Y17
CR2		10 Centavos	HBM	0.750 Silver	260,000	Y18
CR3		25 Centavos	HBM	0.750 Silver	410,000	Y19
CR4		50 Centavos	HBM	0.750 Silver	205,000	—

The 1889 BMR credits THE MINT with "... a silver coinage of $256,722 in pieces of fifty, twenty-five, ten, and five cents." THE MINT's Orderbook shows £3000 each of 5 and 10 centavos, and £12,000 each of 25 and 50 centavos. The above calculated mintages are reasonably consistent with both sources. Although the 50 Centavos piece apparently did not enter circulation, specimens exist in both the Royal Mint Museum and the cabinet of THE MINT.

CR1	1890	5 Centavos	HBM	0.750 Silver	430,500	Y17
CR2		10 Centavos	HBM	0.750 Silver	215,125	Y18
CR3		25 Centavos	HBM	0.750 Silver	395,442	Y19
CR1	1892	5 Centavos	HBM	0.750 Silver	279,731	Y17
CR2		10 Centavos	HBM	0.750 Silver	139,936	Y18
CR3		25 Centavos	HBM	0.750 Silver	440,443	Y19
CR3	1893	25 Centavos	HBM	0.750 Silver	620,000	Y19
CR3	m1894	25 Centavos	HBM	0.750 Silver	50,069	Y19

Many of the 1889–93 25 centavos were reissued following the devaluation of 1923–4 with a counterstamp reading "50 Centavos 1923."

The above mintages are in accord with THE MINT's Orderbook (with the possible exception of the 1890 mintages, for which the Orderbook shows £3000 each of the 5 and 10 centavos, and £14,000 of the 25 centavos) and with the 1890–3 BMRs. By calculation, they generally confirm the 1889 mintages shown herein.

CYPRUS Cyprus was acquired by Great Britain in 1878, and their coinage within the Empire began in 1879.

CY1	1881	¼ Piastre	H	Bronze	108,000	Y1
CY2		½ Piastre	H	Bronze	72,000	Y2
CY3		1 Piastre	H	Bronze	36,000	Y3
CY1	1882	¼ Piastre	H	Bronze	36,000	Y1

[24]The actual mintmark is HEATON BIRMM on these coins.

Coinage Issues of The Birmingham Mint

No.	Date	Denomination	Mintmark	Metal	Mintage	Ref.

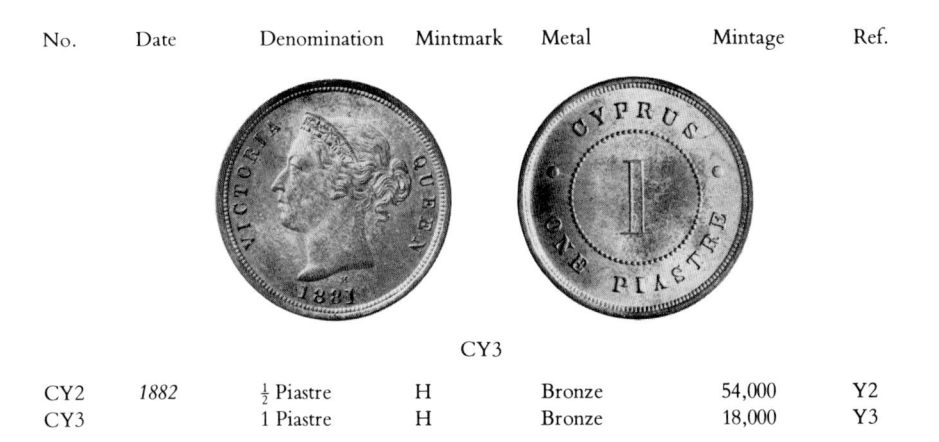

CY3

| CY2 | 1882 | ½ Piastre | H | Bronze | 54,000 | Y2 |
| CY3 | | 1 Piastre | H | Bronze | 18,000 | Y3 |

DOMINICAN REPUBLIC The coinage of the Dominican Republic has been supplied by various American and European mints and sometimes, as in the case of the 1888 coinages, by several mints in the same year.

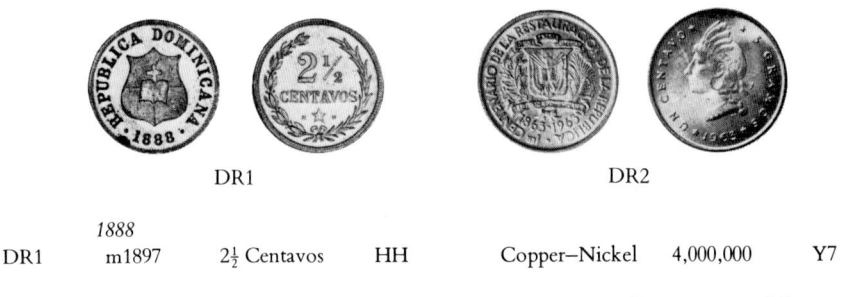

DR1   DR2

| DR1 | 1888 m1897 | 2½ Centavos | HH | Copper–Nickel | 4,000,000 | Y7 |

For some reason, perhaps symmetry, two Hs appear on the reverse of this coin, one on either side of a small star.

The agent for this transaction was Isadore Mendel of Paris.

The 1904 BMR notes that a mint exists at San Salvador, but has not been generally used for want of a competent staff.

| DR2 | 1963 | 1 Centavo | None | Bronze$_5$ | 13,000,000 | Y23 |
| DR3 | | 5 Centavos | None | Copper–Nickel | 4,000,000 | Y24 |

This special one-year type was struck to commemorate the centennial year of the restoration of the Republic. The entire issue was produced by THE MINT in 1963.

DR4   DR5
(courtesy Krause Publications)

No.	Date	Denomination	Mintmark	Metal	Mintage	Ref.
DR4	1968	1 Centavo	None	Bronze$_5$	5,000,000	YA16
DR5	1969 m1970	1 Centavo	None	Bronze$_5$	5,000,000	Y29

This issue was produced under the aegis of the Food and Agriculture Organization of the United Nations.

East Africa and Uganda Protectorates (Now KENYA, UGANDA, *et al.*) Coinage for this administrative group dates from 1897, although THE MINT's participation began only in 1911.

EA3

EA4
(courtesy Krause Publications)

EA4	1910 m1911	25 Cents	H	0.800 Silver	200,000	Y7
EA1	1911	1 Cent	H	Copper–Nickel	25,000,000	Y9
EA3		10 Cents	H	Copper–Nickel	1,250,000	Y11
EA1	1912	1 Cent	H	Copper–Nickel	20,000,000	Y9
EA3		10 Cents	H	Copper–Nickel	1,050,000	Y11
EA2	1913	5 Cents	H	Copper–Nickel	300,000	Y10

This was the first appearance of the 5 cent denomination in the coinage of the Protectorate.

EA6

EA1	1914	1 Cent	H	Copper–Nickel	2,500,000	Y9
EA5		25 Cents	H	0.800 Silver	80,000	Y12
EA6		50 Cents	H	0.800 Silver	180,000	Y13

Also in 1914 the King's Norton Metal Co. struck 1,240,000 5 cent pieces with a K mintmark. This was their first coinage for the British Empire, but hereafter THE

No.	Date	Denomination	Mintmark	Metal	Mintage	Ref.

MINT would have to share the overflow from the Royal Mint, rather than continue to enjoy a monopoly position.

No.	Date	Denomination	Mintmark	Metal	Mintage	Ref.
EA1	1916	1 Cent	H	Copper–Nickel	1,824,000	Y9
EA1	1917	1 Cent	H	Copper–Nickel	3,176,000	Y9
EA1	1918	1 Cent	H	Copper–Nickel	10,000,000	Y9
EA3		10 Cents	H	Copper–Nickel	400,000	Y11
EA5		25 Cents	H	0.800 Silver	40,000	Y12
EA6		50 Cents	H	0.800 Silver	60,000	Y13
EA2	1919	5 Cents	H	Copper–Nickel	200,000	Y10

East Africa Two changes took place between 1919 and 1920. First, the name was changed to East Africa. Secondly, the currency base was shifted from the Rupee to the Florin = 100 Cents.

EA11

No.	Date	Denomination	Mintmark	Metal	Mintage	Ref.
	1920					
EA7	m1921	1 Cent	H	Copper–Nickel	2,908,000	Y14
EA8	m1921	5 Cents	H	Copper–Nickel	550,000	Y15
EA9		10 Cents	H	Copper–Nickel	450,000	Y16
EA9	m1921	10 Cents	H	Copper–Nickel	250,000	Y16
EA10		25 Cents	H	0.500 Silver	424,000	Y17
EA10	m1921	25 Cents	H	0.500 Silver	324,000	Y17
EA11	m1921	50 Cents/ 1 Shilling	H	0.500 Silver	62,000	Y18
EA12		1 Florin	H	0.500 Silver	6,701,000	Y19
EA12	m1921	1 Florin	H	0.500 Silver	2,988,000	Y19

The above issues were authorized by the East Africa and Uganda Order in Council, 1920, which designated the Florin as the new standard. However, coincidental with THE MINT's copper–nickel issues, the Royal Mint was striking bronze 5 and 10 cent pieces in accord with the 1921 Coinage Order, and the 1920/21 BMR reports that these "two ten-cent pieces, one of white metal and the other of bronze, are now circulating concurrently in East Africa." Note that the 1920/21 BMR does *not* record the issue of the 50 Cents/1 Shilling; a specimen is in the cabinet of THE MINT, but these *may* have been only included in specimen sets.

Also in 1921 THE MINT struck shillings as per the 1921 Coinage Order, which constituted the shilling of 0.250 silver as the new standard of the Protectorates.

No.	Date	Denomination	Mintmark	Metal	Mintage	Ref.
EA16	1921	1 Shilling	H	0.250 Silver	4,240,000	Y24
EA13	1922	1 Cent	H	Bronze	36,750,000	Y20

No.	Date	Denomination	Mintmark	Metal	Mintage	Ref.
	1922					
EA13	m1923	1 Cent	H	Bronze$_1$	7,000,000	Y20
EA16		1 Shilling	H	0.250 Silver$_1$	19,880,000	Y24
EA16	m1923	1 Shilling	H	0.250 Silver$_1$	172,000	Y24
EA13	1924	1 Cent	H	Bronze$_1$	13,276,000	Y20
EA13	m1925	1 Cent	H	Bronze$_1$	4,224,000	Y20
EA13	1928	1 Cent	H	Bronze$_1$	7,100,000	Y20
EA13	m1929	1 Cent	H	Bronze$_1$	4,900,000	Y20
EA14	1936	5 Cents	H	Bronze$_1$	1,504,000	Y25
EA14	m1937	5 Cents	H	Bronze$_1$	1,996,000	Y25
EA15		10 Cents	H	Bronze$_1$	3,580,000	Y26
EA15	m1937	10 Cents	H	Bronze$_1$	750,000	Y26

These 1936 issues were among the first — and last — to honour Edward VIII. The mintages shown for 1936 and beyond have been checked against Royal Mint records and are believed to be completely accurate.

No.	Date	Denomination	Mintmark	Metal	Mintage	Ref.
EA17	1937	5 Cents	H	Bronze$_1$	2,880,000	Y28
EA17	m1938	5 Cents	H	Bronze$_1$	120,000	Y28
EA18		10 Cents	H	Bronze$_1$	1,308,000	Y29
EA18	m1938	10 Cents	H	Bronze$_1$	1,192,000	Y29
EA18a		10 Cents	H	Copper–Nickel	Unknown	–
EA19		50 Cents	H	0.250 Silver$_1$	704,000	Y30
EA19	m1938	50 Cents	H	0.250 Silver$_1$	3,296,000	Y30
EA20		1 Shilling	H	0.250 Silver$_1$	2,088,000	Y31
EA20	m1938	1 Shilling	H	0.250 Silver$_1$	5,584,000	Y31

EA20

The 25% silver shilling and 50 cents of George VI have the distinction of being the only Empire coins to bear the full Latin spelling of the Indian titles: GEORGIUS VI REX ET INDIAE IMPERATOR.[25] In 1945 the title became simply GEORGIUS SEXTUS REX as India moved toward independence. EA18a was struck on a British West Africa one penny blank.

No.	Date	Denomination	Mintmark	Metal	Mintage	Ref.
EA17	1939	5 Cents	H	Bronze$_1$	424,000	Y28
EA17	m1940	5 Cents	H	Bronze$_1$	1,576,000	Y28
EA18		10 Cents	H	Bronze$_1$	712,000	Y29
EA18	m1940	10 Cents	H	Bronze$_1$	1,288,000	Y29

[25]Thomas E. Klunzinger, "The Regal Coinage of British East Africa," *The Numismatist*, Vol. 85 (August 1972), pp. 1195–1202.

Coinage Issues of The Birmingham Mint 131

No.	Date	Denomination	Mintmark	Metal	Mintage	Ref.
	1942					
EA19	m1943	50 Cents	H	0.250 Silver$_1$	5,000,000	Y30
EA20		1 Shilling	H	0.250 Silver$_1$	1,326,000	Y31
EA20	m1943	1 Shilling	H	0.250 Silver$_1$	3,000,000	Y31
EA20	m1944	1 Shilling	H	0.250 Silver$_1$	104,000	Y31
EA20	*1944*	1 Shilling	H	0.250 Silver$_1$	9,384,000	Y31
EA20	m1945	1 Shilling	H	0.250 Silver$_1$	616,000	Y31

The 1944 shillings were THE MINT's last silver coinages for East Africa. The silver 1 shilling was struck in the Pretoria Mint in both 1945 and 1946, but thereafter the precious metals were no longer used in East African coinage. From 1906 through 1919 the 25 and 50 cent pieces were of 0.800 silver; in the single year 1920 the fineness was reduced to 0.500; then for twenty-five years through 1946 the alloy included only 25% silver. Finally, debasement became complete in 1948 when nickel was substituted for the silver.

EA24	*1949*	1 Shilling	H	Copper–Nickel	8,496,000	Y36
EA24	m1950	1 Shilling	H	Copper–Nickel	4,088,000	Y36
EA24	*1950*	1 Shilling	H	Copper–Nickel	11,824,000	Y36
EA24	m1951	1 Shilling	H	Copper–Nickel	592,000	Y36
EA21	*1951*	1 Cent	H	Bronze$_1$	6,072,000	Y32
EA21	m1952	1 Cent	H	Bronze$_1$	2,928,000	Y32
EA22		5 Cents	H	Bronze$_1$	6,000,000	Y33

In 1942 the bronze coinage of East Africa was produced by the Royal Mint and the Bombay Mint with a new alloy containing 97% copper, 2½% zinc, and ½% tin, because of the reduced availability of tin due to World War II. When bronze coinage was resumed after the war, it reverted to the standard British alloy which had been adopted in 1923, and this continued until 1961 when the wartime alloy was again used for the minor coinage.

EA21	*1952*	1 Cent	H	Bronze$_1$	7,440,000	Y32
EA21	m1953	1 Cent	H	Bronze$_1$	5,560,000	Y32
EA23	m1953	10 Cents	H	Bronze$_1$	2,000,000	Y34
EA24	m1953	1 Shilling	H	Copper–Nickel	3,752,000	Y36
EA24	m1954	1 Shilling	H	Copper–Nickel	1,864,000	Y36
EA24	m1955	1 Shilling	H	Copper–Nickel	2,408,000	Y36

These were the last shillings struck for East Africa, and the issues dated 1952 were the last of the George VI coinage.

EA25	*1955*	1 Cent	H	Bronze$_1$	6,384,000	Y37
EA26		5 Cents	H	Bronze$_1$	4,000,000	Y38
EA27		50 Cents	H	Copper–Nickel	752,000	Y40
EA27	m1956	50 Cents	H	Copper–Nickel	848,000	Y40
EA25	*1956*	1 Cent	H	Bronze$_1$	14,936,000	Y37
EA25	m1957	1 Cent	H	Bronze$_1$	680,000	Y37
EA26		5 Cents	H	Bronze$_1$	984,000	Y38
EA26	m1957	5 Cents	H	Bronze$_1$	2,016,000	Y38

No.	Date	Denomination	Mintmark	Metal	Mintage	Ref.

EA25   EA27

EA27	1956	50 Cents	H	Copper–Nickel	2,000,000	Y40
EA25	1957	1 Cent	H	Bronze$_1$	4,056,000	Y37
EA25	m1958	1 Cent	H	Bronze$_1$	944,000	Y37
EA26		5 Cents	H	Bronze$_1$	5,000,000	Y38
EA27	1958	50 Cents	H	Copper–Nickel	2,600,000	Y40
EA25	1959	1 Cent	H	Bronze$_1$	10,000,000	Y37
EA25	1961	1 Cent	H	Bronze$_4$	1,800,000	Y37
EA26		5 Cents	H	Bronze$_4$	4,000,000	Y38
EA25	1962	1 Cent	H	Bronze$_4$	10,320,000	Y37
EA28	1964	10 Cents	H	Bronze$_4$	10,002,000	Y42

It is perhaps surprising that the 1964 issue was struck, because starting in 1960 the East Africa Protectorate gradually fell apart. British Somaliland was first, gaining independence in July 1960 and becoming part of the Somali Republic. Tanganyika was next, achieving independence in 1961. Uganda became an independent country in 1962, closely followed by Kenya and Zanzibar in 1963. In 1964 Tanganyika and Zanzibar united to form Tanzania. Except for Somalia, all remained within the Commonwealth, and all continued to receive coinages produced in Birmingham by THE MINT.

For further comment on East African numismatics, see THE REGAL COINAGE OF BRITISH EAST AFRICA by Thomas Klunzinger in the August 1972 *The Numismatist*, and EAST AFRICA SHILLING BILKS NATIVES by Bob Berman in *World Coins*, October 1969.

ECUADOR Until 1872 Ecuador was on the Real system, and all coinage was from the Quito Mint. With the advent of the decimal system, all subsequent coinage was from foreign mints, of which Heatons' 1872 issue was the first.

EC1   EC4

Coinage Issues of The Birmingham Mint

No.	Date	Denomination	Mintmark	Metal	Mintage	Ref.
EC1	1872	1 Centavo	HEATON	Bronze	Unknown	Y21
EC2		2 Centavos	HEATON	Bronze	Unknown	Y23
EC3	1884	½ Centavo	HB[26]	Copper–Nickel	600,000	Y24
EC4		1 Centavo	HB	Copper–Nickel	500,000	Y25
EC5		½ Decimo	HB	Copper–Nickel	600,000	Y26
EC6		1 Decimo	HB	0.900 Silver	50,000	Y28
EC7		2 Decimos	HB	0.900 Silver	25,000	Y29
EC8		½ Sucre	HB	0.900 Silver	20,000	Y30
EC9		1 Sucre	HB	0.900 Silver	250,000	Y31
	1886					
EC3	m1884	½ Centavo	HB	Copper–Nickel	400,000	Y24
EC4		1 Centavo	HB	Copper–Nickel	1,000,000	Y25
EC5		½ Decimo	HB	Copper–Nickel	600,000	Y26
EC9	1888	1 Sucre	HB	0.900 Silver	100,000	Y31
EC6	1889	1 Decimo	HB	0.900 Silver	100,000	Y28
EC7		2 Decimos	HB	0.900 Silver	50,000	Y29
EC9		1 Sucre	HB	0.900 Silver	150,000	Y31

EC6

EC11
(courtesy Krause Publications)

The 1889 BMR shows a Heaton mintage of 220,000 sucres total. This is assumed to be in error, since records at THE MINT show the above. Three separate orders were received during the year, all from the Paris firm of Osa & Diaz, which was functioning as agent for the Banco Internacional of Guayaquil.

EC10	1890	½ Centavo	H	Copper	2,000,000	Y20
EC11		1 Centavo	H	Copper	2,000,000	Y21
EC6		1 Decimo	HB	0.900 Silver	150,000	Y28
EC7		2 Decimos	HB	0.900 Silver	75,000	Y29
EC7	m1894	2 Decimos	HB	0.900 Silver	1,000,000	Y29
EC9		1 Sucre	HB	0.900 Silver	12,000	Y31

THE MINT records show the above 1894 order from Rothschild & Sons of London for 2 Decimos. It is considered likely that the order was cancelled, but since surviving records do not show a cancellation, it is tentatively included above. The records also show that 12,000 Peruvian Sols were provided by Ecuador for the 1890 Sucre coinage.

EC9	1892	1 Sucre	HB	0.900 Silver	60,000	Y31
EC9	1895	1 Sucre	HB	0.900 Silver	102,073	Y31

[26] The actual mintmark on these coins is HEATON BIRMINGHAM.

No.	Date	Denomination	Mintmark	Metal	Mintage	Ref.

Through 1889, all Ecuador orders were placed through their Paris Agent, the firm of Osa & Diaz. Thereafter, several firms acted as Ecuador's agent, including Fredk. R. Huth & Co., Baring Brothers, and Rothschild & Sons, all of London.

EC12	1899	10 Sucres	B[27]	0.900 Gold	50,000	Fr10
EC12a		10 Sucres	B[27]	Copper	Unknown	–
EC12	1900	10 Sucres	B[27]	0.900 Gold	50,000	Fr10

The Coinage Law of 3 November 1898 approved a gold coin to be called a "Condor Ecuatoriano". The orders were placed on THE MINT by Huth in 1899 and Rothschild in 1900, and the gold blanks were made in the Royal Mint. The order included a requirement for "matrices and punches", which were duly furnished.

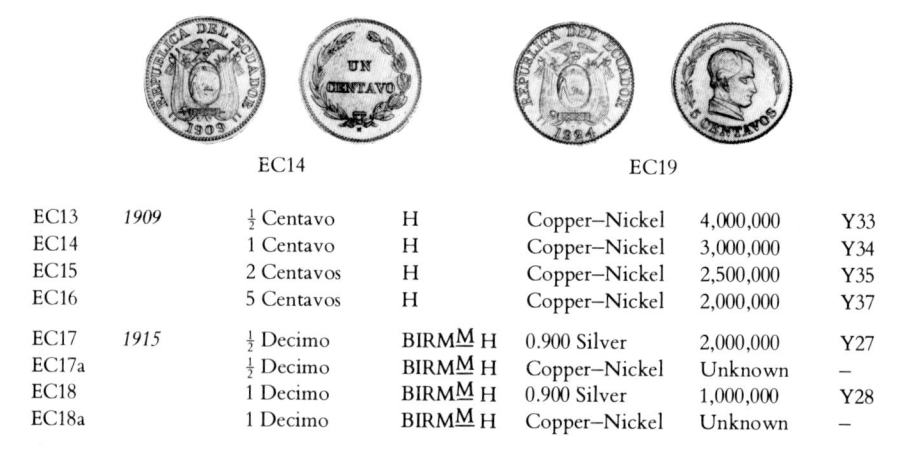

EC14   EC19

EC13	1909	½ Centavo	H	Copper–Nickel	4,000,000	Y33
EC14		1 Centavo	H	Copper–Nickel	3,000,000	Y34
EC15		2 Centavos	H	Copper–Nickel	2,500,000	Y35
EC16		5 Centavos	H	Copper–Nickel	2,000,000	Y37
EC17	1915	½ Decimo	BIRM$\underline{M}$ H	0.900 Silver	2,000,000	Y27
EC17a		½ Decimo	BIRM$\underline{M}$ H	Copper–Nickel	Unknown	–
EC18		1 Decimo	BIRM$\underline{M}$ H	0.900 Silver	1,000,000	Y28
EC18a		1 Decimo	BIRM$\underline{M}$ H	Copper–Nickel	Unknown	–

The Paramount auction sale of August 1975 listed a copper–nickel 1915 1 Decimo. Note that these decimos differ from those of previous years by virtue of the changed mintmark. THE MINT has both copper–nickel pieces.

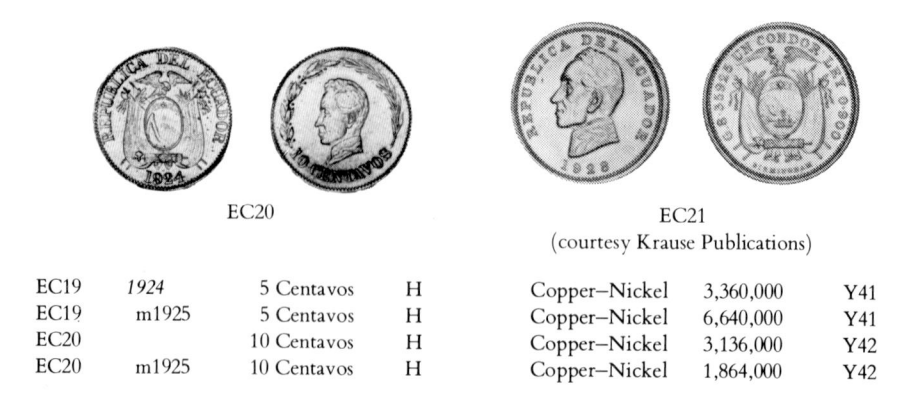

EC20   EC21
(courtesy Krause Publications)

EC19	1924	5 Centavos	H	Copper–Nickel	3,360,000	Y41
EC19	m1925	5 Centavos	H	Copper–Nickel	6,640,000	Y41
EC20		10 Centavos	H	Copper–Nickel	3,136,000	Y42
EC20	m1925	10 Centavos	H	Copper–Nickel	1,864,000	Y42

[27] The actual mintmark is BIRMINGHAM on these coins.

No.	Date	Denomination	Mintmark	Metal	Mintage	Ref.
EC21	*1928*	1 Condor	B[27]	0.900 Gold	20,000	Fr11

With its first coinage for Ecuador, THE MINT ushered in the era of decimal coinage for that country. With its last coinage, it ushered out the era of gold coinage.

EGYPT A general currency reform took place in Egypt in 1886, ordered by a decree of the Khedive dated 14 November 1885.[28] From then until 1903, almost all of Egypt's coinage was struck in the Berlin Mint, but starting in 1904 THE MINT enjoyed a near monopoly on Egyptian coinage. During this period Egypt, although strongly influenced by the British, was nominally subject to the Porte in Constantinople, and so its coins were markedly similar to Turkish coins. Regnal Year dating was used, with Year 1 beginning on 1 September 1876.

Accession Year AH*1293* – Abdul Hamid II (Reigned: 1 September 1876– 26 April 1909).

EG2 EG9

	Yr29(1904)					
EG7	m1904	1 Guerche	H	0.833 Silver	100,000	Y18
EG8	m1904	2 Guerche	H	0.833 Silver	1,250,000	Y19
EG9	m1904	5 Guerche	H	0.833 Silver	3,465,365	Y20
EG10	m1904	10 Guerche	H	0.833 Silver	2,950,000	Y21
EG11	m1904	20 Guerche	H	0.833 Silver	425,000	Y22
	Yr30(1905)					
EG8	m1905	2 Guerche	H	0.833 Silver	250,000	Y19
EG9	m1905	5 Guerche	H	0.833 Silver	1,213,365	Y20
EG10	m1905	10 Guerche	H	0.833 Silver	1,000,000	Y21
EG11	m1905	20 Guerche	H	0.833 Silver	200,000	Y22
	Yr31(1906)					
EG1	m1906	1/40 Guerche	H	Bronze	2,400,000	Y12
EG2	m1906	1/20 Guerche	H	Bronze	3,000,000	Y13
EG3	m1906	1/10 Guerche	H	Copper–Nickel	3,000,000	Y14
EG4	m1906	2/10 Guerche	H	Copper–Nickel	1,000,000	Y15
EG9	m1906	5 Guerche	H	0.833 Silver	1,958,604	Y20
EG10	m1906	10 Guerche	H	0.833 Silver	1,250,000	Y21
EG11	m1906	20 Guerche	H	0.833 Silver	250,000	Y22

[28] For a more complete discussion of this currency reform, see the 1886 BMR, pages 37–8 and 80–6.

No.	Date	Denomination	Mintmark	Metal	Mintage	Ref.
	Yr32(1907)					
EG1	m1907	1/40 Guerche	H	Bronze	Included	Y12
EG2	m1907	1/20 Guerche	H	Bronze	in the	Y13
EG3	m1907	1/10 Guerche	H	Copper–Nickel	Year 33	Y14
EG9	m1907	5 Guerche	H	0.833 Silver	totals	Y20
EG10	m1907	10 Guerche	H	0.833 Silver	below[a]	Y21
EG11	m1907	20 Guerche	H	0.833 Silver		Y22
	Yr33(1908)					
EG1	m1907	1/40 Guerche	H	Bronze	1,200,000[a]	Y12
EG2	m1907	1/20 Guerche	H	Bronze	1,400,000[a]	Y13
EG3	m1907	1/10 Guerche	H	Copper–Nickel	2,000,000[a]	Y14
EG4	m1907	2/10 Guerche	H	Copper–Nickel	1,500,000	Y15
EG5	m1907	5/10 Guerche	H	Copper–Nickel	1,000,000	Y16
EG6	m1907	1 Guerche	H	Copper–Nickel	1,000,000	Y17
EG7	m1907	1 Guerche	H	0.833 Silver	100,000	Y18
EG8	m1907	2 Guerche	H	0.833 Silver	450,000	Y19
EG9	m1907	5 Guerche	H	0.833 Silver	2,800,000[a]	Y20
EG10	m1907	10 Guerche	H	0.833 Silver	2,400,000[a]	Y21
EG11	m1907	20 Guerche	H	0.833 Silver	300,000[a]	Y22
	YR35(1910)					
EG1	m1909	1/40 Guerche	H	Bronze	1,200,000	Y12
EG2	m1909	1/20 Guerche	H	Bronze	1,400,000	Y13
EG3	m1909	1/10 Guerche	H	Copper–Nickel	2,000,000	Y14
EG4	m1909	2/10 Guerche	H	Copper–Nickel	750,000	Y15

Abdul Hamid II was dethroned and imprisoned for life in April 1909. This was in the middle of his 34th reign year, and so the coins dated Year 35 must have been struck in the early part of 1909. His Year 35 would have started about August 1909.

Abdul Hamid II was succeeded by Mehmed V. His tenuous control over Egypt ended in 1914 when the Khedive was deposed and a British Protectorate established. During this period the Turkish style coinage continued, as did Egypt's almost complete dependence on THE MINT for its coinage.

Accession Year AH*1327* – Mehmed V (Reigned: 26 April 1909–3 July 1918).

EG16

No.	Date	Denomination	Mintmark	Metal	Mintage	Ref.
	Yr2(1910)					
EG12	m1910	1/40 Guerche	H	Bronze	2,000,000	Y23
EG13	m1910	1/20 Guerche	H	Bronze	2,000,000	Y24
EG14	m1910	1/10 Guerche	H	Copper–Nickel	3,000,000	Y25
EG15	m1910	2/10 Guerche	H	Copper–Nickel	1,000,000	Y26
EG16	m1910	5/10 Guerche	H	Copper–Nickel	2,130,673	Y27

Coinage Issues of The Birmingham Mint

No.	Date	Denomination	Mintmark	Metal	Mintage	Ref.

EG21

No.	Date	Denomination	Mintmark	Metal	Mintage	Ref.
	Yr2(1910)					
EG17	m1910	1 Guerche	H	Copper–Nickel	1,000,000	Y28
EG18	m1910	1 Guerche	H	0.833 Silver	250,943	Y29
EG19	m1910	2 Guerche	H	0.833 Silver	250,000	Y30
EG20	m1910	5 Guerche	H	0.833 Silver	574,336	Y31
EG21	m1910	10 Guerche	H	0.833 Silver	300,000	Y32
EG22	m1910	20 Guerche	H	0.833 Silver	75,000	Y33
	Yr3(1911)					
EG12	m1911	1/40 Guerche	H	Bronze	2,000,000	Y23
EG13	m1911	1/20 Guerche	H	Bronze	2,000,000	Y24
EG18	m1911	1 Guerche	H	0.833 Silver	171,070	Y29
EG19	m1911	2 Guerche	H	0.833 Silver	300,000	Y30
EG20	m1911	5 Guerche	H	0.833 Silver	2,400,000	Y31
EG21	m1911	10 Guerche	H	0.833 Silver	1,300,000	Y32
EG22	m1911	20 Guerche	H	0.833 Silver	600,000	Y33

In addition to the above, 2.8 million copper–nickel pieces were also struck by the Vienna Mint in denominations of 1/10 to 1 guerche.

No.	Date	Denomination	Mintmark	Metal	Mintage	Ref.
	Yr4(1912)					
EG12	m1913	1/40 Guerche	H	Bronze	1,200,000	Y23
EG13	m1912	1/20 Guerche	H	Bronze	1,000,000	Y24
EG13	m1913	1/20 Guerche	H	Bronze	1,400,000	Y24
EG14	m1912	1/10 Guerche	H	Copper–Nickel	3,000,000	Y25
EG15	m1912	2/10 Guerche	H	Copper–Nickel	1,000,000	Y26
EG16	m1912	5/10 Guerche	H	Copper–Nickel	3,327,439	Y27
EG17	m1912	1 Guerche	H	Copper–Nickel	500,000	Y28
EG20	m1912	5 Guerche	H	0.833 Silver	1,000,000	Y31
EG20	m1913	5 Guerche	H	0.833 Silver	350,923	Y31
EG21	m1912	10 Guerche	H	0.833 Silver	300,000	Y32
EG22	m1912	20 Guerche	H	0.833 Silver	100,000	Y33
	Yr6(1914)					
EG12	m1914	1/40 Guerche	H	Bronze	1,200,000	Y23
EG13	m1914	1/20 Guerche	H	Bronze	1,400,000	Y24
EG14	m1914	1/10 Guerche	H	Copper–Nickel	3,000,000	Y25
EG15	m1914	2/10 Guerche	H	Copper–Nickel	1,000,000	Y26
EG16	m1916	5/10 Guerche	H	Copper–Nickel	3,000,000	Y27
EG17	m1915	1 Guerche	H	Copper–Nickel	2,000,000	Y28
EG17	m1916	1 Guerche	H	Copper–Nickel	500,000	Y28
EG20	m1915	5 Guerche	H	0.833 Silver	5,800,000	Y31

No.	Date	Denomination	Mintmark	Metal	Mintage	Ref.
	Yr6(1914)					
EG20	m1916	5 Guerche	H	0.833 Silver	1,600,000	Y31
EG21	m1915	10 Guerche	H	0.833 Silver	2,847,000	Y32
EG21	m1916	10 Guerche	H	0.833 Silver	1,365,000	Y32
EG22	m1915	20 Guerche	H	0.833 Silver	825,000	Y33
EG22	m1916	20 Guerche	H	0.833 Silver	50,000	Y33

By Law No. 25 of 18 October 1916, a new coinage was mandated with the name of Sultan Hussein and his Accession Year AH1333 (AD1915). Both THE MINT and the Bombay Mint struck coins to the new design, as well as King's Norton (in 1921). These bear both Mohammedan and Christian dates, and English and Arabic values. The silver coins' designer was John Harvey Rowntree of the Egyptian Survey Dept.; the nickel coins were by Hamid Effendi Sirry of the Government Assay Office, Egypt.

EG24   EG28

No.	Date	Denomination	Mintmark	Metal	Mintage	Ref.
	AH1335/1916					
EG24	m1916	2 Milliemes	H	Copper–Nickel	300,000	Y36
EG25	m1916	5 Milliemes	H	Copper–Nickel	3,000,000	Y37
EG26	m1916	10 Milliemes	H	Copper–Nickel	1,000,000	Y38
	AH1335/1917					
EG23	m1917	1 Millieme	H	Copper–Nickel	4,000,000	Y35
EG23	m1918	1 Millieme	H	Copper–Nickel	135,000	Y35
EG23	m1919	1 Millieme	H	Copper–Nickel	5,705,000	Y35
EG23	m1920	1 Millieme	H	Copper–Nickel	2,160,000	Y35
EG24	m1917	2 Milliemes	H	Copper–Nickel	3,000,000	Y36
EG24	m1918	2 Milliemes	H	Copper–Nickel	1,752,500	Y36
EG24	m1919	2 Milliemes	H	Copper–Nickel	4,247,500	Y36
EG25	m1917	5 Milliemes	H	Copper–Nickel	3,000,000	Y37
EG25	m1918	5 Milliemes	H	Copper–Nickel	5,164,000	Y37
EG25	m1919	5 Milliemes	H	Copper–Nickel	10,836,000	Y37
EG25	m1920	5 Milliemes	H	Copper–Nickel	15,008,000	Y37
EG25	m1921	5 Milliemes	H	Copper–Nickel	2,992,000	Y37
EG26	m1917	10 Milliemes	H	Copper–Nickel	1,000,000	Y38
EG26	m1918	10 Milliemes	H	Copper–Nickel	3,000,000	Y38
EG26	m1919	10 Milliemes	H	Copper–Nickel	2,000,000	Y38
EG26	m1920	10 Milliemes	H	Copper–Nickel	5,000,000	Y38
EG27	m1919	2 Piastres	H	0.833 Silver	2,180,000	Y39
EG28	m1917	5 Piastres	H	0.833 Silver	4,452,000	Y40
EG28	m1918	5 Piastres	H	0.833 Silver	548,000	Y40
EG29	m1917	10 Piastres	H	0.833 Silver	1,223,000	Y41
EG29	m1918	10 Piastres	H	0.833 Silver	777,000	Y41

Coinage Issues of The Birmingham Mint 139

No.	Date	Denomination	Mintmark	Metal	Mintage	Ref.
	AH1335/1917					
EG30	m1917	20 Piastres	H	0.833 Silver	160,500	Y42
EG30	m1918	20 Piastres	H	0.833 Silver	89,500	Y42

In 1917 Sultan Hussein was succeeded by Sultan Fuad I, whose name and accession year (AH1335) appear on the issues of 1920.

EG32

	AH1338/1920					
EG31	m1920	2 Piastres	H	0.833 Silver	2,545,000	Y44
EG31	m1921	2 Piastres	H	0.833 Silver	275,000	Y44
EG32	m1920	5 Piastres	H	0.833 Silver	400,000	Y45
EG32	m1921	5 Piastres	H	0.833 Silver	600,000	Y45
EG33	m1920	10 Piastres	H	0.833 Silver	30,000	Y46
EG33	m1921	10 Piastres	H	0.833 Silver	470,000	Y46

EG33

Finally, in 1922 Egypt became an independent kingdom under Fuad, whose portrait thereafter adorned Egypt's coinage. The double dating continued to appear, but with the British no longer politically involved both dates (Mohammedan and Christian) now appear in Arabic.

EG36

140   *Catalogue*

No.	Date	Denomination	Mintmark	Metal	Mintage	Ref.
	AH*1341/1923*					
EG35	m1925	5 Piastres	H	0.833 Silver	800,000	Y53
EG35	m1926	5 Piastres	H	0.833 Silver	1,000,000	Y53
EG36	m1925	10 Piastres	H	0.833 Silver	500,000	Y54
EG36	m1926	10 Piastres	H	0.833 Silver	500,000	Y54
EG37	m1925	20 Piastres	H	0.833 Silver	50,000	Y55
	AH*1342/1923*					
EG34	m1924	2 Piastres	H	0.833 Silver	2,500,000	Y52

In 1923 the Royal Mint struck coins for Egypt. The 1923 BMR states that it was "... the first undertaking for many years in this department for an independent state...". It was a significant expansion of the Royal Mint role, but certainly an unfortunate event for THE MINT, because here was a potent new competitor in the commercial minting business. Note that THE MINT received no more orders for silver coinage for Egypt.

EG39   EG43

	AH*1342/1924*					
EG38	m1925	½ Millieme	H	Bronze$_1$	2,000,000	Y47
EG38	m1926	½ Millieme	H	Bronze$_1$	1,000,000	Y47
EG39	m1925	1 Millieme	H	Bronze$_1$	3,000,000	Y48
EG39	m1926	1 Millieme	H	Bronze$_1$	3,500,000	Y48
EG40	m1925	2 Milliemes	H	Copper–Nickel	3,000,000	Y49
EG40	m1929	2 Milliemes	H	Copper–Nickel	1,500,000	Y49

Following the establishment of the Kingdom, the first coinage was struck in 1923–6 with the portrait of Fuad facing right. The second coinage, with the royal portrait facing left, was struck during the years 1929–35. The entire coinage dated 1929, with BP mintmark, was struck in Budapest.

	AH*1351/1932*					
EG41	m1932	½ Millieme	H	Bronze$_1$	1,000,000	Y60
EG42	m1932	1 Millieme	H	Bronze$_1$	2,500,000	Y61
	AH*1352/1933*					
EG42x	m1934	1 Millieme	H	Bronze$_1$	5,110,000	Y61
EG43x	m1934	2½ Milliemes	None	Copper–Nickel	4,000,000	Y63

This was Egypt's only octagonal coin, and it was struck in only the one year.

EG44x	m1934	5 Milliemes	H	Copper–Nickel	3,000,000	Y64
EG45x	m1934	10 Milliemes	H	Copper–Nickel	1,500,000	Y65

Coinage Issues of The Birmingham Mint

No.	Date	Denomination	Mintmark	Metal	Mintage	Ref.

The 1352 issues, as well as the 1354 and 1357 issues, were placed with THE MINT, who partially subcontracted them out to Imperial Chemical Industries (formerly King's Norton). The mintage figures shown here are the totals for the issues, half of which was produced by each mint. The H mintmark was on the emissions of both mints.

AH1354/1935

EG42x	m1935	1 Millieme	H	Bronze$_1$	8,000,000	Y61
EG42x	m1936	1 Millieme	H	Bronze$_1$	10,000,000	Y61
EG44x	m1935	5 Milliemes	H	Copper–Nickel	2,000,000	Y64
EG44x	m1936	5 Milliemes	H	Copper–Nickel	4,000,000	Y64
EG44x	m1937	5 Milliemes	H	Copper–Nickel	2,000,000	Y64
EG45x	m1935	10 Milliemes	H	Copper–Nickel	1,000,000	Y65
EG45x	m1936	10 Milliemes	H	Copper–Nickel	2,000,000	Y65
EG45x	m1937	10 Milliemes	H	Copper–Nickel	1,000,000	Y65

Fuad died in 1936, and was succeeded by his son Farouk I. Farouk's first minor coinage was the 1938 issue, struck by THE MINT and ICI without mintmarks. Several of the denominations were struck in both bronze and copper–nickel during the next few years.

EG44   EG51

AH1357/1938

EG46x	m1939	½ Millieme	None	Bronze$_1$	4,000,000	Y74
EG47x	m1938	1 Millieme	None	Bronze$_1$	820,000	Y75
EG47x	m1939	1 Millieme	None	Bronze$_1$	9,180,000	Y75
EG47x	m1942	1 Millieme	None	Bronze$_1$	12,400,000	Y75
EG47x	m1943	1 Millieme	None	Bronze$_1$	3,840,000	Y75
EG48x	m1938	1 Millieme	None	Copper–Nickel	1,980,000	Y79
EG48x	m1939	1 Millieme	None	Copper–Nickel	1,520,000	Y79
EG49x	m1939	2 Milliemes	None	Copper–Nickel	2,500,000	Y80
EG50x	m1938	5 Milliemes	None	Copper–Nickel	1,600,000	Y81
EG50x	m1939	5 Milliemes	None	Copper–Nickel	5,400,000	Y81
EG51x	m1938	10 Milliemes	None	Copper–Nickel	252,000	Y82
EG51x	m1939	10 Milliemes	None	Copper–Nickel	3,248,000	Y82

AH1360/1941

EG50x	m1941	5 Milliemes	None	Copper–Nickel	1,520,000	Y81
EG50x	m1942	5 Milliemes	None	Copper–Nickel$_1$	8,480,000	Y81
EG50x	m1943	5 Milliemes	None	Copper–Nickel$_1$	1,500,000	Y81
EG51x	m1941	10 Milliemes	None	Copper–Nickel	644,000	Y82
EG51x	m1942	10 Milliemes	None	Copper–Nickel$_1$	3,676,000	Y82
EG51x	m1943	10 Milliemes	None	Copper–Nickel$_1$	1,002,000	Y82

142   Catalogue

No.   Date   Denomination   Mintmark   Metal   Mintage   Ref.

These last issues by THE MINT for Egypt were ill-fated, because at least 1,360,000 1 milliemes and 294,000 10 milliemes were lost in transit from England to Egypt as a result of enemy action in January and February of 1943.

EIRE

ER1

	1968					
ER1x	m1969	1 Penny	None	Bronze$_4$	21,000,000	Y11
ER2x	m1969	3 Pence	None	Copper–Nickel	4,000,000	Y12a

ER2

This was the last issue before decimalization came to Eire, and it was THE MINT's first for that country. Percy Metcalfe designed the coins, which date back to 1928.

EL SALVADOR   Although Salvador became independent in about 1839, its first distinctive coinage was produced by THE MINT in 1889. The order was placed through G. Bryson, the Birmingham consul for Ecuador.

SD2

SD1	1889	1 Centavo	H	Copper–Nickel	1,500,000	Y1
SD2		3 Centavos	H	Copper–Nickel	333,333	Y2
	1911					
SD3	m1912	5 Centavos	None	0.835 Silver	1,000,000	Y22
SD4	m1912	10 Centavos	None	0.835 Silver	1,000,000	Y23
SD5	m1912	25 Centavos	None	0.835 Silver	600,000	Y24

Coinage Issues of The Birmingham Mint 143

No.	Date	Denomination	Mintmark	Metal	Mintage	Ref.

SD5

| SD1 | 1913 | 1 Centavo | H | Copper–Nickel | 2,500,000 | Y1 |
| SD2 | | 3 Centavos | H | Copper–Nickel | 1,000,000 | Y2 |

Henceforth until the 1970s, all of Salvador's coinages were struck in U.S. mints, with the exception of the 1 colon of 1925, which was struck in Mexico.

ETHIOPIA The modern coinages of Ethiopia have been struck principally at Paris and Addis Ababa, but with the accession of Haile Selassie in 1930 outside mints were called on to supplement the output of the Addis Ababa Mint. This was particularly so with the large new coinage that took place after 1944.

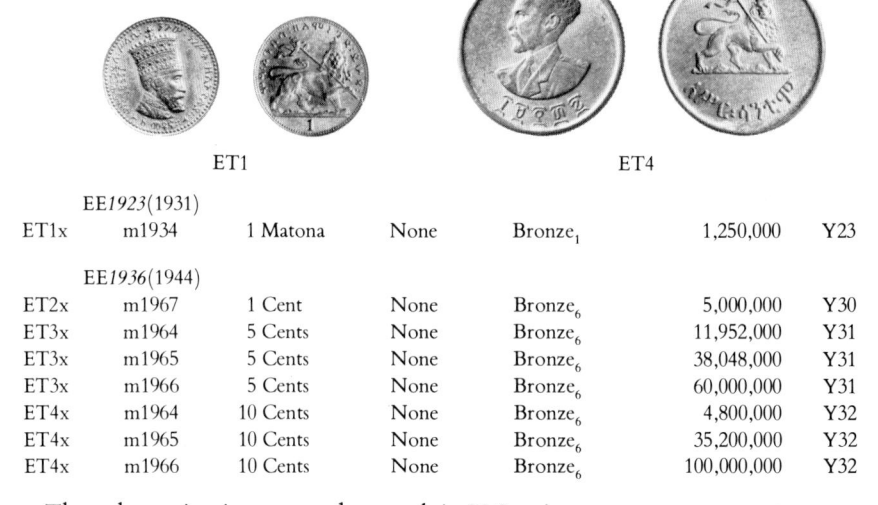

ET1   ET4

	EE*1923*(1931)					
ET1x	m1934	1 Matona	None	Bronze$_1$	1,250,000	Y23
	EE*1936*(1944)					
ET2x	m1967	1 Cent	None	Bronze$_6$	5,000,000	Y30
ET3x	m1964	5 Cents	None	Bronze$_6$	11,952,000	Y31
ET3x	m1965	5 Cents	None	Bronze$_6$	38,048,000	Y31
ET3x	m1966	5 Cents	None	Bronze$_6$	60,000,000	Y31
ET4x	m1964	10 Cents	None	Bronze$_6$	4,800,000	Y32
ET4x	m1965	10 Cents	None	Bronze$_6$	35,200,000	Y32
ET4x	m1966	10 Cents	None	Bronze$_6$	100,000,000	Y32

These denominations were also struck in U.S. mints.

FIJI The reverse designs of this new decimal coinage are by Geoffrey Colley from original work by J. K. Payne. The obverses are by Arnold Machin.

FJ1 rev.   FJ2

No.	Date	Denomination	Mintmark	Metal	Mintage	Ref.
	1969					
FJ1	m1968	1 Cent	None	Bronze$_4$	11,000,000	Y27
FJ2	m1968	2 Cents	None	Bronze$_4$	8,000,000	Y28

FINLAND On gaining independence following World War I, Finland's coinage needs exploded, and the Mint at Helsinki was unable to meet the demand. Accordingly, the copper–nickel coinage was contracted out to THE MINT, while the Helsinki Mint busied itself with the new bronze coinage.

FN3

FN1	1921	25 Penniä	H	Copper–Nickel	20,096,000	Y36
FN2		50 Penniä	H	Copper–Nickel	10,072,000	Y37
FN3		1 Markka	H	Copper–Nickel	10,048,000	Y38

Compared with all previous issues, these were huge mintages, made necessary by the inflation-born requirement of replacing the silver coins previously struck in these denominations.

This was THE MINT's only coinage contract with Finland. An H mintmark on Finnish coinage in the 1950s continues to be confused for coinage by THE MINT. For an explanation, see Appendix V.

FRANCE Bronze as a coinage metal was reintroduced by the French in 1791 when they legislated a loosely-defined mixture of copper and bell-metal.[29] This went through various permutations until finally rigidly fixed by law dated 6 May 1852, a law which ushered in the modern bronze age – at least as far as coinage was concerned. That same law decreed a general recoinage for France, and by participating under contract to the French Government in that recoinage, Heatons became one of the first minters to produce modern bronze coins. (See Appendix I for complete details of Heatons' participation).

FR4

[29] See BMR 1923, pp. 51–2.

Coinage Issues of The Birmingham Mint

No.	Date	Denomination	Mintmark	Metal	Mintage	Ref.
FR1	1853	1 Centime	MA	Bronze	224,966	Y14
FR2		2 Centimes	MA	Bronze	162,823	Y15
FR3		5 Centimes	MA	Bronze	1,654,175	Y16
FR4		10 Centimes	MA	Bronze	889,145	Y17
FR1	1854	1 Centime	MA	Bronze	1,976,110	Y14
FR2		2 Centimes	MA	Bronze	1,311,775	Y15
FR3		5 Centimes	MA	Bronze	14,834,662	Y16
FR4		10 Centimes	MA	Bronze	7,994,737	Y17
FR1	1855	1 Centime	MA	Bronze	2,838,936	Y14
FR2		2 Centimes	MA	Bronze	2,437,805	Y15
FR3		5 Centimes	MA	Bronze	15,417,041	Y16
FR4		10 Centimes	MA	Bronze	11,309,128	Y17
FR1	1856	1 Centime	MA	Bronze	305,227	Y14
FR2		2 Centimes	MA	Bronze	2,780,834	Y15
FR3		5 Centimes	MA	Bronze	16,996,668	Y16
FR4		10 Centimes	MA	Bronze	10,936,634	Y17
FR1	1857	1 Centime	MA	Bronze	1,500,000	Y14
FR2		2 Centimes	MA	Bronze	1,250,001	Y15
FR3		5 Centimes	MA	Bronze	4,187,969	Y16
FR4		10 Centimes	MA	Bronze	2,051,927	Y17

These mintages are per Harris.[30] Records in THE MINT show the total value of this coinage to have been 6,200,000 francs, which exactly checks the above total.

French Indo-China In 1863 the French established a Protectorate relation with Cambodia, and by 1887 had persuaded Cambodia to become part of the French Indo-China Federation. Beginning then in 1887 the coinage of the area was generally produced in Paris, and bore French Indo-China designations. Nevertheless, between 1879 and 1889 Heatons received several orders for bronze coins for Cambodia, the last of which was referenced by the 1889 BMR as follows: "... for the French Dependency of Cambodia, a copper [sic] coinage of 26,500 kilograms in ten-cent pieces and 4000 kilograms in five-cent pieces." It is possible that earlier orders (than 1879) were also received by Heatons; records at THE MINT are less than complete.

FC1

---

[30] Robert P. Harris, *A Guidebook of Modern European Coins*, 1st Edition, Racine, Wisc., Western Publishing Company, Inc., 1965.

Catalogue

No.	Date	Denomination	Mintmark	Metal	Mintage	Ref.
	1860					
FC1x	m1879	5 Centimes	None	Bronze	9,000,000	Y2
FC1x	m1882	5 Centimes	None	Bronze	1,666,667	Y2
FC1x	m1889	5 Centimes	None	Bronze	800,000	Y2
FC2x	m1879	10 Centimes	None	Bronze	6,000,000	Y3
FC2x	m1882	10 Centimes	None	Bronze	1,666,667	Y3
FC2x	m1889	10 Centimes	None	Bronze	2,600,000	Y3

The 1879 and 1882 orders were placed by Oeschger Mesdach & Co. of Paris, they furnishing the blanks for the 1882 coinage. The 1889 order was placed by the successor firm Eschger Ghesquière & Co., who furnished both blanks and dies to Heatons.

Following World War I, when the French Mint was busy producing massive coinages for use in France proper, THE MINT received a contract for manufacture of trade coins for French Indo-China.

FC3

| FC3 | *1921* | 1 Piastre | H | 0.900 Silver | 3,580,000 | Y9a |
| FC3 | *1922* | 1 Piastre | H | 0.900 Silver | 7,420,289 | Y9a |

GHANA Formerly the Gold Coast and a part of British West Africa (q.v.), Ghana became an independent republic within the British Commonwealth on 6 March 1957. It was the first black country south of the Sahara to shake off colonial rule.

GH1

| GH1x | *1958* | 2 Shillings | None | Copper–Nickel | 15,000,000 | Y6 |

Coinage Issues of The Birmingham Mint 147

No.   Date   Denomination   Mintmark   Metal   Mintage   Ref.

This was part of a large new coinage ordered from the Royal Mint. The issue was designed to correspond to the superseded currency of British West Africa. P. Vincze was responsible for the obverse design, the reverse being engraved in the Royal Mint.

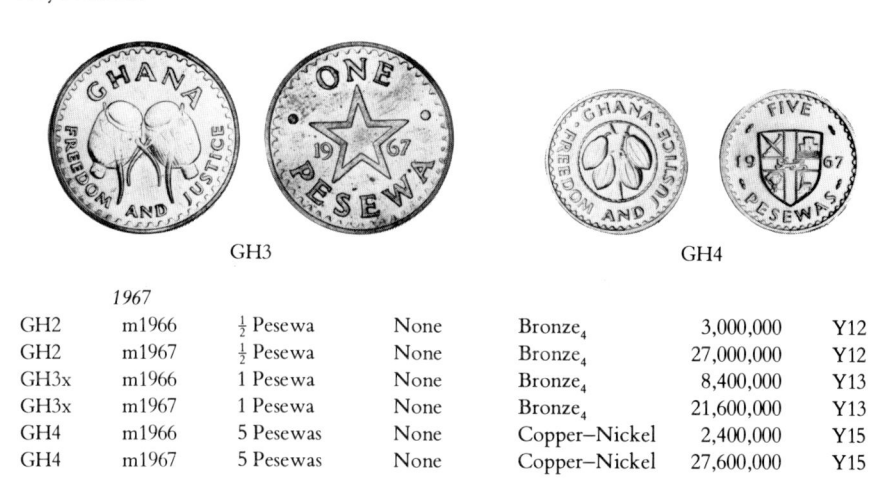

GH3   GH4

	1967					
GH2	m1966	½ Pesewa	None	Bronze$_4$	3,000,000	Y12
GH2	m1967	½ Pesewa	None	Bronze$_4$	27,000,000	Y12
GH3x	m1966	1 Pesewa	None	Bronze$_4$	8,400,000	Y13
GH3x	m1967	1 Pesewa	None	Bronze$_4$	21,600,000	Y13
GH4	m1966	5 Pesewas	None	Copper–Nickel	2,400,000	Y15
GH4	m1967	5 Pesewas	None	Copper–Nickel	27,600,000	Y15

Michael Rizzello produced both the obverse and reverse designs of the 1967 coinage.

Ghurfah (Al-Ghuraf)   This small village sultanate near the Wadi Hadramawt in what is now The People's Democratic Republic of Yemen, then under British protection, issued its own currency in denominations slightly different from those used by its neighbour Tarim (q.v.). The total issue was produced by THE MINT.

GU5

	AH*1344*(1925/1926)					
GU1	m1926	4 Chomsihs	None	0.900 Silver	5,000	Y4
GU2	m1926	8 Chomsihs	None	0.900 Silver	5,000	Y6
GU3	m1926	15 Chomsihs	None	0.900 Silver	5,000	Y8
GU3	m1927	15 Chomsihs	None	0.900 Silver	5,000	Y8
GU4	m1926	30 Chomsihs	None	0.900 Silver	5,000	Y10
GU4	m1927	30 Chomsihs	None	0.900 Silver	5,000	Y10
GU5	m1926	45 Chomsihs	None	0.900 Silver	5,000	Y11
GU5	m1927	45 Chomsihs	None	0.900 Silver	5,000	Y11
GU6	m1926	60 Chomsihs	None	0.900 Silver	5,000	Y12
GU6	m1927	60 Chomsihs	None	0.900 Silver	5,000	Y12

No.	Date	Denomination	Mintmark	Metal	Mintage	Ref.

GREAT BRITAIN By the mid-nineteenth century, the Royal Mint on Little Tower Hill was still equipped with the old screw presses that were manufactured by Matthew Boulton in 1805. The output of the old presses was quite limited in terms of the needs of the times, and the Royal Mint's melting and blanking operations were also inadequate. Thus when the very heavy demand for Imperial coinage in all three metals (copper, silver, and gold) arose in 1853, The Royal Mint found it necessary to farm out large quantities of copper coinage to Heaton & Sons.

Numismatic references do not indicate exactly what mintages were provided by Heatons, but clues are available which admit of a reasonable conclusion. First, in his testimony before the Decimal Coinage Commission on 30 July 1857, Thomas Graham (Master of the Royal Mint) stated that "... the coin has been executed by one contractor (Heaton) for the last five or six years".[31] Second, in a feature article on the Heaton Mint in their 15 September 1967 issue, the *Birmingham Post* wrote: "During the same period (1853–57 when Ralph Heaton III was managing the Marseilles Mint) Ralph Heaton II made 500 tons of copper pennies, halfpennies, and farthings for the Royal Mint." Third, in their book of testimonials[32] Heatons showed pictures of all the Imperial copper coins of 1853, implicitly accepting responsibility for participation in this coinage. Add to these clues the fact that the copper coinage of 1853–7 totals just under 500 tons, and it appears that Heatons must have produced most of the copper coinage in that period while the Royal Mint busied itself producing an extraordinarily large output of silver and gold Imperial coinage. Mr. G. P. Dyer of the Royal Mint confirms that Heatons did indeed produce all of the 1853–6 Imperial copper coinage except for 11.15 tons that were struck by the Royal Mint in 1854, although an element of doubt necessarily attaches to the exact mintage figures due to the inadequacy of surviving Mint records. Heatons' contribution is calculated to be as follows:

GB2
(courtesy British Museum)

GB4
(courtesy Krause Publications)

No.	Date	Denomination	Mintmark	Metal	Mintage	Ref.
GB1	1853	¼ Farthing	None	Copper	1,926,048	Y1[33]
GB2		½ Farthing	None	Copper	955,296	Y2[33]
GB3		Farthing	None	Copper	1,028,436	Y1
GB4		Halfpenny	None	Copper	1,559,040	Y2
GB5		Penny	None	Copper	1,021,440	Y3
GB2	1854	½ Farthing	None	Copper	677,376	Y2[33]

[31] Ralph Heaton & Sons, *Testimonials*, 1st Edition, *ca* 1879.
[32] Ibid, Plate II.
[33] These numbers are as listed under Sri Lanka in Yeoman.

Coinage Issues of The Birmingham Mint

No.	Date	Denomination	Mintmark	Metal	Mintage	Ref.
GB3x	1854	Farthing	None	Copper	4,945,920	Y1
GB4x		Halfpenny	None	Copper	12,257,280	Y2
GB5x		Penny	None	Copper	6,558,720	Y3
GB3	1855	Farthing	None	Copper	3,440,640	Y1
GB4		Halfpenny	None	Copper	7,455,837	Y2
GB5		Penny	None	Copper	5,273,856	Y3

Heatons' first coinage contract with the Royal Mint was completed in August 1855, and was soon followed by a contract for 50 tons of copper coins in 1856, completed in December 1856.

No.	Date	Denomination	Mintmark	Metal	Mintage	Ref.
GB2	1856	½ Farthing	None	Copper	913,920	Y2[33]
GB3		Farthing	None	Copper	1,771,392	Y1
GB4		Halfpenny	None	Copper	1,942,080	Y2
GB5		Penny	None	Copper	1,212,288	Y3

Toward the end of the 1850s, Great Britain made the decision to convert from copper to bronze coins – a change that France had made eight years earlier. France had found it necessary to contract for additional minting by private industry (Heatons produced 620 tons of the new bronze coinage in the Marseilles Mint in the period 1853–7), and the Royal Mint had to do likewise in order to effectuate the changeover in an expeditious manner. Continued heavy demands for gold and silver coinage caused the Royal Mint to let out a contract for 1720 tons of bronze coins, and bids by private minters were invited. Heatons' previous experience with bronze and their previous satisfactory contract performance for the Royal Mint certainly gave them reason to expect to receive the contract – except that a lower bid was submitted by the firm of James Watt & Co., a survivor of the Boulton & Watt enterprises of half a century earlier. Because Watt was unable to get production out as rapidly as needed, Heatons were given in 1861 a small contract for 60 tons of bronze coins. This was in addition to the order for coinage dies that the Royal Mint had separately placed on Heatons. This latter function was mentioned in an 1861 letter from Arthur Ryland, Mayor of Birmingham, who stated that "Messrs Heaton & Sons are now engaged in preparing the dies for and in manufacturing part of the new Bronze coinage of this kingdom...".[34] Heatons' actual coinage contribution, according to information furnished by Mr. G. P. Dyer of the Royal Mint, amounted to only 42 tons of the some 1950 tons of bronze struck in the 1860–3 period. This must have been a great disappointment to Heatons, who could logically feel that they had earned the right to this potentially lucrative contract.

No.	Date	Denomination	Mintmark	Metal	Mintage	Ref.
GB6x	1861	Farthing	None	Bronze	716,800	Y16
GB7x		Halfpenny	None	Bronze	1,433,600	Y17
GB8x		Penny	None	Bronze	3,333,120	Y18

Peck[35] commented on this period as follows: "From 1863 to 1873 inclusive all

---

[34] Ralph Heaton & Sons, *Testimonials*, 1st Edition, ca. 1879.
[35] C. Wilson Peck, *English Copper, Tin and Bronze Coins in the British Museum*, London, 1960.

imperial bronze coins were struck in London, but in 1874 and on several later occasions when the Mint was particularly hard-pressed, the coining of part or all . . . of the bronze was again entrusted to Heaton, under Mint supervision." According to the 1874 BMR, ". . . this renewed demand came at a time when the Mint was fully occupied with the coinage of silver. . .", and so the Mint turned to Heatons for the 1874 bronze coinage.

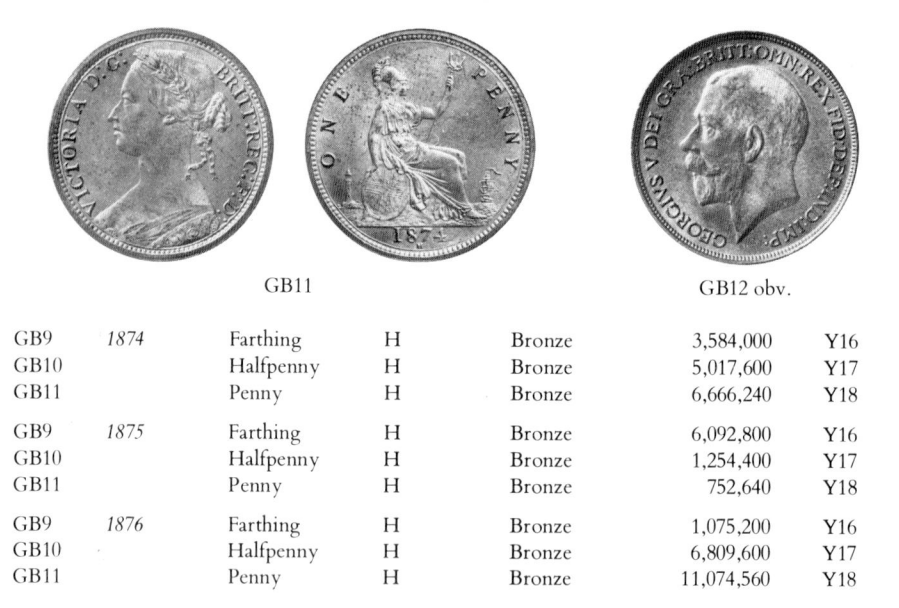

GB11

GB12 obv.

No.	Date	Denomination	Mintmark	Metal	Mintage	Ref.
GB9	1874	Farthing	H	Bronze	3,584,000	Y16
GB10		Halfpenny	H	Bronze	5,017,600	Y17
GB11		Penny	H	Bronze	6,666,240	Y18
GB9	1875	Farthing	H	Bronze	6,092,800	Y16
GB10		Halfpenny	H	Bronze	1,254,400	Y17
GB11		Penny	H	Bronze	752,640	Y18
GB9	1876	Farthing	H	Bronze	1,075,200	Y16
GB10		Halfpenny	H	Bronze	6,809,600	Y17
GB11		Penny	H	Bronze	11,074,560	Y18

A breakdown of its ancient machinery shut down the Royal Mint's coinage activities for five months in 1876, as a result of which Heatons furnished all the bronze coinage that year.

GB9	1881	Farthing	H	Bronze	1,792,000	Y16
GB10		Halfpenny	H	Bronze	1,792,000	Y17
GB11		Penny	H	Bronze	3,763,200	Y18
GB9	1882	Farthing	H	Bronze	1,792,000	Y16
GB10		Halfpenny	H	Bronze	4,480,000	Y17
GB11		Penny	H	Bronze	7,526,400	Y18

In 1882 all the Colonial coinages, as well as all of the Imperial bronze coinage, were produced by Heatons. In this year a new Royal Mint was constructed, and new and rehabilitated machinery installed therein. As a result of the greatly increased capacity, the contracting of Imperial and Colonial coinages became unnecessary until 1889, when demand once again exceeded capacity and Heatons were called on to help with the Colonial requirements.

GB12	1912	Penny	H	Bronze	16,800,000	Y63

Passage of the National Insurance Act on 1 July 1911, which forced employers to

Coinage Issues of The Birmingham Mint

No.   Date   Denomination   Mintmark   Metal   Mintage   Ref.

pay in "broken wages", created an unusually heavy requirement for silver and bronze coins. To help meet the need, THE MINT supplied a portion of that year's Imperial bronze coinage.

| GB12 | 1918 | Penny | H | Bronze | 2,572,800 | Y63 |
| GB12 | 1919 | Penny | H | Bronze | 4,526,034 | Y63 |

These mintages are calculated based on Royal Mint and THE MINT records, and are believed by the Royal Mint to be accurate.

Finally, sixty-five years after it began, THE MINT's participation in the manufacture of Imperial coinage came to an end as the Royal Mint achieved self-sufficiency. For the whole period, THE MINT accounted directly for only about 145 million English coins, but indirectly it contributed importantly to England's total money supply by virtue of the minting machinery and the extensive quantities of coinage metal furnished to the Royal Mint.

GREECE   Shortly before he was pressured into resigning in favour of his eldest son George, Constantine I issued a Royal Decree dated 14 June 1922 authorizing the minting and circulation of coins of copper–nickel and other metals. Orders were immediately placed with two Birmingham firms, King's Norton and THE MINT, for a total of 28 million coins, and both firms filled their orders in the year 1922.

GR1

| GR1 | 1921 m1922 | 50 Lepta | H | Copper–Nickel | 14,000,000 | Y30 |

These coins were never put into circulation. By the time the shipment reached Greece, the market value of the metal was in excess of the face value of the coins, so they were placed in storage in the vaults of the Ministry of Finance in Athens. Four years later they were delivered to Arthur Krupp of Bredore, Austria, for use in the production of the 2 drachmai coins of 1926. Somehow in the interim a few pieces escaped into the hands of collectors. One story has it that while the kegs of coins sat on the loading dock awaiting shipment to Austria, a keg broke open, spilling a few coins on the dock, several of which were liberated by dock employees. A more likely theory is that Finance Ministry personnel gave away a few specimens while the coins were stored in their care.[36][37]

152   *Catalogue*

| No. | Date | Denomination | Mintmark | Metal | Mintage | Ref. |

GR2 dies

In addition, THE MINT received an order on 5 October 1920 for coins of 5 lepta weighing 3 grams and having a diameter of 19 mm. Dies were prepared, but the order was cancelled before production was begun. The dies remain in THE MINT collection. Assuming that specimens were struck for approval, the piece is included in this listing. It is similar to Yeoman No. 19, except that there is a garland on the reverse in place of the owl on Y19.

	1921					
GR2	m1920	5 Lepta	None	Copper–Nickel	Unknown	–

George II took over from his father in September 1922, but left Greece in December 1923; the monarchy was ended by the National Assembly in March 1924. It was restored in October 1935, and George II returned to the throne. His return was memorialized with the following MINT issue.

GR3a

GR4a

[36] James A. Simek, "Greek 1921 50-Lepta Rare", *Coin World*, 5 March 1975, p. 81.
[37] Costas Chr. Hadziotis, "Greece's Mysterious 50 Lepta Coin", *World Coins*, March 1975, p. 62.

Coinage Issues of The Birmingham Mint

No.	Date	Denomination	Mintmark	Metal	Mintage	Ref.
	1935					
GR3	m1939	20 Drachmai	None	0.900 Gold	200	Fr11
GR3a	m1939	20 Drachmai	None	Copper	Unknown	–
GR4	m1939	100 Drachmai	None	0.900 Gold	140	Fr10
GR4a	m1939	100 Drachmai	None	0.900 Silver	500	YA37
GR4b	m1939	100 Drachmai	None	Bronze	Unknown	–

The order was placed in 1939 through Spink & Son, the intention being to commemorate the fifth anniversary of the Restoration of the Monarchy. Regardless, it is the only issue of George II.

The cabinet of THE MINT contains a 20 drachmai in copper, and at least two bronze 100 drachmai have appeared on the market in recent years.

GUATEMALA Until the 1890s, all of Guatemala's coinage needs were supplied by the Casa de Moneda in Guatemala City. Thereafter, the increasing needs were met by countermarking coins of other countries, and by contracting with outside mints. In the years 1894 to 1924 THE MINT was the sole outside supplier. At least during the early years of this relationship, the contracts were placed through the firm of Chalmers, Guthrie & Co. of London, acting as Agent for the Republic of Guatemala. The first order, totalling two million pesos, was executed in 1894 and 1895.

GA1   GA5

GA1	1894	¼ Real	H	0.835 Silver	600,000	Y74
GA2		½ Real	H	0.835 Silver	900,000	Y75
GA3		1 Real	H	0.835 Silver	600,000	Y77
GA4		2 Reales	H	0.835 Silver	900,000	Y82
GA5		4 Reales	H	0.900 Silver	500,000	Y83

GA8

154   *Catalogue*

No.	Date	Denomination	Mintmark	Metal	Mintage	Ref.
GA5s	1894	4 Reales	H/H	0.900 Silver	In above	Y83a
GA6		1 Peso	H	0.900 Silver	875,000	Y84
GA7p		5 Pesos	None	0.900 Gold	17	Fr47
GA7a		5 Pesos	None	Copper	Unknown	–
GA8p		10 Pesos	None	0.900 Gold	17	Fr46

A letter to Heaton[38] dated 16 May 1895 from the Paris Legation of Guatemala included the following: "The engraving of the matrices for the gold and silver coins was . . . well executed, the designs being both pleasing and artistic, and the specimen gold coins highly satisfactory." This refers to THE MINT having provided dies of new designs for 4 reales, 1 peso, 5 and 10 pesos (GA9p, GA10p, GA7p, GA8p), along with the specimen gold pieces. THE MINT cabinet contains trial strikes of all four pieces, as well as the copper strike of GA7a. (See also Lot 225 of the Paramount 8 August 1975 auction of Birmingham material.)

GA9

GA1	1895	¼ Real	H	0.835 Silver	200,000	Y74
GA2		½ Real	H	0.835 Silver	300,000	Y75
GA3		1 Real	H	0.835 Silver	200,000	Y77
GA4		2 Reales	H	0.835 Silver	300,000	Y82
GA9p		4 Reales	H	0.900 Silver	Unknown	–
GA6		1 Peso	H	0.900 Silver	375,000	Y84
GA10p		1 Peso	H	0.900 Silver	Unknown	–

In 1899 a rapid debasement of the coinage took place, ending with a change to copper–nickel in 1900. Then until 1915 all coinage was in copper–nickel, and all was produced by THE MINT except for the silver 1 real of 1900 which was struck in the Casa de Moneda. Note: The Wayte Raymond collection contained an 1894 proof set (GA1–6), and specimens of both GA9p and GA10p.

GA11   GA13

[38] The Mint, Birmingham, Ltd., *Testimonials*, 5th Edition, 1904, p. 15.

No.	Date	Denomination	Mintmark	Metal	Mintage	Ref.
GA11	1900	¼ Real	H	Copper–Nickel	2,944,000	Y85
GA12		½ Real	None	Copper–Nickel	5,348,000	Y86
GA13		1 Real	None	Copper–Nickel	4,612,000	Y87
GA11	1901	¼ Real	H	Copper–Nickel	5,056,000	Y85
GA12		½ Real	None	Copper–Nickel	6,652,000	Y86
GA13		1 Real	None	Copper–Nickel	7,388,000	Y87
GA13m	THE MINT collection contains a nickel–brass piece of GA13 with a double obverse.					
GA13	1910	1 Real	None	Copper–Nickel	4,000,000	Y87
GA13	1911	1 Real	None	Copper–Nickel	2,000,000	Y87
GA13	1912	1 Real	None	Copper–Nickel	8,000,000	Y87

GUERNSEY Although a possession of Great Britain, Guernsey has enjoyed a special status within the Commonwealth. It has its own laws, and is exempt from English law unless specifically cited in the wording of the law. This peculiar status has, among other things, meant that Guernsey has responsibility for making its own mintage decisions, and from 1830 through 1949 Guernsey placed all its coinage contracts with Birmingham firms. The 1830 issue, its first, was apparently produced by Boulton & Watt. The 1858 through 1874 issues are sometimes credited to Heatons, but this is probably wrong. They are not referenced in the Heaton Orderbook, nor does the Heaton Cabinet contain any specimens. Lowsley[39] states that Sir Charles Fremantle. (Deputy Master of the Royal Mint from 1868 to 1894) told him that the early issues were by Boulton, Henry Jay, and Partridge & Co., but these last two firms are now difficult to trace. Hawkins[40] has uncovered Directory references to a Henry Toy & Co., diesinkers, etc., whom he concludes could have produced the 1858 and 1864 issues. He also located a Partridge & Co., furnishing ironmongers, whom he concludes may have been the agents for the Guernsey issues of 1868 and 1874, but were probably not the minters. Who actually did the minting remains a mystery, but it is certain that thereafter, until the issue of 1956, THE MINT was sole supplier to the Channel Island of Guernsey.

GE2

GE1	1885	1 Double	H	Bronze	56,016	Y1
GE2		2 Doubles	H	Bronze	71,280	Y2
GE3		4 Doubles	H	Bronze	69,696	Y3
GE4		8 Doubles	H	Bronze	69,696	Y4

[39] Lt.-Col. B. Lowsley, *The Coinage of the Channel Islands*, London, 1897.
[40] R. N. P. Hawkins, *Coin and Medal Bulletin*, B. A. Seaby, London, April 1970, p. 127.

Catalogue

No.	Date	Denomination	Mintmark	Metal	Mintage	Ref.

GE4

No.	Date	Denomination	Mintmark	Metal	Mintage	Ref.
GE1	1889	1 Double	H	Bronze	56,016	Y1
GE1	m1890	1 Double	H	Bronze	56,016	Y1
GE2		2 Doubles	H	Bronze	35,616	Y2
GE3		4 Doubles	H	Bronze	52,224	Y3
GE3	m1890	4 Doubles	H	Bronze	52,224	Y3
GE4		8 Doubles	H	Bronze	104,496	Y4
GE4	m1890	8 Doubles	H	Bronze	117,600	Y4
GE1	1893	1 Double	H	Bronze	56,016	Y1
GE3		4 Doubles	H	Bronze	52,224	Y3
GE4		8 Doubles	H	Bronze	117,600	Y4
GE1	1899	1 Double	H	Bronze	56,000	Y1
GE2		2 Doubles	H	Bronze	35,636	Y2
	1902					
GE1	m1901	1 Double	H	Bronze	84,000	Y1
GE2	m1901	2 Doubles	H	Bronze	17,818	Y2
GE3	m1901	4 Doubles	H	Bronze	104,534	Y3
GE4	m1901	8 Doubles	H	Bronze	235,200	Y4
GE1	1903	1 Double	H	Bronze	112,000	Y1
GE2		2 Doubles	H	Bronze	17,818	Y2
GE3		4 Doubles	H	Bronze	52,265	Y3
GE4		8 Doubles	H	Bronze	117,600	Y4
GE2	1906	2 Doubles	H	Bronze	17,820	Y2
GE3		4 Doubles	H	Bronze	52,266	Y3
	1908					
GE2	m1907	2 Doubles	H	Bronze	17,780	Y2
GE3	m1907	4 Doubles	H	Bronze	25,760	Y3
GE3	1910	4 Doubles	H	Bronze	52,267	Y3
GE4		8 Doubles	H	Bronze	91,467	Y4
GE1	1911	1 Double	H	Bronze	44,800	Y1
GE5		1 Double	H	Bronze	89,600	Y1a
GE2		2 Doubles	H	Bronze	28,509	Y2
GE3		4 Doubles	H	Bronze	52,267	Y3
GE4		8 Doubles	H	Bronze	78,400	Y4

Minor design detail changes took place in 1911 and 1914.

Coinage Issues of The Birmingham Mint 157

No.	Date	Denomination	Mintmark	Metal	Mintage	Ref.

GE7

No.	Date	Denomination	Mintmark	Metal	Mintage	Ref.
GE5	1914	1 Double	H	Bronze	44,800	Y1a
GE6		2 Doubles	H	Bronze	28,509	Y2a
GE7		4 Doubles	H	Bronze	209,067	Y3a
GE8		8 Doubles	H	Bronze	156,800	Y5
GE6	1917	2 Doubles	H	Bronze	14,524	Y2a
GE6	1918	2 Doubles	H	Bronze	57,018	Y2a
GE7		4 Doubles	H	Bronze	156,800	Y3a
GE8		8 Doubles	H	Bronze	156,800	Y5
GE6	1920	2 Doubles	H	Bronze	57,018	Y2a
GE7		4 Doubles	H	Bronze	156,800	Y3a
GE8		8 Doubles	H	Bronze	156,800	Y5
GE5	1929	1 Double	H	Bronze	79,100	Y1a
GE6		2 Doubles	H	Bronze	79,100	Y2a
GE5	1933	1 Double	H	Bronze	96,000	Y1a
GE8	1934	8 Doubles	H	Bronze	120,000	Y5
GE8	m1935	8 Doubles	H	Bronze	3,600	Y5
GE9	m1935	8 Doubles	H	Bronze	500	Y5

These 500 Mint Specimen pieces, to be struck on polished planchets, were ordered to commemorate the Silver Jubilee of George V, and also the centenary of the eight doubles piece.[41]

No.	Date	Denomination	Mintmark	Metal	Mintage	Ref.
GE5	1938	1 Double	H	Bronze$_1$	96,000	Y1a
GE8		8 Doubles	H	Bronze$_1$	120,000	Y5
GE7	1945	4 Doubles	H	Bronze$_4$	96,000	Y3a
GE8		8 Doubles	H	Bronze$_4$	192,000	Y5
GE8	1947	8 Doubles	H	Bronze$_1$	240,000	Y5
GE7	1949	4 Doubles	H	Bronze$_1$	19,200	Y3a
GE8		8 Doubles	H	Bronze$_1$	230,400	Y5

This was the last issue by THE MINT for Guernsey. At this time the cost of production exceeded the face value of the coins. The people of Guernsey were unwilling to subsidize the minting costs, and THE MINT, not being an eleemosynary institution, could of course not do so. So the Royal Mint took over and thereafter produced Guernsey's coinage.

---

[41] Jerome Remick, *British Commonwealth Coins*, p. 266.

158   *Catalogue*

No.	Date	Denomination	Mintmark	Metal	Mintage	Ref.

GUYANA   As a British possession, this country obtained all its coinage from the Royal Mint. It attained independence in 1966, remaining within the Commonwealth, and continued to use the services of the Royal Mint. The following issues were subcontracted out to THE MINT.

GY1

| GY1 | 1969 | 1 Cent | None | Nickel–Brass | 4,000,000 | Y1 |
| GY1 | 1970 | 1 Cent | None | Nickel–Brass | 6,000,000 | Y1 |

William Gardner modelled the obverse designs for this series.

HAITI   With no national mint, Haiti relied entirely on contract minting for its coinage requirements. Two issues were provided by Heatons, of which at least the 1863 issue was placed through the London firm of Irving, Ebsworth, & Holmes.

HA3

HA1	1863	5 Centimes	HEATON	Bronze	1,000,000	YA1
HA2		10 Centimes	HEATON	Bronze	1,000,000	YB1
HA3		20 Centimes	HEATON	Bronze	1,000,000	YC1

HA5

| HA4 | 1881 | 1 Centime | None | Bronze | 830,000 | Y1 |
| HA5 | | 2 Centimes | None | Bronze | 830,000 | Y2 |

Hedjaz   The first regular coinage of Hedjaz, aside from the previous counterstamped issues, was dated AH1334 Year 5 (AD1920). The 1923 BMR (page

Coinage Issues of The Birmingham Mint 159

No.   Date   Denomination   Mintmark   Metal   Mintage   Ref.

30) states that some machinery had been supplied to Hedjaz from England to enable them to strike coins for local circulation. The following pattern or trial strike in the cabinet of THE MINT suggests that they produced dies to Hedjaz designs for use with the new machinery for striking the 20 piastres or 1 riyal piece; however, the circulation coins that were finally struck in 1923 (Y25) were of a modified design. Note that this pattern bears the date AH1340 Yr 1, whereas all Hedjaz circulation coins bear the accession year AH1334 and the regnal year 5, 8, or 9.

HE1

AH*1340/Yr1*(1922)
| HE1p | m1922 | 20 Piastres | None | Bronze | Unknown | – |

HONG KONG As a Crown Colony, Hong Kong's coinage would normally have been supplied by the Royal Mint. These first issues struck specifically for the Colony came at a time, however, when the Royal Mint was quite busy, and so both Heatons and James Watt were called on to augment the Royal Mint's output.

HK1   HK3 rev.

HK1x	*1863*	1 Mil	None	Bronze	19,000,000	Y1
HK1	*1865*	1 Mil	None	Bronze	40,000,000	Y1
HK2x		1 Cent	None	Bronze	1,000,000	Y2
HK3	*1866*	1 Mil	None	Bronze	20,000,000	Y1a[42]

From 1866 through 1868 a mint operated in Hong Kong, but thereafter for the next ten or twelve years Heatons supplied most of Hong Kong's needs.

| HK4 | *1872* | 5 Cents | H | 0.800 Silver | 136,000 | Y3 |
| HK5 | | 10 Cents | H | 0.800 Silver | 88,000 | Y4 |

[42] The Chinese value designation on the reverse was changed from WEN 文 on HK1 to CH'IEN 千 on HK3.

Catalogue

No.	Date	Denomination	Mintmark	Metal	Mintage	Ref.

HK6

No.	Date	Denomination	Mintmark	Metal	Mintage	Ref.
HK6	1872	20 Cents	H	0.800 Silver	64,000	Y5
HK4	1873	5 Cents	H	0.800 Silver	256,000	Y3
HK5		10 Cents	H	0.800 Silver	128,000	Y4
HK6		20 Cents	H	0.800 Silver	64,000	Y5
HK4	1874	5 Cents	H	0.800 Silver	280,000	Y3
HK5		10 Cents	H	0.800 Silver	200,000	Y4
HK6		20 Cents	H	0.800 Silver	70,000	Y5
HK4	1875	5 Cents	H	0.800 Silver	280,000	Y3
HK5		10 Cents	H	0.800 Silver	200,000	Y4
HK6		20 Cents	H	0.800 Silver	70,000	Y5

HK2

No.	Date	Denomination	Mintmark	Metal	Mintage	Ref.
HK2	1876	1 Cent	None	Bronze	1,000,000	Y2
HK4		5 Cents	H	0.800 Silver	480,000	Y3
HK5		10 Cents	H	0.800 Silver	480,000	Y4
HK6		20 Cents	H	0.800 Silver	120,000	Y5
HK4	1877	5 Cents	H	0.800 Silver	240,000	Y3
HK5		10 Cents	H	0.800 Silver	240,000	Y4
HK6		20 Cents	H	0.800 Silver	60,000	Y5
HK2	1880	1 Cent	None	Bronze	1,000,000	Y2
HK4		5 Cents	H	0.800 Silver	300,000	Y3
HK5		10 Cents	H	0.800 Silver	300,000	Y4
HK6		20 Cents	H	0.800 Silver	25,000	Y5
HK4	1882	5 Cents	H	0.800 Silver	600,000	Y3
HK5		10 Cents	H	0.800 Silver	500,000	Y4
HK6		20 Cents	H	0.800 Silver	100,000	Y5
HK4	1883	5 Cents	H	0.800 Silver	250,000	Y3
HK5		10 Cents	H	0.800 Silver	250,000	Y4
HK6		20 Cents	H	0.800 Silver	62,500	Y5

The 1885 BMR spoke of the Hong Kong coinage as follows: "The nominal

No.	Date	Denomination	Mintmark	Metal	Mintage	Ref.

value of the subsidiary silver coins struck at the Mint, and by Messrs. Ralph Heaton & Sons, of Birmingham, for the government of Hong Kong during the last five years has been no less than 1,090,000 dollars, an amount which at once seems to be in excess of the requirements of a Colony with so small a population. From an interesting report, however, by the Colonial Treasurer, it would appear that these coins are in great demand for circulation in China, and are exported in large quantities, almost as soon as they reach Hong Kong, for use in the interior of that country. At all times they command a steady premium of one per cent., and at certain seasons the wholesale price for ten-cent pieces is double, and for five-cent pieces as much as four times, their par value."

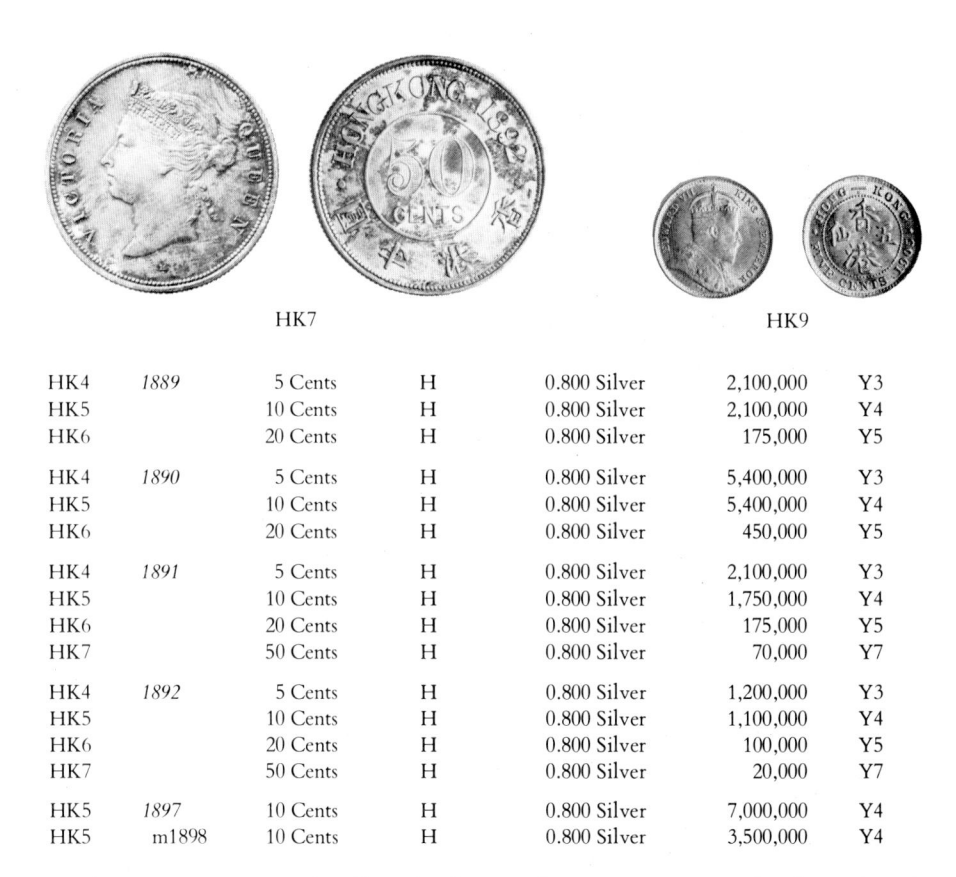

HK7   HK9

HK4	1889	5 Cents	H	0.800 Silver	2,100,000	Y3
HK5		10 Cents	H	0.800 Silver	2,100,000	Y4
HK6		20 Cents	H	0.800 Silver	175,000	Y5
HK4	1890	5 Cents	H	0.800 Silver	5,400,000	Y3
HK5		10 Cents	H	0.800 Silver	5,400,000	Y4
HK6		20 Cents	H	0.800 Silver	450,000	Y5
HK4	1891	5 Cents	H	0.800 Silver	2,100,000	Y3
HK5		10 Cents	H	0.800 Silver	1,750,000	Y4
HK6		20 Cents	H	0.800 Silver	175,000	Y5
HK7		50 Cents	H	0.800 Silver	70,000	Y7
HK4	1892	5 Cents	H	0.800 Silver	1,200,000	Y3
HK5		10 Cents	H	0.800 Silver	1,100,000	Y4
HK6		20 Cents	H	0.800 Silver	100,000	Y5
HK7		50 Cents	H	0.800 Silver	20,000	Y7
HK5	1897	10 Cents	H	0.800 Silver	7,000,000	Y4
HK5	m1898	10 Cents	H	0.800 Silver	3,500,000	Y4

The 1898 BMR states that "... the fractional coinage issues ... for the Colonial Government are gradually taking the place, as a circulating medium, of the pieces of silver passing by weight (Sycee) which for so long a period of time have served as money amongst the Chinese...".

HK2	1900	1 Cent	H	Bronze	1,000,000	Y2b
HK4		5 Cents	H	0.800 Silver	7,000,000	Y3
HK5		10 Cents	H	0.800 Silver	41,500,000	Y4

Catalogue

No.	Date	Denomination	Mintmark	Metal	Mintage	Ref.
HK2	1901	1 Cent	H	Bronze	10,000,000	Y2b
HK8	1904	1 Cent	H	Bronze	10,000,000	Y9
HK8	1905	1 Cent	H	Bronze	12,500,000	Y9
HK9		5 Cents	H	0.800 Silver	7,000,000	Y10

There was no further coinage for Hong Kong until 1919, and then for the next twelve years only the bronze one cent coin was struck.

HK10	1919	1 Cent	H	Bronze	2,500,000	Y14

The last silver coins were struck in 1933. Thereafter, various nickel alloys were used.

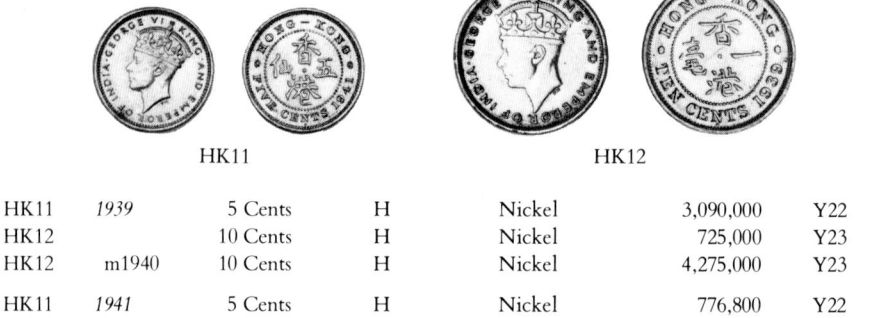

HK11   HK12

No.	Date	Denomination	Mintmark	Metal	Mintage	Ref.
HK11	1939	5 Cents	H	Nickel	3,090,000	Y22
HK12		10 Cents	H	Nickel	725,000	Y23
HK12	m1940	10 Cents	H	Nickel	4,275,000	Y23
HK11	1941	5 Cents	H	Nickel	776,800	Y22

According to Remick[43] and the Royal Mint none of this 1941 issue was sent to Hong Kong. All except a very few copies were melted down.

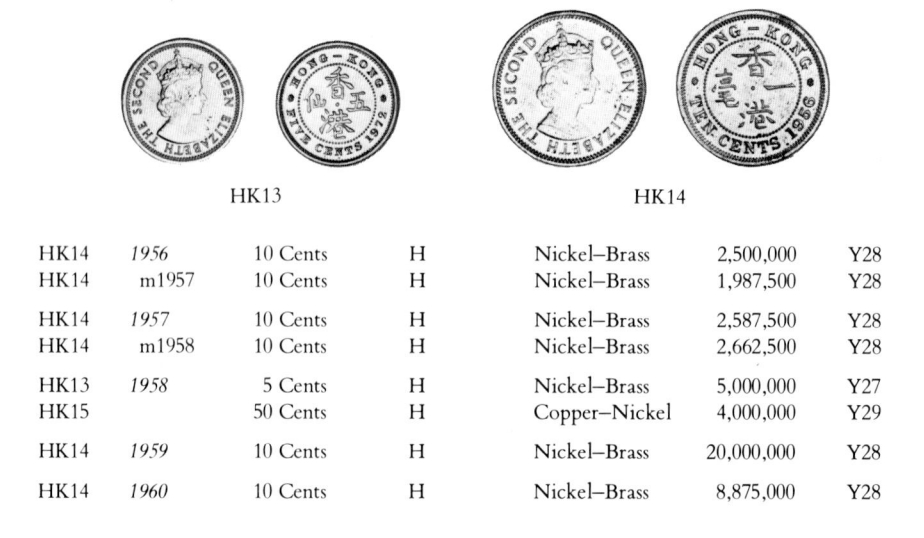

HK13   HK14

No.	Date	Denomination	Mintmark	Metal	Mintage	Ref.
HK14	1956	10 Cents	H	Nickel–Brass	2,500,000	Y28
HK14	m1957	10 Cents	H	Nickel–Brass	1,987,500	Y28
HK14	1957	10 Cents	H	Nickel–Brass	2,587,500	Y28
HK14	m1958	10 Cents	H	Nickel–Brass	2,662,500	Y28
HK13	1958	5 Cents	H	Nickel–Brass	5,000,000	Y27
HK15		50 Cents	H	Copper–Nickel	4,000,000	Y29
HK14	1959	10 Cents	H	Nickel–Brass	20,000,000	Y28
HK14	1960	10 Cents	H	Nickel–Brass	8,875,000	Y28

[43]Remick, *British Commonwealth Coins*, p. 272.

Coinage Issues of The Birmingham Mint

No.	Date	Denomination	Mintmark	Metal	Mintage	Ref.

HK16

No.	Date	Denomination	Mintmark	Metal	Mintage	Ref.
	1960					
HK14	m1961	10 Cents	H	Nickel–Brass	1,125,000	Y28
HK16		1 Dollar	H	Copper–Nickel	32,050,000	Y30
HK16	m1961	1 Dollar	H	Copper–Nickel	7,950,000	Y30
HK14	1961	10 Cents	H	Nickel–Brass	5,000,000	Y28
HK14	1962	10 Cents	H	Nickel–Brass	5,000,000	Y28
HK14	1963	10 Cents	H	Nickel–Brass	7,100,000	Y28
HK14	m1964	10 Cents	H	Nickel–Brass	2,900,000	Y28
HK15		50 Cents	H	Copper–Nickel	7,000,000	Y29
HK15	m1964	50 Cents	H	Copper–Nickel	3,000,000	Y29
	1964					
HK14	m1965	10 Cents	H	Nickel–Brass	21,000,000	Y28
HK13	1965	5 Cents	H	Nickel–Brass	6,000,000	Y27
HK14		10 Cents	H	Nickel–Brass	8,000,000	Y28
HK13	1967	5 Cents	None	Nickel–Brass	10,000,000	Y27
HK14	1968	10 Cents	H	Nickel–Brass	15,000,000	Y28
HK15		50 Cents	H	Copper–Nickel	12,000,000	Y29
	1970					
HK15	m1969	50 Cents	H	Copper–Nickel	4,600,000	Y29
HK16	m1969	1 Dollar	H	Copper–Nickel	15,000,000	Y30
HK13	1971	5 Cents	H	Nickel–Brass	6,000,000	Y27a
HK14	m1970	10 Cents	H	Nickel–Brass	16,000,000	Y28a
HK16	m1970	1 Dollar	H	Copper–Nickel	8,000,000	Y30a
	1972					
HK13	m1971	5 Cents	H	Nickel–Brass	14,000,000	Y27a

The Hong Kong 1972 five cents was the last circulating coin for any country to be produced by THE MINT with the H mintmark. Thus ended a century of use of the H mintmark on coins of the Commonwealth, and coins specifically of Hong Kong. THE MINT's romance with the coinage of Hong Kong certainly has the distinction of extending, in a sustained way, over the longest period of that of all of its many customers. Hong Kong's very first coinage was made by Heatons, and now, well over a hundred years later, THE MINT continues to serve her needs.

Hyderabad – *see* Indian Native States

164   *Catalogue*

No.   Date   Denomination   Mintmark   Metal   Mintage   Ref.

ICELAND Until World War II, Iceland's coinage requirements were supplied by the Copenhagen Mint. In 1940 Iceland turned to the Royal Mint for help, Copenhagen having been taken over by the Germans in April of that year. The 1940 BMR records that "Striking began at daybreak after a night during which the windows and roofs had been wrecked by enemy action; a glacial wind whirled around the coining presses to inaugurate this coinage of Iceland." Thereafter, all of Iceland's coinages were produced by the Royal Mint, with occasional contracts being farmed out to the Birmingham mints.

IC2

| IC1 | 1969 | 10 Aurar | None | Copper–Nickel | 3,200,000 | Y13 |
| IC2 | | 1 Króna | None | Nickel–Brass | 2,000,000 | Y15a |

INDIA The British East India Company was chartered in 1600, and thereafter for two centuries enjoyed monopolistic trading privileges in India and China. It lost its India Monopoly in 1813, and beginning in 1834 became a managing agency, acting as trustees for the British Government in India. It caused many coinages to be produced during and after its trading years, including distinctive issues by Matthew Boulton. The last issues bearing the name of the East India Company were all produced by Heatons, with the exception of an 1860 issue of ¼ annas (dated 1858) by James Watt. A letter dated 3 August 1857 from the East India House in London to Thomas Graham, then Master of the Royal Mint, stated that the East India House had accepted Heatons' bid to supply 300 tons of copper pyce described as "... 100 troy grains, diameter as per sample, denomination ¼ anna." Delivery requirements were 100 tons in 1857 and 200 tons in 1858. The mintages shown below have been calculated from these weights, and it is assumed that the 1858 issue continued to use the 1857 date.

IN1

| IN1 | 1857 | ¼ Anna | None | Copper | 15,680,000 | C67 |
| IN1 | m1858 | ¼ Anna | None | Copper | 31,360,000 | C67 |

On 20 October 1859 the East India House again advised Graham that Heatons'

Coinage Issues of The Birmingham Mint 165

No.	Date	Denomination	Mintmark	Metal	Mintage	Ref.

bid to supply 350 tons of copper pyce, as described above, had been accepted, and that delivery was to be 70 tons in 1859 and 280 tons in 1860.

	1858					
IN1x	m1859	¼ Anna	None	Copper	10,976,000	C67
IN1x	m1860	¼ Anna	None	Copper	43,904,000	C67

In 1860 the India Office advised Heatons by letter dated 10 May that their "... tender of the 15th instance for the supply of 400 tons of copper pyce has been accepted." Records in THE MINT files show that 280 tons were to be delivered in 1860, and 120 tons in 1861.

	1858					
IN1x	m1860	¼ Anna	None	Copper	43,904,000	C67
IN1x	m1861	¼ Anna	None	Copper	18,816,000	C67

This coinage is referred to in a letter dated 2 January 1861 signed by several agents with whom Heatons had been doing business. It states in part: "They [Heatons] are at the present time engaged in ... the coinage of Copper Money for India, and in the preparation of the dies for this Coinage also."

Finally, an item in the *Illustrated Times* of 10 May 1862 refers to the fact that Heatons had obtained "... a recent contract for the Indian Government of the nominal value of £89,600." This would have been practically equivalent to 350 tons of pyce, which is assumed to have been the true dimension of the order.

	1858					
IN1x	m1862/3	¼ Anna	None	Copper	62,720,000	C67

In 1866 Ralph Heaton wrote in a Birmingham publication[44] that Heaton & Sons' coinage since 1849 included 1400 tons for India. The four orders detailed above account in full for that coinage – all of a single coin type. It is interesting that these coins, issued in the name of the East India Company, continued to be struck after the silver coinage had been changed to eliminate reference to the East India Company in 1862.

Note: The cabinet of THE MINT contains a proof set of the new regal coinage of India; all pieces are dated 1861 except the ¼ anna, which is dated 1862. This suggests the possibility that Heatons contributed in some way to the 1862 regal coinage issue, perhaps in the preparation of dies for use in the India mints, and also that Heatons may have been the source of the 1861 proofs which show up on the numismatic market from time to time. Until more definitive evidence is available, this can only be taken as speculation.

Indian Native States The business relation between THE MINT and several of the Native States extended over many years and involved all parts of their coinage business, from furnishing complete minting plants to the preparation of dies, blanks, and coins. Much of it remains obscure, and the part for which there are records is nevertheless doubtful due to the skimpy nature of the records. It is hoped that additional research may help to correct and amplify the following listings.

[44] Ralph Heaton, "Birmingham Coinage", *Industrial History*, etc., p. 556.

No.   Date   Denomination   Mintmark   Metal   Mintage   Ref.

Hyderabad THE MINT provided various minting equipment to Hyderabad in 1893 and 1894, following which the Hyderabad coinage was generally machine-struck in the Hyderabad Mint. Previous to this, however, it appears that THE MINT prepared dies in connection with the proposals for minting equipment; the following piece in the cabinet of THE MINT apparently being a trial strike used to demonstrate the superior quality of machine-struck coinage. It is 30.6 mm in diameter, but otherwise identical with Krause No. KM 32.2 (*Standard Catalog of World Coins*, 5th Edition, page 846).

IN2

	AH*1307*(1889–90)					
IN2s	m1889	1 Rupee	None	0.900 Silver	Unknown	KM32.2

A partial record of MINT orders shows in 1900 the following cryptic entries or orders placed by a John Spencer, Glasgow:

> May 8, 1899: "One pair of matrices and punches made to fit the presses supplied in Sept. 1893..."

> Sept. 11, 1900: Matrices, punches, dies, and collars for 1 rupee (30½ mm), ½ rupee (24 mm), ¼ rupee (19½ mm), and 1/8 rupee (15 mm).

Lacking further evidence, it is tentatively assumed that these were for the second provisional coinage of Hyderabad of 1900. THE MINT collection does contain specimens of the 1 rupee dated AH1312, which were apparently struck with dies provided from Birmingham.

Indore Another of the States which retained its coinage rights was the west central state of Indore, now part of Madya Pradesh. Indore's first machine-struck silver coin, produced in the Indore Mint, was dated VS1956 (AD1899). It is a handsome piece, showing a bust of the ruler, Shariji Rao, on the obverse, and a horse and bull on the reverse, along with other symbols including the traditional sun-face. It was a short-lived series, however, because Indore gave up its coinage rights and closed its mint in 1902. The dies for this rupee coinage were made in THE MINT.

	VS*1955*(1898)					
IN3s	m1898	1 Rupee	None	0.900 Silver	Unknown	Y19

| No. | Date | Denomination | Mintmark | Metal | Mintage | Ref. |

IN3

THE MINT collection contains several specimens of the above piece, probably struck in Birmingham before sending out the dies for the rupee coinage. Observed circulated rupees of this type are dated either VS1956 or VS1958.

In addition, THE MINT collection contains dies for a ½ anna of the type (Yeoman No. 11a3) struck between VS1945 and VS1959, thus suggesting that THE MINT furnished the dies to Indore for that series. No specimen strikes are known, however, and so the piece will only be referenced by this note.

Pudukota This subdivision of the Indian State of Madras has issued only a single coin type since around 1770. It is undated, and bears on the obverse the image of Brahadamba, the Mother Goddess (the Family Deity of the ruler).[45] On the reverse is the single word VIJAYA (Victory) in Tamil. The early coins were rather crude, and were probably struck locally. Since at least 1876 they have been machine-struck. In that year the Indian Government offered to strike the State's coinage free if it would close down its own mints and agree to a uniform coinage.[46] Pudukota chose to retain its rights, but thereafter contracted out its coinage requirements. Until 1914 all machine-struck issues were from THE MINT, but since then Calcutta has also struck these interesting little coins.

IN4

	No date					
IN4x	m1889	1 Ammon Cash	None	Copper	2,000,000	Y1
IN4x	m1897	1 Ammon Cash	None	Copper	1,000,000	Y1
IN4x	m1902	1 Ammon Cash	None	Copper	1,000,000	Y1
IN4x	m1906	1 Ammon Cash	None	Copper	1,000,000	Y1

Travancore This state in southern India also refused to give up its coining privileges, both in 1876 and again around the turn of the century when pressure was again applied by the Indian Government. The coins of Travancore all carry a

---

[45] Remick, *British Commonwealth Coins*, p. 387.
[46] Parmeshwari Lal Gupta, *Coins*, (New Delhi, India, National Book Trust, September 1969), p. 171.

No.	Date	Denomination	Mintmark	Metal	Mintage	Ref.

device resembling a question mark (?). It is a Sanka, or conch, and is sacred by virtue of being one of the four objects usually seen in Vishnu's hands, symbolizing The Battle. THE MINT's contributions to the coinage of Travancore have been broad-based, including actual coinage as well as furnishing both dies and blanks to the Travancore Mint.

IN6

	ME*1057/1881*					
IN5a	m1881?	½ Sovereign	None	White-metal	Unknown	Fr330
IN6a	m1881?	1 Sovereign	None	White-metal	Unknown	Fr329

THE MINT prepared the dies for this issue, and may or may not have struck the regular issue (which otherwise may have been struck in the Travancore Mint), but for sure THE MINT struck these trial pieces in white-metal, which exist in The Birmingham Mint collection.

IN7

	No date					
IN7	m1903	Cash Eight	None	Copper	2,992,367	Y31
IN8	m1903	Chuckram One	None	Copper	1,498,089	Y32
IN8a	m1903	Chuckram One	None	Copper–Nickel	Unknown	–

This copper–nickel specimen in THE MINT cabinet is identical with IN8, except for being only 1.4 mm thick, rather than the normal 2.5 mm. It may have been made to send to Travancore for approval of the dies.

IN8

Coinage Issues of The Birmingham Mint 169

No.	Date	Denomination	Mintmark	Metal	Mintage	Ref.

IN9

	ME*1082*(1907)					
IN9p	m1907?	¼ Rupee	None	0.950 Silver	Unknown	–

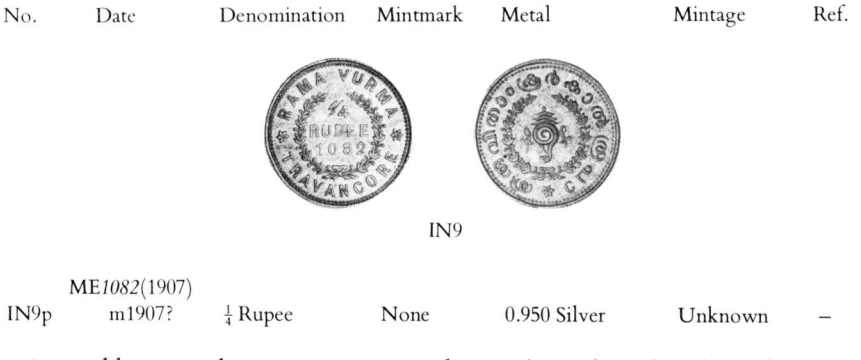

It would appear that THE MINT made samples and produced the dies for the new ¼ rupee issue beginning in 1908. This pattern, similar to IN11 but with minor differences, is in THE MINT collection.

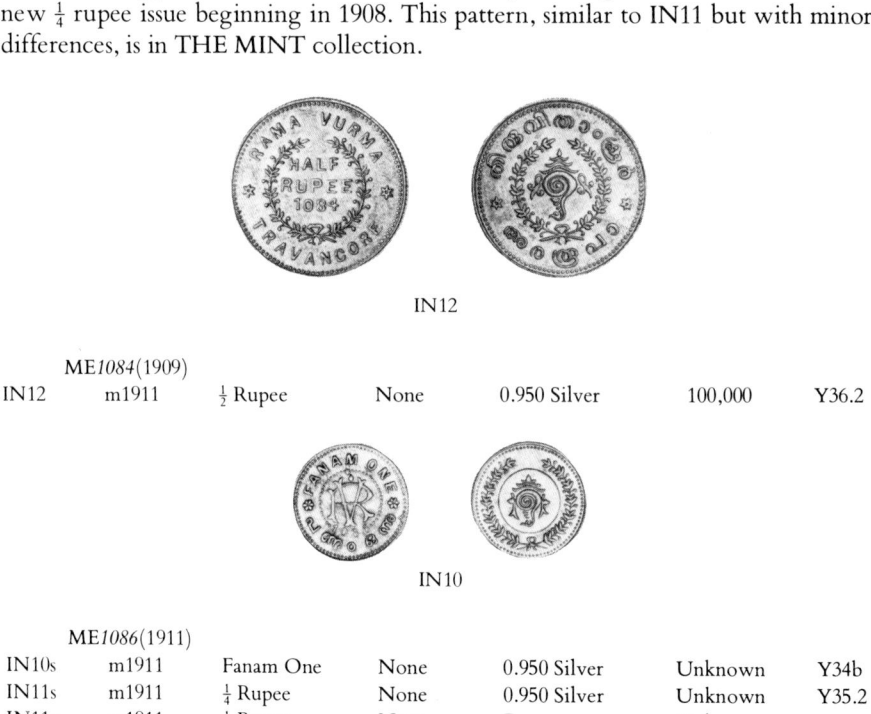

IN12

	ME*1084*(1909)					
IN12	m1911	½ Rupee	None	0.950 Silver	100,000	Y36.2

IN10

	ME*1086*(1911)					
IN10s	m1911	Fanam One	None	0.950 Silver	Unknown	Y34b
IN11s	m1911	¼ Rupee	None	0.950 Silver	Unknown	Y35.2
IN11a	m1911	¼ Rupee	None	Bronze	Unknown	—

Orders for these silver coins were placed on THE MINT on 3 July 1911, with the requirement that samples be submitted for approval. Dies were prepared, and specimens struck (the above silver pieces are in THE MINT cabinet, and the bronze piece was noted in a dealer's coin listing [Format 13, January 1981]), but before actual coinage began, the date requirement was changed to ME1087. There are probably some ½ Rupee specimens extant (dies still exist), but none have so far surfaced.

	ME*1087*(1912)					
IN10	m1911	Fanam One	None	0.950 Silver	200,000	Y34b
IN10	m1912	Fanam One	None	0.950 Silver	900,000	Y34b

No.	Date	Denomination	Mintmark	Metal	Mintage	Ref.
	ME*1087*(1912)					
IN11	m1911	¼ Rupee	None	0.950 Silver	200,000	Y35.2
IN11	m1912	¼ Rupee	None	0.950 Silver	200,000	Y35.2
IN12	m1911	½ Rupee	None	0.950 Silver	100,000	Y36.2
IN12	m1912	½ Rupee	None	0.950 Silver	100,000	Y36.2
	ME*1096*(1921)					
IN10	m1921	Fanam One	None	0.950 Silver	350,000	Y34b
	ME*1099*(1924)					
IN10	m1924	Fanam One	None	0.950 Silver	350,000	Y34b
	ME*1100*(1925)					
IN10	m1925	Fanam One	None	0.950 Silver	700,000	Y34b
	ME*1103*(1928)					
IN10	m1928	Fanam One	None	0.950 Silver	700,000	Y34b
IN11	m1928	¼ Rupee	None	0.950 Silver	200,000	Y35.2
IN12	m1928	½ Rupee	None	0.950 Silver	100,000	Y36.2
	ME*1106*(1930)					
IN10	m1930	Fanam One	None	0.950 Silver	700,000	Y34b
IN11	m1930	¼ Rupee	None	0.950 Silver	200,000	Y35.2
IN12	m1930	½ Rupee	None	0.950 Silver	100,000	Y36.2
	ME*1107*(1931)					
IN12	m1931	½ Rupee	None	0.950 Silver	800,000	Y36.2

It would appear from a study of THE MINT records and Royal Mint reports that most of the silver coinage of Rama Varma VI (AD1885–1924), plus that of the first twelve years of his successor Bala Rama Varma, was produced by THE MINT. The relatively small amount struck in the Travancore Mint was struck with both dies and blanks from Birmingham. In addition, THE MINT generally produced the dies used by the Travancore State Mint for striking their copper coins. THE MINT also furnished the blanks for the copper coins, at least during the period 1900 to 1931. In total in those years, Travancore purchased about 29 million chuckram blanks, 23 million 8 cash blanks, 23 million 4 cash blanks, and 75 million 1 cash blanks from THE MINT. These probably represent their total copper coinage for the period.

Although Bala Rama Varma succeeded Rama Varma VI in 1924, the first coinage with his name did not appear until 1937, when THE MINT produced this issue.

IN14

	ME*1112*(1937)					
IN13	m1937	One Fanam	None	0.950 Silver	350,000	Y45

Coinage Issues of The Birmingham Mint

No.	Date	Denomination	Mintmark	Metal	Mintage	Ref.
	ME*1112*(1937)					
IN14	m1937	¼ Rupee	None	0.950 Silver	200,000	Y46
IN15	m1937	½ Rupee	None	0.950 Silver	200,000	Y47

IN16

It is likely that THE MINT participated one last time in Travancore's coinage in 1938/39 when it produced the dies for Travancore's chuckram coins of 1939. Specimens of these are in THE MINT collection.

	ME*1114*(1939)					
IN16s	m1938?	One Chuckram	None	Copper	Unknown	Y44

Hereafter, until it ended, Travancore's coinage was produced in the Bombay Mint.

Indore – *see* Indian Native States

Ionian Islands (Under Great Britain) Heatons' book of Testimonials includes an illustration of the Ionian 1 lepton of 1853.[47] Mr. G. P. Dyer of the Royal Mint advises that a manuscript note of 1853 states that 2½ tons of copper coin were "...about to be coined at Birmingham." The mintage below derives from that figure. This coinage was part of the 500 tons of Imperial coinage contracted to Heatons by the Royal Mint in 1853. (*See* Great Britain)

II1
(courtesy British Museum)

II1	*1853*	1 Letpton	None	Copper	1,344,000	C24

IRAN A modern mint was established in Tehran in 1877, which thereafter produced gold, silver, and copper coins. In 1898, an order for matrices and punches and 5 pairs of working dies for two gold denominations was placed on THE MINT. The following gold-plated specimen strikes from those dies exist in the cabinet of THE MINT.

[47] Ralph Heaton & Sons, *Testimonials*, 1st Edition, *ca.* 1879.

172   Catalogue

No.	Date	Denomination	Mintmark	Metal	Mintage	Ref.

IR2

	AH1316(1898)					
IR1s	m1898	½ Toman	None	Brass	Unknown	Fr70
IR2s		1 Toman	None	Brass	Unknown	Fr69

During the years 1877 to 1890, Tehran struck such huge quantities of copper coins that by 1900 the shahi (50 dinars), nominally 20 to the kran, was passing at up to 80 to the kran. In 1900 a currency reform took place; the copper pieces were replaced by copper–nickel 50 and 100 dinar pieces which were struck exclusively at Brussels from 1900 to 1909, and exclusively by THE MINT from 1914 through 1929.

IR4

	AH1332(1914)					
IR3	m1914	50 Dinars	None	Copper–Nickel	6,000,000	Y23
IR4	m1914	100 Dinars	None	Copper–Nickel	5,000,000	Y24
	AH1337(1919)					
IR3	m1919	50 Dinars	None	Copper–Nickel	5,600,000	Y23
IR3	m1920	50 Dinars	None	Copper–Nickel	1,400,000	Y23
IR4	m1919	100 Dinars	None	Copper–Nickel	5,200,000	Y24
IR4	m1920	100 Dinars	None	Copper–Nickel	1,300,000	Y24
	SH1305(1926)					
IR5	m1926	50 Dinars	None	Copper–Nickel	11,000,000	Y95
IR6	m1926	100 Dinars	None	Copper–Nickel	4,500,000	Y96

The Tehran Mint has generally struck all of Iran's gold and silver coinages. The 1900 BMR reported that "... the outturn does not suffice for the requirements of the country, and silver coin is in consequence appreciated in value. This is in great measure due to the flow of Persian silver coin, in spite of prohibition by Ukase, into Russian territory, some of which finds its way into Afghanistan, where it is probably reminted. But a large amount is hoarded, and the outflow from Tehran into the South, North East, and North West Districts does not in the main reappear."

Coinage Issues of The Birmingham Mint

No.   Date   Denomination   Mintmark   Metal   Mintage   Ref.

Nevertheless, on only two occasions did Tehran place outside contracts for silver coinages. In 1926 an order was placed on the Leningrad Mint for silver 2000 and 5000 dinars, of which 7.5 and 3 million respectively were delivered in 1928. The other case was an order placed on THE MINT in 1927 for similar denominations, which were struck in 1928 and 1929.

Coincidentally, these two orders marked the first, and last, appearance of mintmarks on the coins of Iran. As compared with the Heaton "H", the Leningrad strikes carry a letter "L".

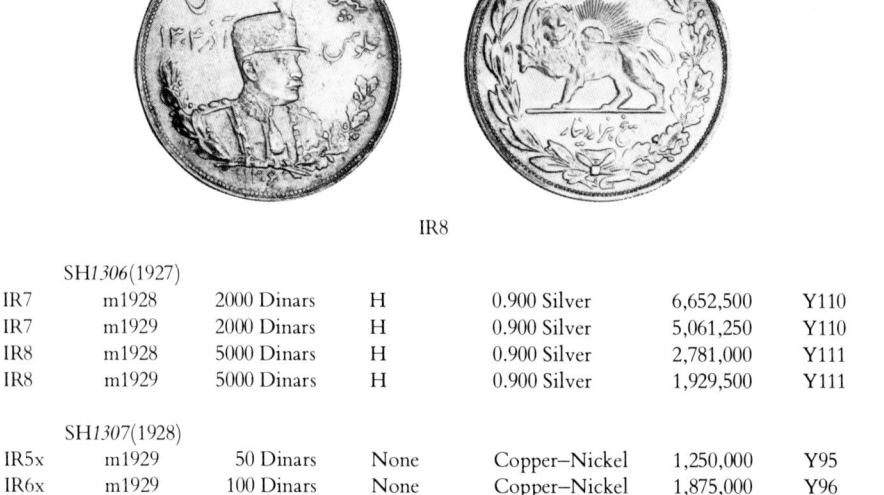

IR8

	SH1306(1927)					
IR7	m1928	2000 Dinars	H	0.900 Silver	6,652,500	Y110
IR7	m1929	2000 Dinars	H	0.900 Silver	5,061,250	Y110
IR8	m1928	5000 Dinars	H	0.900 Silver	2,781,000	Y111
IR8	m1929	5000 Dinars	H	0.900 Silver	1,929,500	Y111
	SH1307(1928)					
IR5x	m1929	50 Dinars	None	Copper–Nickel	1,250,000	Y95
IR6x	m1929	100 Dinars	None	Copper–Nickel	1,875,000	Y96

ICI produced an equal quantity of the above two pieces.

IRAQ   Most of the coinages for Iraq during this period were provided by the British Royal Mint, shared in relatively small degree by the Birmingham and Bombay Mints.

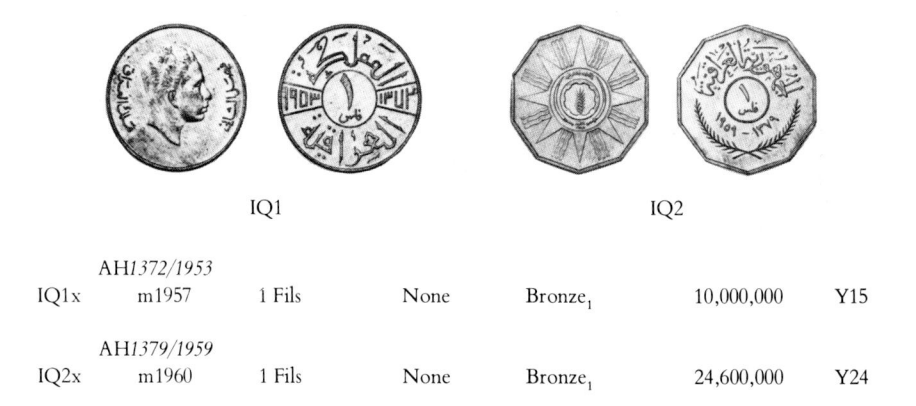

IQ1   IQ2

	AH1372/1953					
IQ1x	m1957	1 Fils	None	Bronze$_1$	10,000,000	Y15
	AH1379/1959					
IQ2x	m1960	1 Fils	None	Bronze$_1$	24,600,000	Y24

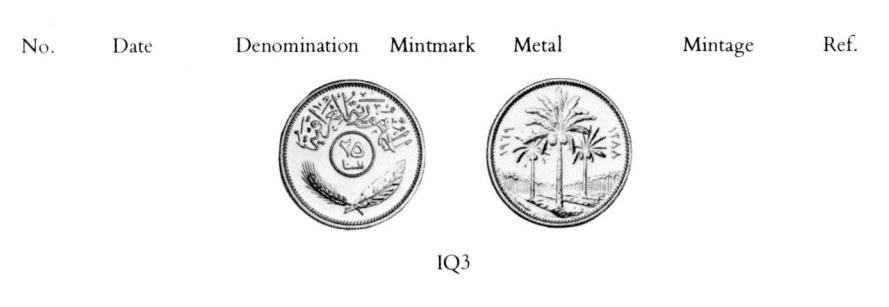

174   *Catalogue*

No.	Date	Denomination	Mintmark	Metal	Mintage	Ref.

IQ3

	AH*1388/1969*					
IQ3	m1969	25 Fils	None	Copper–Nickel	6,000,000	Y33

IRELAND – *see* Eire

ISRAEL   The modern state of Israel came into being on 5 May 1948, and only shortly thereafter caused a new issue of 25 Mils to be struck locally in Jeruselem. This was technically and economically a failure, and so the second series was contracted with the Imperial Chemical Industries Mint (ICI), who in turn sub-contracted a large part of the order with THE MINT.

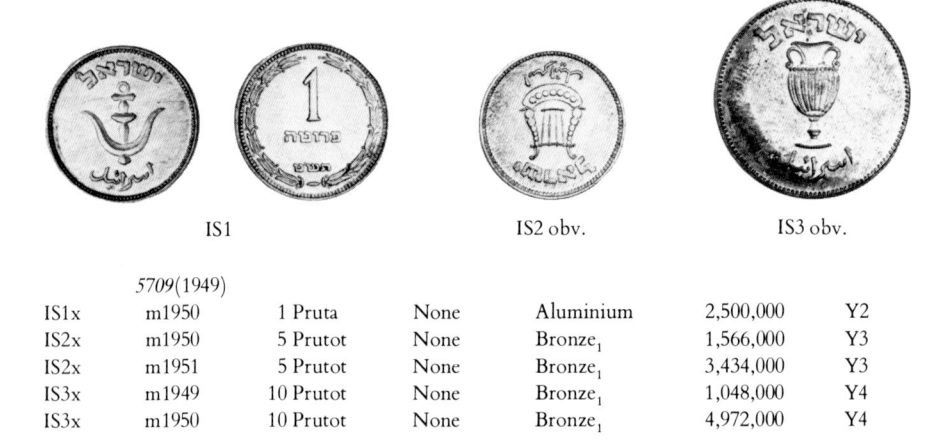

IS1   IS2 obv.   IS3 obv.

	5709(1949)					
IS1x	m1950	1 Pruta	None	Aluminium	2,500,000	Y2
IS2x	m1950	5 Prutot	None	Bronze$_1$	1,566,000	Y3
IS2x	m1951	5 Prutot	None	Bronze$_1$	3,434,000	Y3
IS3x	m1949	10 Prutot	None	Bronze$_1$	1,048,000	Y4
IS3x	m1950	10 Prutot	None	Bronze$_1$	4,972,000	Y4

20,000 of the above 10 prutot coins were struck in proof.

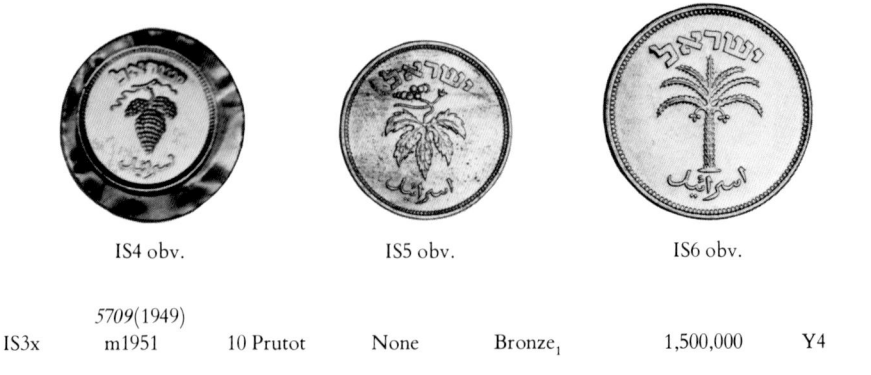

IS4 obv.   IS5 obv.   IS6 obv.

	5709(1949)					
IS3x	m1951	10 Prutot	None	Bronze$_1$	1,500,000	Y4

Coinage Issues of The Birmingham Mint 175

No.	Date	Denomination	Mintmark	Metal	Mintage	Ref.
	5709(1949)					
IS4x	m1949	25 Pruta	None	Copper–Nickel	1,360,000	Y6
IS4x	m1950	25 Pruta	None	Copper–Nickel	1,140,000	Y6
IS5x	m1949	50 Pruta	None	Copper–Nickel	6,000,000	Y8
IS6x	m1949	100 Pruta	None	Copper–Nickel	3,000,000	Y10
IS6x	m1950	100 Pruta	None	Copper–Nickel	20,000	Y10

These 100 Pruta were struck in proof in 1950, but entered circulation and so now are difficult to distinguish from the non-proof issues by THE MINT and ICI.[48]

IS7 obv.   IS9 obv.

No.	Date	Denomination	Mintmark	Metal	Mintage	Ref.
	5709(1949)					
IS7x	m1950	250 Pruta	None	Copper–Nickel	524,000	Y12
IS8	m1951	250 Pruta	H	0.500 Silver	18,175	Y13
IS8	m1952	250 Pruta	H	0.500 Silver	25,950	Y13
IS9	m1951	500 Pruta	None	0.500 Silver	15,025	Y14
IS9	m1952	500 Pruta	None	0.500 Silver	4,825	Y14
IS9	m1953	500 Pruta	None	0.500 Silver	13,962	Y14

Only THE MINT struck the proof 500 pruta coins, and like the silver proof 250 pruta coins, these were intended purely for numismatic purposes. The 250 pruta are the only pruta coins to be mintmarked.

Some of the coins of the pruta series have a small dot, or "pearl", below the horizontal bar at the bottom of the reverse. All such are emissions of ICI, none of the dies used by THE MINT having had the dot. This does not suffice for a mintmark, however, since some ICI coins also have no dot.

IS10

No.	Date	Denomination	Mintmark	Metal	Mintage	Ref.
	5721(1961)					
IS10x	m1961	5 Agorot	None	Aluminium–bronze	5,000,000	Y24

[48] For an excellent study of Israel's coins, see *The History of Modern Israel's Money* by Silvia Haffner.

No.	Date	Denomination	Mintmark	Metal	Mintage	Ref.

These were struck in THE MINT on blanks supplied by ICI. The 1961 BMR indicates the alloy to be "aluminium–nickel–bronze".

ITALY (Provisional Government of Tuscany 1859–61) During this period Tuscany was in a state of transition, having allegiance to Victor Emmanuel, but not yet a part of United Italy. The coinage that was then issued included a silver issue minted in Florence, and a copper issue by Heatons. The order for the latter was placed on Heatons by R. Raphael & Sons as Agent for the Provisional Government of Tuscany.

IT3

IT1	*1859*	1 Centesimo	None	Copper	25,000,000	C81
IT2		2 Centesimi	None	Copper	12,500,000	C82
IT3		5 Centesimi	None	Copper	10,000,000	C83

According to an English publication, *The Ironmonger*, dated March 1860, page 186, Heatons supplied 47,000 [*sic*] coins for Tuscany. The above breakdown is from the official authority dated 5 June 1860.

ITALY On attaining unification, it became necessary for Italy to replace the State's coinage with a new Imperial coinage. This was a major job, eventually involving many mints. Heatons contracted to operate the Milan Mint, and in 1861–2 produced large quantities of bronze Imperial coins using planchets from Birmingham. This was Italy's first use of bronze for coinage.

IT7

IT4	*1861*	1 Centesimo	M	Bronze$_2$	75,000,000	Y6
IT5		2 Centesimi	M	Bronze$_2$	37,500,000	Y7
IT6		5 Centesimi	M	Bronze$_2$	210,000,000	Y8
IT7	*1862*	10 Centesimi	M	Bronze$_2$	40,000,000	Y9

Coinage Issues of The Birmingham Mint

| No. | Date | Denomination | Mintmark | Metal | Mintage | Ref. |

The above mintages, which are the total mintages for 1861 per the Paris Mint Report for 1900, are believed to represent correctly the Heatons' output based on the following corroborating facts. First, a letter from the Italian Minister of Agriculture, Industry and Commerce dated 27 November 1862 to Heaton & Sons acknowledges their mintage of "... the value of twelve millions of Italian Lira (nominal value) in pieces ... of ten Centesimi."[49]

Second, the Heaton Orderbook for 1861 indicates a nominal value of 9 million francs, which was the amount of the first order except for the 10 centesimi pieces. Third, an 1866 article by Ralph Heaton in the Birmingham press indicated a total weight of 1600 tons, which also agrees with the sum of the Paris Mint figures.

| IT7 | 1866 | 10 Centesimi | H | Bronze$_2$ | 40,000,000 | Y9 |
| IT7 | 1867 m1868 | 10 Centesimi | H | Bronze$_2$ | 50,000,000 | Y9 |

IT8   IT9

| IT8 | 1893 | 10 Centesimi | BI | Bronze$_2$ | 28,000,000 | Y25 |
| IT9p | | 20 Centesimi | None | Copper–Nickel | Unknown | – |

It appears that THE MINT quoted for the 1894 20 centesimi coinage which was produced in Rome, because their cabinet contains the above anachronistic piece, differing from the Rome strikes in several details.

| IT8 | 1894 | 10 Centesimi | BI | Bronze$_2$ | 32,000,000 | Y25 |

JAMAICA Although the Royal Mint produced most of Jamaica's coins, Heatons participated frequently by the production of blanks for use in the Royal Mint.

JA3

[49]Ralph Heaton & Sons, *Testimonials*, 1st Edition, *ca.* 1879.

Catalogue

No.	Date	Denomination	Mintmark	Metal	Mintage	Ref.

These coins, equivalent in value to the corresponding British bronze pieces, were struck in copper–nickel because the Jamaicans did not like bronze. The alloy, an 80–20 ratio of copper and nickel, was peculiar to Jamaica's coins.

JA1	1882	Farthing	H	Copper–Nickel₁	384,000	Y1
JA2		Halfpenny	H	Copper–Nickel₁	96,000	Y2
JA3		Penny	H	Copper–Nickel₁	48,000	Y3
JA4		Penny	None	Copper–Nickel₁	In above	Y3

The reason for these non-mintmarked pennies is unknown. The dies came from the Royal Mint without mintmark, so a few may have been made by mistake before the error was discovered.

JA1	1890	Farthing	H	Copper–Nickel₁	96,000	Y1
JA2		Halfpenny	H	Copper–Nickel₁	120,000	Y2
JA3		Penny	None	Copper–Nickel₁	36,000	Y3

After 1906, Jamaican coins were of the usual copper–nickel ratio of 75:25.

JA5 obv.

JA5	1916	Farthing	H	Copper–Nickel	480,000	Y10
JA6		Halfpenny	H	Copper–Nickel	192,000	Y11
JA7		Penny	H	Copper–Nickel	24,000	Y12

JAPAN In 1868 Japan purchased the decommissioned Hong Kong mint equipment, with which they began a modern minting operation in Osaka. They soon realized that the six old Watt presses from Hong Kong were not adequate, so they placed an order on Heatons for ten new lever presses, also ordering designs and dies for new coin denominations. Details about this order are unavailable, but a set of the coins in THE MINT cabinet attest to their having been produced. Three are illustrated in the book of Testimonials,[50] as shown below.

JP1 obv.   JP2 obv.

[50] Ralph Heaton & Sons, *Testimonials*, 1st Edition, *ca.* 1879.

Coinage Issues of The Birmingham Mint   179

No.	Date	Denomination	Mintmark	Metal	Mintage	Ref.
	No date					
JP1p	m1869?	1 Fun	None	Copper	Unknown	–
JP2p	m1869?	5 Fun	None	Copper	Unknown	–
JP3p	m1869?	1 Monme	None	Copper	Unknown	–

JP3

Identification of these pieces was made by Mr. M. Oka (Tokyo) from pictures in Heatons' book of Testimonials.[50]

JERSEY All of Jersey's rather limited coinage was struck by the Royal Mint except the 1877 issue. In that year Heatons struck most of the Colonial coins, including the new issue for Jersey. These new denominations replaced the 1/52nd, 1/26th, and 1/13th shilling coins that had previously been used.

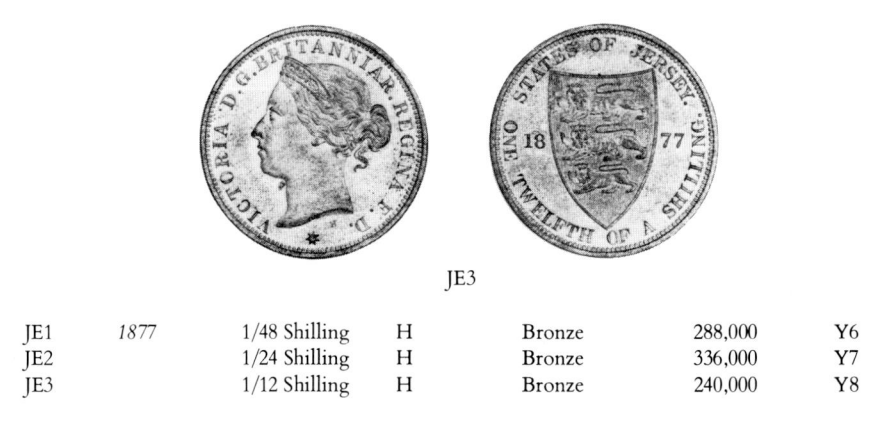

JE3

JE1	1877	1/48 Shilling	H	Bronze	288,000	Y6
JE2		1/24 Shilling	H	Bronze	336,000	Y7
JE3		1/12 Shilling	H	Bronze	240,000	Y8

This first farthing was a short-lived coin. This was the only year it was struck, and of the £300 minted, £260 were melted down and re-coined into pence in 1881, leaving only about 38,000 pieces extant.

JORDAN Having had earlier ties to the Commonwealth, Jordan has continued to rely on British mints for its coinage, the first of which was dated 1949.

180   Catalogue

No.	Date	Denomination	Mintmark	Metal	Mintage	Ref.

JO2

	AH1390/1970					
JO1	m1970	5 Fils	None	Bronze₄	1,400,000	Y14
JO2	m1970	10 Fils	None	Bronze₄	1,000,000	Y15

KENYA A product of the dissolution of East Africa (q.v.), Kenya remained within the British Commonwealth and issued its first distinctive coinage in 1966. Both obverse and reverse of this series are by Norman Sillman.

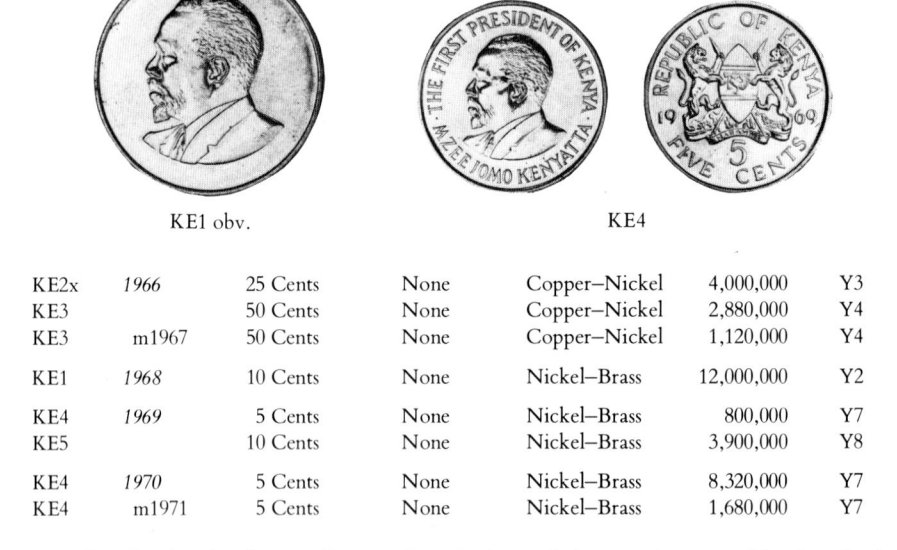

KE1 obv.   KE4

KE2x	1966	25 Cents	None	Copper–Nickel	4,000,000	Y3
KE3		50 Cents	None	Copper–Nickel	2,880,000	Y4
KE3	m1967	50 Cents	None	Copper–Nickel	1,120,000	Y4
KE1	1968	10 Cents	None	Nickel–Brass	12,000,000	Y2
KE4	1969	5 Cents	None	Nickel–Brass	800,000	Y7
KE5		10 Cents	None	Nickel–Brass	3,900,000	Y8
KE4	1970	5 Cents	None	Nickel–Brass	8,320,000	Y7
KE4	m1971	5 Cents	None	Nickel–Brass	1,680,000	Y7

Latvia During its short existence, Latvia depended on various world mints for its entire coinage needs.

LA2

Coinage Issues of The Birmingham Mint

No.	Date	Denomination	Mintmark	Metal	Mintage	Ref.
LA2	1926	2 Santimi	None	Bronze	4,100,000	Y2
LA2	m1925	2 Santimi	None	Bronze	900,000	Y2
LA2	1928	2 Santimi	None	Bronze	5,000,000	Y2
LA1x	1935	1 Santims	None	Bronze	2,500,000	Y1

LIBERIA THE MINT's part in the coinage of Liberia must be considered significant, since it struck all of Liberia's coinage between 1862 and 1937, and the first Liberian silver issues in 1896 and 1906; denominations which were not struck again until 1960.

LB2

LB1	1896	1 Cent	H	Bronze	358,400	Y4
LB2		2 Cents	H	Bronze	322,560	Y5
LB3		10 Cents	H	0.925 Silver	20,000	Y6
LB4		25 Cents	H	0.925 Silver	15,000	Y7
LB5		50 Cents	H	0.925 Silver	5,000	Y8
LB1	1906	1 Cent	H	Bronze	179,200	Y4
LB1	m1908	1 Cent	H	Bronze	1,000	Y4
LB2		2 Cents	H	Bronze	107,522	Y5
LB2	m1908	2 Cents	H	Bronze	500	Y5
LB3		10 Cents	H	0.925 Silver	35,000	Y6
LB4		25 Cents	H	0.925 Silver	34,000	Y7
LB5		50 Cents	H	0.925 Silver	24,000	Y8
LB6	1968	1 Cent	None	Bronze$_6$	3,000,000	Y12

LB4 rev.   LB6

In addition to the above, 6 red leather cased sets, inscribed "Manufactured by The Mint Birmingham Ltd.", were provided to H. Hayman, Esq., the London Agent for Liberia, in both 1896 and 1906. An 1896 set showed up as Lot 2364 in the 7 December 1977 Wayte Raymond auction by NASCA.

182   *Catalogue*

No.   Date   Denomination   Mintmark   Metal   Mintage   Ref.

Lundy   The story of the Lundy coinage is an oft-told tale. These issues, struck for a London businessman who owned the island of Lundy, were declared illegal by the British Government in 1930. They are included here only because of their broad collector interest.

LU1 rev.   LU2

| LU1 | 1929 | ½ Puffin | None | Bronze₁ | 50,000 | Y1 |
| LU2 | | 1 Puffin | None | Bronze₁ | 50,000 | Y2 |

Madagascar   In 1887, at a time when the French were seeking to control the affairs of the island but the native ruler was still resisting and the British had not yet recognized France's claim, the Oriental Bank Corporation Ltd. of Threadneedle St., London, ordered dies and specimen coins for a proposed new denomination, equivalent to a shilling, for Madagascar. Heatons supplied samples weighing 100 grains troy in two alloys, but the denomination was never adopted for use. The cabinet of THE MINT contains a specimen of this interesting piece.

MD1

| MD1p | 1888 | 1 Kiroba | None | 0.800 Silver | 20 | – |
| MD1p | 1888 | 1 Kiroba | None | 0.750 Silver | 20 | – |

MALAGASY REPUBLIC – *see* Madagascar

Malaya and British Borneo   This administrative Federation, initially under Britain, was the successor to the separate entities of Malaya (previously Straits Settlements) and British North Borneo. The Royal Mint, King's Norton Mint (ICI), and THE MINT were all involved in its coinage.

MB4	1955	50 Cents	H	Copper–Nickel	2,560,000	Y4
MB4	m1956	50 Cents	H	Copper–Nickel	1,440,000	Y4
MB1	1957	5 Cents	H	Copper–Nickel	2,520,000	Y1
MB1	m1958	5 Cents	H	Copper–Nickel	7,480,000	Y1

Coinage Issues of The Birmingham Mint

No.	Date	Denomination	Mintmark	Metal	Mintage	Ref.

MB4

No.	Date	Denomination	Mintmark	Metal	Mintage	Ref.
MB2	1957	10 Cents	H	Copper–Nickel	10,000,000	Y2
MB3		20 Cents	H	Copper–Nickel	2,500,000	Y3
MB4		50 Cents	H	Copper–Nickel	2,000,000	Y4
MB1	1958	5 Cents	H	Copper–Nickel	10,000,000	Y1
MB4		50 Cents	H	Copper–Nickel	2,460,000	Y4
MB4	m1959	50 Cents	H	Copper–Nickel	1,540,000	Y4
MB1	1961	5 Cents	H	Copper–Nickel	5,000,000	Y1
MB2		10 Cents	H	Copper–Nickel	5,000,000	Y2
MB2	m1962	10 Cents	H	Copper–Nickel	10,000,000	Y2
MB2	m1963	10 Cents	H	Copper–Nickel	15,000,000	Y2
MB2	m1964	10 Cents	H	Copper–Nickel	28,600,000	Y2
MB2	m1965	10 Cents	H	Copper–Nickel	10,620,000	Y2
MB3		20 Cents	H	Copper–Nickel	13,000,000	Y3
MB3	m1965	20 Cents	H	Copper–Nickel	10,000,000	Y3
MB4		50 Cents	H	Copper–Nickel	4,000,000	Y4

MALAYSIA See also British North Borneo, Malaya and British Borneo, Sarawak, and Straits Settlements.

Although Malaysia gained independence in 1963, the old coinage of Malaya and British Borneo continued to circulate, and indeed to be minted, until an official Malaysian currency was introduced in 1967.

MA3

No.	Date	Denomination	Mintmark	Metal	Mintage	Ref.
MA1x	1967	1 Sen	None	Bronze$_4$	10,000,000	Y1
MA3x		20 Sen	None	Copper–Nickel	7,000,000	Y4
MA3x	m1968	20 Sen	None	Copper–Nickel	12,560,000	Y4
MA2x	1968	10 Sen	None	Copper–Nickel	2,400,000	Y3
MA2x	m1969	10 Sen	None	Copper–Nickel	17,600,000	Y3
MA3x		20 Sen	None	Copper–Nickel	30,440,000	Y4
MA3x	m1969	20 Sen	None	Copper–Nickel	5,000,000	Y4

184   *Catalogue*

No.	Date	Denomination	Mintmark	Metal	Mintage	Ref.

MALTA

ML1
(courtesy British Museum)

| ML1 | *1866* | 1/3 Farthing | None | Bronze | 576,000 | Y2(GB) |

This issue is included speculatively, based entirely on the fact that Heatons' book of Testimonials includes an illustration of this coin. The mintage is relatively small, making it unlikely that more than one mint would have been involved. One other possibility is that Heatons furnished the blanks for this coinage.

Maria Theresa Thaler   From 1936 through 1961 the Royal Mint, as a service to British business interests, minted on request these Maria Theresa Thalers. Occasionally THE MINT was called on to produce these when the Royal Mint was otherwise occupied. On the first such occasion, both the dies and the silver were furnished to THE MINT by Samuel Montagu, a London bullion dealer.

MT1

	1780					(Austria)
MT1x	m1949	Thaler	None	0.833 Silver	475,000	Y55
MT1x	m1953	Thaler	None	0.833 Silver	180,000	Y55
MT1x	m1954	Thaler	None	0.833 Silver	2,434,000	Y55
MT1x	m1955	Thaler	None	0.833 Silver	339,500	Y55

Finally, in 1961 the British Government acceded to the desire of the Austrian Government to re-establish the monopoly they had enjoyed before 1936 in minting the Thalers. The Royal Mint ceased making the Maria Theresa Thalers, thus ending it also for THE MINT.

MAURITIUS   Although Great Britain acquired control over Mauritius in 1810, the first coinage of a Colonial type was the Heaton-produced issue of 1877.

Coinage Issues of The Birmingham Mint 185

No.	Date	Denomination	Mintmark	Metal	Mintage	Ref.

Thereafter, most of the coinage was struck in the Royal Mint, with only occasional participation by Heatons and the Pretoria Mint.

MU3

MU1	1877	1 Cent	H	Bronze	700,000	Y1
MU2		2 Cents	H	Bronze	350,000	Y2
MU3		5 Cents	H	Bronze	140,000	Y3
MU4		10 Cents	H	0.800 Silver	250,000	Y4
MU5		20 Cents	H	0.800 Silver	375,000	Y5

The mintages of the 10 and 20 cents shown above, which are at variance with the figures in the 1877 BMR, were taken from Heatons' Orderbook entry for that year.

MU1	1882	1 Cent	H	Bronze	300,000	Y1
MU2		2 Cents	H	Bronze	150,000	Y2
MU3		5 Cents	H	Bronze	60,000	Y3
MU4		10 Cents	H	0.800 Silver	30,000	Y4
MU5		20 Cents	H	0.800 Silver	15,000	Y5
MU4	1889	10 Cents	H	0.800 Silver	500,000	Y4
MU5		20 Cents	H	0.800 Silver	250,000	Y5
MU1	1890	1 Cent	H	Bronze	500,000	Y1
MU2		2 Cents	H	Bronze	250,000	Y2
MU3		5 Cents	H	Bronze	100,000	Y3

MU6

| MU6 | 1970 | 1 Cent | None | Bronze$_4$ | 1,500,000 | Y25 |

MEXICO In 1905 a general currency reform was begun in Mexico. All of the branch mints were closed, and the metal content of particularly the gold and silver coins was changed to meet current needs. To satisfy the large requirement for this new coinage, it was necessary to farm out a major part of the work, and so THE MINT became a participant in Mexico's coinage for a few years.

186   *Catalogue*

No.	Date	Denomination	Mintmark	Metal	Mintage	Ref.

ME2

ME1x	*1906*	1 Centavo	None	Bronze	50,000,000	KM415
ME2x		2 Centavos	None	Bronze	5,000,000	KM419
ME3x		5 Centavos	None	Nickel	6,000,000	KM421

These coins were identical with those produced by the Mexico City Mint, including the M mintmark. Since the function of a mintmark is to identify the mint, and in this case it does not do so, the M here cannot be properly called a mintmark. Thus the "None" in the listing above. Note also that this was the first pure nickel coinage struck by THE MINT, as well as the first used by Mexico.

ME3 rev.

ME3	*1907*	5 Centavos	None	Nickel	4,000,000	KM421
ME3	*1909*	5 Centavos	None	Nickel	2,051,600	KM421
ME3	*1910*	5 Centavos	None	Nickel	4,113,200	KM421
ME3	m1909	5 Centavos	None	Nickel	2,068,000	KM421
ME3x	*1911*	5 Centavos	None	Nickel	4,086,250	KM421
ME3	*1914*	5 Centavos	None	Nickel	5,004,600	KM421

After 1914 Mexico no longer used nickel in its coinage, thereafter issuing bronze 5 centavos instead. By far the greatest portion of the nickel coinage between 1905 and 1914 was made in THE MINT.

Mombasa (Now part of KENYA)   This coral island just off the coast of Kenya was ceded to the Imperial British East Africa Company by the Sultan of Zanzibar in 1888. Its only coinage was produced by THE MINT, except for a small 1888 issue struck in the Calcutta Mint.

| MO1 | *1888*
m1889 | 1 Pice | H | Copper | 1,724,900 | Y1.2 &
Y1.3 |
| MO1 | m1890 | 1 Pice | H | Copper | 627,300 | Y1.2 &
Y1.3 |

Coinage Issues of The Birmingham Mint

No.	Date	Denomination	Mintmark	Metal	Mintage	Ref.

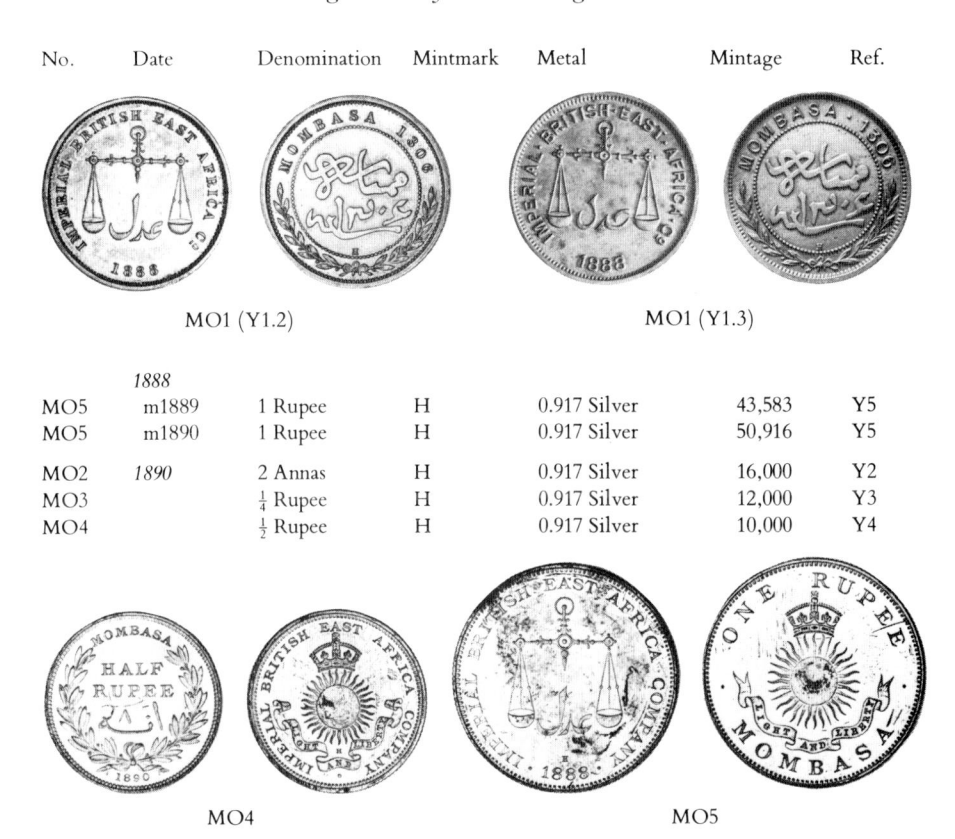

MO1 (Y1.2)   MO1 (Y1.3)

	1888					
MO5	m1889	1 Rupee	H	0.917 Silver	43,583	Y5
MO5	m1890	1 Rupee	H	0.917 Silver	50,916	Y5
MO2	1890	2 Annas	H	0.917 Silver	16,000	Y2
MO3		¼ Rupee	H	0.917 Silver	12,000	Y3
MO4		½ Rupee	H	0.917 Silver	10,000	Y4

MO4   MO5

According to the 1890 BMR, the combined coinage of the 1890 dated coins was Rs 10,300. Records at THE MINT show the above quantities, totalling Rs 10,000.

Note that the 1 pice bears both the Mohammedan calendar date 1306 and the Christian Era date 1888. There are two varieties, the difference being in the size of the lettering and the presence or absence of serifs.

MOROCCO During the reign of Sultan Abdul Aziz I (1894–1908), a currency reform took place in Morocco. The mint at Fez continued to be used for bronze coinage, but all of the silver and much additional bronze coinage was produced for Morocco by mints in Paris, Berlin, and Birmingham. The Tangiers firm of Moses Pariente acted as Morocco's agent in placing orders on THE MINT through the London firm of Samuel Montagu & Co.

MR4   MR5

Catalogue

No.	Date	Denomination	Mintmark	Metal	Mintage	Ref.

MR8

No.	Date	Denomination	Mintmark	Metal	Mintage	Ref.
	AH*1320*(1902)					
MR1	m1903	1 Mazuna	ضرب بباريس	Bronze	3,000,000	Y14
MR2	m1903	2 Mazunas	ضرب بباريس	Bronze	1,500,000	Y15
MR3	m1903	5 Mazunas	ضرب بباريس	Bronze	2,400,000	Y16
MR4	m1903	10 Mazunas	ضرب بباريس	Bronze	1,200,000	Y17
MR5	m1903	1/20 Rial	ضرب بباريس	0.835 Silver	3,920,000	Y18
MR6	m1903	1/10 Rial	ضرب بباريس	0.835 Silver	2,940,000	Y19
MR7	mxt03	¼ Rial	ضرب بباريس	0.835 Silver	3,056,000	Y20
MR8	m1903	½ Rial	ضرب بباريس	0.835 Silver	900,000	Y21
MR9	m1903	1 Rial	ضرب بباريس	0.900 Silver	333,333	Y22
	AH*1321*(1903)					
MR1	m1904	1 Mazuna	ضرب بباريس	Bronze	900,000	Y14
MR2	m1904	2 Mazunas	ضرب بباريس	Bronze	450,000	Y15
MR3	m1904	5 Mazunas	ضرب بباريس	Bronze	720,000	Y16
MR4	m1904	10 Mazunas	ضرب بباريس	Bronze	360,000	Y17
MR5	m1904	1/20 Rial	ضرب بباريس	0.835 Silver	1,665,000	Y18
MR5	m1905	1/20 Rial	ضرب بباريس	0.835 Silver	440,000	Y18
MR6	m1904	1/10 Rial	ضرب بباريس	0.835 Silver	760,000	Y19
MR6	m1905	1/10 Rial	ضرب بباريس	0.835 Silver	10,000	Y19
MR7	m1904	¼ Rial	ضرب بباريس	0.835 Silver	1,224,500	Y20
MR7	m1905	¼ Rial	ضرب بباريس	0.835 Silver	484,000	Y20
MR7	m1906	¼ Rial	ضرب بباريس	0.835 Silver	180,000	Y20
MR8	m1904	½ Rial	ضرب بباريس	0.835 Silver	455,250	Y21
MR8	m1905	½ Rial	ضرب بباريس	0.835 Silver	496,000	Y21
MR8	m1906	½ Rial	ضرب بباريس	0.835 Silver	90,000	Y21
MR10p	?	½ Rial	ضرب بباريس	0.835 Silver	Unknown	—

MR9

Coinage Issues of The Birmingham Mint

MR10p is a proof pattern of different design from the preceding regular issue coins. It appeared as Lot 2623 in the 7 December 1977 Wayte Raymond auction by NASCA.

The mint designation on these coins is written somewhat differently on the silver and bronze coins. Nevertheless, all were produced by The Birmingham Mint.

MOZAMBIQUE In 1894 the Companhia do Nyassa was given a charter by the Lisbon Government to administer the 73,292 square miles of the northern end of the Colony of Mozambique. One of their first acts was to commission a distinctive coinage for use in the Colony, and this was produced by THE MINT that same year.[51]

MZ1

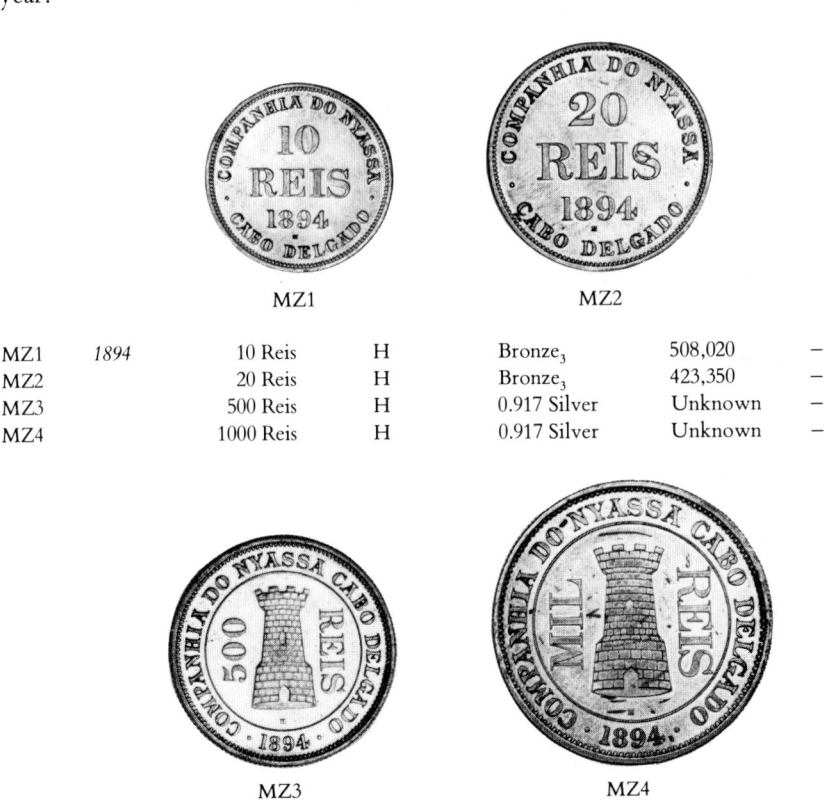

MZ2

No.	Date	Denomination	Mintmark	Metal	Mintage	Ref.
MZ1	1894	10 Reis	H	Bronze$_3$	508,020	–
MZ2		20 Reis	H	Bronze$_3$	423,350	–
MZ3		500 Reis	H	0.917 Silver	Unknown	–
MZ4		1000 Reis	H	0.917 Silver	Unknown	–

MZ3

MZ4

These coins are among the very few official coinages bearing identical obverse and reverse impressions. The 1894 BMR records the existence of the bronze pieces, but not the silver pieces. All are in the cabinet of The Birmingham Mint, and the dies as well, although their Orderbook does not mention the silver pieces. It is reasonable to conclude that they were struck as presentation pieces as a favour to officials of the Companhia.

[51] Thomas Faistauer, "The Coinage of Portuguese Africa", *The Numismatist*, Vol. 86, May 1973, pp. 735–42.

No.	Date	Denomination	Mintmark	Metal	Mintage	Ref.

No further coinages were commissioned by the Companhia do Nyassa, despite the fact that their charter continued in force until 1929.

Muscat and Oman (now OMAN) This Sultanate at the eastern end of the Arabian peninsula is one of the few remaining absolute monarchies. Prior to 1940 its only national coinage consisted of an issue of 1/12 annas in the years 1893–4, and several issues of ¼ annas in the period 1893–8. Except for the Birmingham strikes, most of the ¼ annas are rather crude pieces, indicative of a primitive source.

MS2

	AH*1315*(1897)				Weight (Grains)		
MS1	m1898	¼ Anna	None	Copper	89.6	2,187,500	YA3
MS2	m1898	¼ Anna	None	Copper	85.7	8,784,000	YA3
MS3	m1898	¼ Anna	None	Copper	80.8	6,208,000	YA3
MS4	m1899	¼ Anna	None	Copper	81.2	1,930,000	YA3

It was no accident that the above issues varied in weight. Three separate orders were placed on THE MINT in 1898 by E. W. Carling & Co., London, and for each order a different weight was specified. In addition, the agent changed the weight during the production run of the last order, causing manufacture to be extended into 1899. Carling also ordered 3 tons of copper blanks, each 89.5 grains (total of 595,585 pieces) in September 1898. These would probably have been used for the AH1316 issue (Y3.7) of ¼ annas minted locally.

MS7

	AH*1390*(1970)					
MS5	m1969	2 Baizah	None	Bronze	2,000,000	Y18
MS5	m1970	2 Baizah	None	Bronze	2,000,000	Y18
MS6	m1969	5 Baizah	None	Bronze	2,000,000	Y19
MS6	m1970	5 Baizah	None	Bronze	1,400,000	Y19
MS7	m1969	10 Baizah	None	Bronze	2,000,000	Y20
MS7	m1970	10 Baizah	None	Bronze	2,500,000	Y20

Coinage Issues of The Birmingham Mint

No.	Date	Denomination	Mintmark	Metal	Mintage	Ref.

Nedj – *see* SAUDI ARABIA

NEPAL Although the documentation is sketchy, it is clear that THE MINT furnished dies and other minting accessories to Nepal in the period from 1905 to 1931, and probably even earlier. The only coins known to have been furnished, however, were a few specimen coins in connection with an order of 11 April 1905 which included "1 set of punches from dies in our possession . . . 6 silver coins same as sample with milled edges. . . .". Dies and coins in THE MINT collection identify that order as follows:

NP1

| NP1x | Sa1826(1904) m1905 | 1 Mohar | None | Silver | Unknown | Y15.2 |

Additional dies were made for Nepal again in 1914 (probably for the 1 and 4 mohars of that year – YB26 and Y36) but no evidence of specimen coins having been produced has shown up.

New Brunswick – *see* CANADA

Newfoundland – *see* CANADA

NICARAGUA Beginning in 1880 the major part of Nicaragua's coinage for forty years was furnished by THE MINT. The first two issues were handled for Nicaragua by the London firm of J. Hart & Co., who wrote on 10 July 1883 saying: "The Central American Coinage struck in your mint has, so far as we are aware, given every satisfaction to the Government abroad."

NC3

NC1	1880	5 Centavos	H	0.800 Silver	200,000	Y4
NC1	m1884	5 Centavos	H	0.800 Silver	56,000	Y4
NC2		10 Centavos	H	0.800 Silver	200,000	Y5

Catalogue

No.	Date	Denomination	Mintmark	Metal	Mintage	Ref.
	1880					
NC2	m1881	10 Centavos	H	0.800 Silver	250,000	Y5
NC2	m1884	10 Centavos	H	0.800 Silver	102,000	Y5
NC3		20 Centavos	H	0.800 Silver	100,000	Y6
NC3	m1881	20 Centavos	H	0.800 Silver	125,000	Y6
NC3	m1884	20 Centavos	H	0.800 Silver	62,500	Y6

The 1884 BMR records the above issue, but there is no final proof that the 1884 issue was dated 1880. However, no 1884 dates are in THE MINT cabinet, nor do any popular references record an 1884 date, so it is assumed that they were struck as indicated above.

NC6

NC4	1887	5 Centavos	H	0.800 Silver	1,000,000	Y7
NC5		10 Centavos	H	0.800 Silver	1,500,000	Y8
NC6		20 Centavos	H	0.800 Silver	1,000,000	Y9

The 1887 issue was placed through Isaac & Samuel of London.

NC9

NC7	1912	½ Centavo	H	Bronze	900,000	Y10
NC8		1 Centavo	H	Bronze	450,000	Y11
NC9		5 Centavos	H	Copper–Nickel	460,000	Y12
NC10		10 Centavos	H	0.800 Silver	230,000	Y13
NC11		25 Centavos	H	0.800 Silver	320,000	Y14
NC12		50 Centavos	H	0.800 Silver	260,000	Y15
NC13		1 Cordoba	H	0.900 Silver	35,000	Y16

Harris[52] notes that only 7000 of the 1912 1 cordoba pieces entered circulation; this according to the Banco Nacional de Nicaragua.

NC8	1914	1 Centavo	H	Bronze	300,000	Y11
NC9		5 Centavos	H	Copper–Nickel	300,000	Y12
NC10		10 Centavos	H	0.800 Silver	220,000	Y13
NC11		25 Centavos	H	0.800 Silver	100,000	Y14
NC7	1915	½ Centavo	H	Bronze	320,000	Y10

[52] Robert P. Harris, *Modern Latin American Coins*.

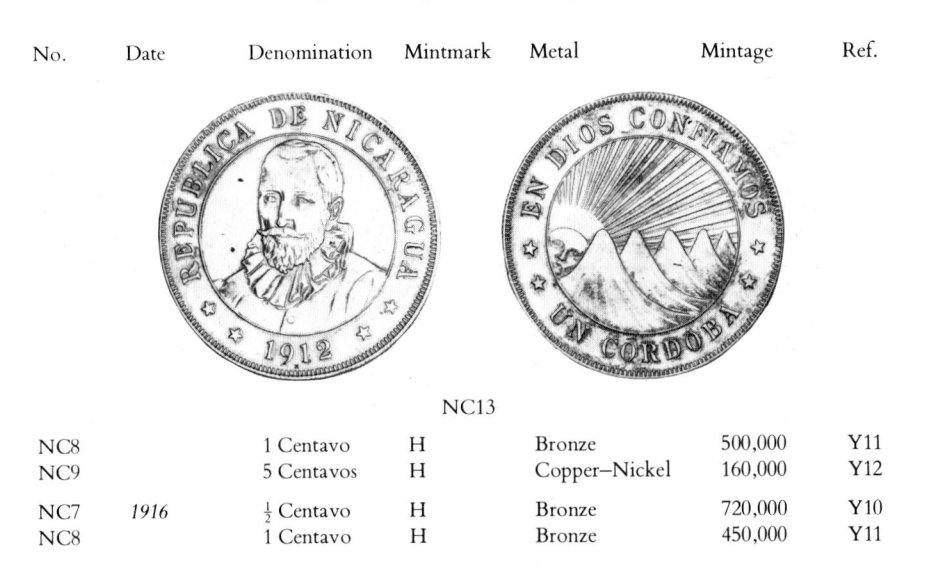

Coinage Issues of The Birmingham Mint

No.	Date	Denomination	Mintmark	Metal	Mintage	Ref.

NC13

NC8		1 Centavo	H	Bronze	500,000	Y11
NC9		5 Centavos	H	Copper–Nickel	160,000	Y12
NC7	1916	½ Centavo	H	Bronze	720,000	Y10
NC8		1 Centavo	H	Bronze	450,000	Y11

From 1917 through 1943 all Nicaraguan coins were minted in the Philadelphia Mint, and thereafter through at least 1965 in the Royal Mint in London.

Nigeria British West Africa – *see* British West Africa

NIGERIA   Until 1960 Nigeria used the coinage of British West Africa. On 1 October 1960, Nigeria became an independent Federation, remaining in the Commonwealth. Thereafter, a distinctive Nigerian coinage replaced the BWA coins.

NG2

	1959					
NG1x	m1963	1 Halfpenny	None	Bronze$_4$	9,600,000	Y1
NG1x	m1964	1 Halfpenny	None	Bronze$_4$	23,160,000	Y1
NG1x	m1965	1 Halfpenny	None	Bronze$_4$	20,040,000	Y1
NG1m	?	1 Halfpenny	None	Bronze$_4$	Unknown	–

Specimens of this double-obverse halfpenny are in THE MINT cabinet.

NG3 rev.   NG4

No.	Date	Denomination	Mintmark	Metal	Mintage	Ref.
	1959					
NG2x	m1959	1 Penny	None	Bronze₄	2,526,000	Y2
NG2x	m1960	1 Penny	None	Bronze₄	2,472,000	Y2
NG2x	m1961	1 Penny	None	Bronze₄	8,472,000	Y2
NG2x	m1962	1 Penny	None	Bronze₄	9,846,000	Y2
NG2x	m1963	1 Penny	None	Bronze₄	17,492,400	Y2
NG2x	m1964	1 Penny	None	Bronze₄	9,378,000	Y2
NG2x	m1965	1 Penny	None	Bronze₄	43,182,000	Y2
NG3x	m1964	3 Pence	None	Nickel–Brass	25,200,000	Y3
NG3x	m1965	3 Pence	None	Nickel–Brass	26,800,000	Y3
NG4x	m1961	6 Pence	None	Copper–Nickel	19,000,000	Y4
NG4x	m1970	6 Pence	None	Copper–Nickel	16,000,000	Y4
NG5x	m1959	1 Shilling	None	Copper–Nickel	8,580,000	Y5
NG5x	m1960	1 Shilling	None	Copper–Nickel	9,420,000	Y5
NG6	m1961	2 Shillings	None	Copper–Nickel	15,000,000	Y6

NG5 rev.   NG6 rev.

The 2 shilling pieces produced by THE MINT have safety (security) edges. Specimens with reeded edges were made by ICI.

NG5x	1961	1 Shilling	None	Copper–Nickel	45,200,000	Y5
NG5x	m1962	1 Shilling	None	Copper–Nickel	5,384,000	Y5
NG5x	1962	1 Shilling	None	Copper–Nickel	39,416,000	Y5

Nova Scotia – *see* CANADA

Nyasaland – *see* MOZAMBIQUE

OMAN – *see* Muscat and Oman

PARAGUAY   Aside from the 1/12 real of 1845, the first Paraguayan coins were

Coinage Issues of The Birmingham Mint 195

| No. | Date | Denomination | Mintmark | Metal | Mintage | Ref. |

those of 1870, which were ordered from Heatons by Paraguay's Birmingham agent, Chas. J. Shaw & Co. (See also Uruguay in this connection.)

PA1	1870	1 Centesimo	None	Bronze	Unknown	Y2
PA2		2 Centesimos	None	Bronze	Unknown	Y3
PA3		4 Centesimos	None	Bronze	Unknown	Y4

Persia – *see* IRAN

PERU Most of Peru's coins were produced in the Lima Mint. Occasionally it became necessary for Peru to use outside mints, but not until 1966 did THE MINT contribute to Peruvian coinage.

PE1

| PE1 | 1965 m1966 | ½ Sol | None | Brass | 10,000,000 | Y56 |

This coin was struck in commemoration of the 400th anniversary of the Lima Mint. It is interesting that it was struck outside the mint.

POLAND Following World War I, newly independent Poland found it necessary to create and issue a suitable coinage. Appropriate laws and regulations were enacted in 1924, and contracts were placed with various world mints. THE MINT tendered for 1 zloty and 2 zlote pieces, and was awarded a contract for twelve million 2 zlote coins. Production proceeded with difficulties, and the 1924 BMR reports that: "In the autumn of the same year (1924), in consequence of a difficulty which had arisen in connection with that part of the Polish coinage which was in course of manufacture by a private firm in England...", the Deputy Master of the Royal Mint went to Warsaw and resolved the difficulty. In 1925 the Royal Mint produced the remaining 10,800,000 2 zlote of THE MINT's contract. The problem at THE MINT had been one of quality control – a rare occurrence for the Birmingham firm.

PO1 obv.   PO2

No.	Date	Denomination	Mintmark	Metal	Mintage	Ref.
PO1s	1924	1 Zloty	H	0.750 Silver	Unknown	Y15
PO2		2 Zlote	H	0.750 Silver	1,200,000	Y16

A specimen 1 zloty, evidently prepared in connection with their tender, is in the cabinet of THE MINT.

Pudukota – *see* Indian Native States

ROMANIA Being without a State Mint, Romania obtained its coinage from several European mints, including especially the Brussels Mint. However, the first issues of both Carol I and Carol II, and the complete coinage of Mihai I, were struck in Birmingham.

RO4

RO1	1867	1 Banu	H	Bronze	(3,000,000)[53]	Y1
RO2		2 Bani	HEATON	Bronze	3,383,000	Y2
RO2	m1868	2 Bani	HEATON	Bronze	(3,000,000)	Y2
RO3		5 Bani	HEATON	Bronze	10,002,500	Y3
RO3	m1868	5 Bani	HEATON	Bronze	(7,000,000)	Y3
RO4		10 Bani	HEATON	Bronze	(18,000,000)	Y4

The dies for this coinage were engraved by the medallist Moore of Birmingham. The mintage was a very large one for the times, and so some 10,000 kilos were subcontracted by Heatons to James Watt & Co. Watt experienced severe quality problems, resulting in many complaints by the Romanian authorities and the necessity of melting down much of the Watt output. The order was finally completed in 1868 to the satisfaction of the Romanian Government, as shown by a July 1868 letter from the Director General of the Romanian Treasury: "... I now hasten to congratulate you for the careful and enlightened manner in which you have accomplished this fabrication. . . .".

RO5p	1869	50 Bani	None	0.835 Silver	Unknown	–
RO5a		50 Bani	None	White-metal	Unknown	–
RO5b		50 Bani	None	Brass	Unknown	–
RO6p		1 Leu	None	0.835 Silver	Unknown	–
RO6a		1 Leu	None	White-metal	Unknown	–

[53] The figures shown in parentheses are the total struck that year; the author has not been able to determine the portion struck by each of the two mints.

Coinage Issues of The Birmingham Mint

No.	Date	Denomination	Mintmark	Metal	Mintage	Ref.

RO7

No.	Date	Denomination	Mintmark	Metal	Mintage	Ref.
RO7p	1869	2 Lei	None	0.835 Silver	Unknown	–
RO7a		2 Lei	None	White-metal	Unknown	–

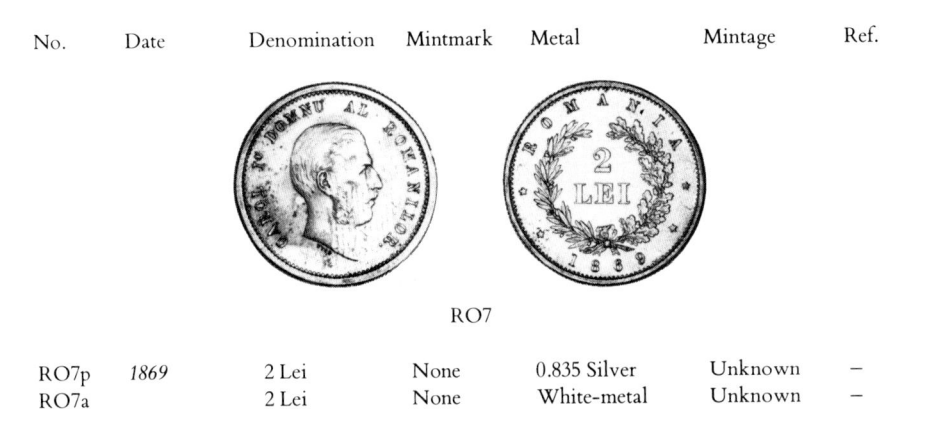

These patterns, with a youthful bust of Carol I by L. C. Wyon, were struck with dies ordered by Romania in connection with their new minting plant, but never used there. In fact, this bust did not appear at all until the 40th Anniversary issue of 1906. It can be guessed that the design was not used because the image was felt to look too immature. An 1870 issue displayed a quite mature bust of the King.

Silver specimens are in THE MINT collection, and also appeared in Lot 2503 of the Palace Collections of Egypt auction in 1954. The brass and white-metal 50 bani and 2 lei were also in the Farouk auction. The white-metal 1 Leu is speculative.

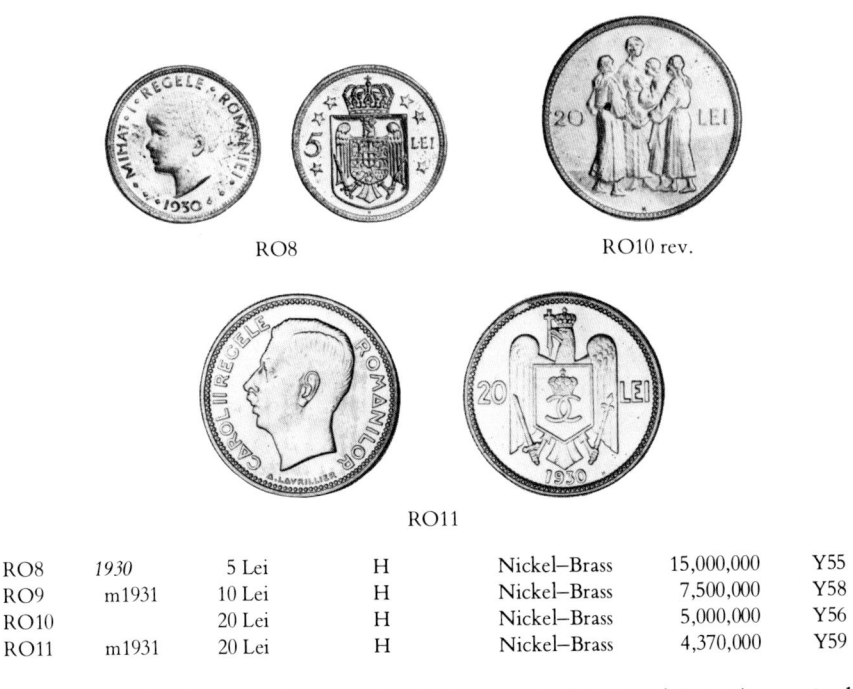

RO8   RO10 rev.

RO11

No.	Date	Denomination	Mintmark	Metal	Mintage	Ref.
RO8	1930	5 Lei	H	Nickel–Brass	15,000,000	Y55
RO9	m1931	10 Lei	H	Nickel–Brass	7,500,000	Y58
RO10		20 Lei	H	Nickel–Brass	5,000,000	Y56
RO11	m1931	20 Lei	H	Nickel–Brass	4,370,000	Y59

The artist for the coins bearing Carol II's portrait (RO9 and RO11) was Andre Lavrillier. Mr. Percy Metcalfe produced the portrait of the boy-king Mihai I on RO8 and RO10.

198   *Catalogue*

No.   Date   Denomination   Mintmark   Metal   Mintage   Ref.

RUSSIA The accession of Nicholas II coincided with a need for a coinage of unprecedented dimension. The facilities of the St. Petersburg Mint were inadequate, so other mints also had to be employed. In 1897 and 1898 Russia's entire copper coinage was struck by THE MINT; certain silver issues were struck in Paris and Brussels.

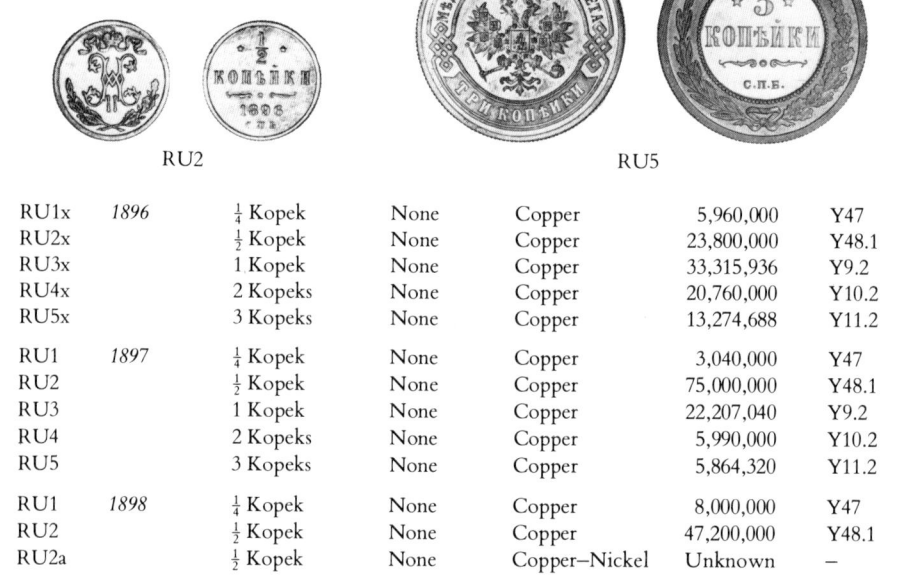

RU2   RU5

No.	Date	Denomination	Mintmark	Metal	Mintage	Ref.
RU1x	1896	¼ Kopek	None	Copper	5,960,000	Y47
RU2x		½ Kopek	None	Copper	23,800,000	Y48.1
RU3x		1 Kopek	None	Copper	33,315,936	Y9.2
RU4x		2 Kopeks	None	Copper	20,760,000	Y10.2
RU5x		3 Kopeks	None	Copper	13,274,688	Y11.2
RU1	1897	¼ Kopek	None	Copper	3,040,000	Y47
RU2		½ Kopek	None	Copper	75,000,000	Y48.1
RU3		1 Kopek	None	Copper	22,207,040	Y9.2
RU4		2 Kopeks	None	Copper	5,990,000	Y10.2
RU5		3 Kopeks	None	Copper	5,864,320	Y11.2
RU1	1898	¼ Kopek	None	Copper	8,000,000	Y47
RU2		½ Kopek	None	Copper	47,200,000	Y48.1
RU2a		½ Kopek	None	Copper–Nickel	Unknown	—

This off-metal piece was probably struck on a Siam 2½ satang blank as used on the Siam coinage dated RS116 (SM4).

RU3	1898	1 Kopek	None	Copper	47.008,144	Y9.2
RU4		2 Kopeks	None	Copper	14,500,000	Y10.2
RU5		3 Kopeks	None	Copper	6,783,952	Y11.2

These copper coinages bear the designation of the St. Petersburg Mint (СПБ), which in this case obviously cannot be considered a mintmark. It is interesting to

RU6

Coinage Issues of The Birmingham Mint   199

No.   Date   Denomination   Mintmark   Metal   Mintage   Ref.

note that on 4 January 1898 THE MINT recorded an order for 30 specimens each of the 1896 and 1897 coins – for the collection of His Imperial Highness Grand Duke George – which may account for the proof coins which appear from time to time.

| RU6x | 1924 | 5 Kopeks | None | Copper | 2,500,000 | Y79 |

Several mints struck the 1924 5 kopeks. Birmingham issues are not reeded.

SALVADOR – *see* EL SALVADOR

Sarawak   Sir James Brooke, an English adventurer (used here in the best sense), acquired control of Sarawak in 1841, and thereafter he and his family ruled this corner of the island of Borneo for the next century. Except for a single issue in 1841, all of Sarawak's coinage was contracted to THE MINT.

SR3

SR1	1863	¼ Cent	None	Copper	Unknown	Y2
SR2		½ Cent	None	Copper	Unknown	Y3
SR3		1 Cent	None	Copper	Unknown	Y4

Although James Brooke had ruled Sarawak for twenty-two years, it was not until he finally returned to England in 1863, leaving control in his nephew's hands, that the above coinage with his portrait by the Birmingham diesinker Joseph Moore was issued.

SR6

	1870					
SR4	m1871	¼ Cent	None	Copper	Unknown	Y5
SR5	m1871	½ Cent	None	Copper	Unknown	Y6
SR6	m1871	1 Cent	None	Copper	Unknown	Y7

No.	Date	Denomination	Mintmark	Metal	Mintage	Ref.

Charles Brooke became Rajah in 1868, and three years later had the above coinage struck bearing his own portrait.

No.	Date	Denomination	Mintmark	Metal	Mintage	Ref.
SR5	1879	½ Cent	None	Copper	640,000	Y6
SR6	1879	1 Cent	None	Copper	750,000	Y7
SR6	1880	1 Cent	None	Copper	1,070,000	Y7
SR6	1882	1 Cent	None	Copper	1,070,000	Y7
SR6	1884	1 Cent	None	Copper	1,070,000	Y7
SR6	1885	1 Cent	None	Copper	2,140,000	Y7
SR6	1886	1 Cent	None	Copper	3,210,000	Y7
SR6	1887	1 Cent	None	Copper	1,605,000	Y7
SR6	1888	1 Cent	None	Copper	2,140,000	Y7
SR6	1889	1 Cent	None	Copper	535,000	Y7
SR7	1889	1 Cent	H	Copper	2,675,000	Y7
SR7	1890	1 Cent	H	Copper	3,210,000	Y7
SR6	1891	1 Cent	None	Copper	535,000	Y7
SR7	1891	1 Cent	H	Copper	1,070,000	Y7

Sarawak came under British protection in 1888, with Charles Brooke continuing as Rajah. Previously, all coin orders had been placed through the Birmingham firm of Smith & Wright, distinguished by lack of any mintmark. Beginning in 1889 the orders were placed by the Borneo Company of London, all of which bear the H mintmark. Note that small orders by Smith & Wright were placed in both 1889 and 1891, but none thereafter.

SR8

No.	Date	Denomination	Mintmark	Metal	Mintage	Ref.
SR8	1892	1 Cent	H	Copper	2,177,776	Y8

This unusual perforated coin with a miniature bust of Charles Brooke shows two equi-positioned flags symbolic of the new relationship between Sarawak and Great Britain. Its weight was made to conform with the British North Borneo cent.

No.	Date	Denomination	Mintmark	Metal	Mintage	Ref.
SR8	1893	1 Cent	H	Copper	1,633,888	Y8
SR8	1894	1 Cent	H	Copper	1,632,776	Y8

Coinage Issues of The Birmingham Mint

No.	Date	Denomination	Mintmark	Metal	Mintage	Ref.
	1896					
SR4	m1895	¼ Cent	H	Copper	283,093	Y5
SR5	m1895	½ Cent	H	Copper	326,646	Y6
SR8		1 Cent	H	Copper	2,177,640	Y8
SR8	*1897*	1 Cent	H	Copper	1,088,820	Y8

Starting in 1900 Sarawak's coinage changed to reflect the growing prosperity of the country, an evolution that came about despite the Brooke dynasty's efforts to protect the natives from the encroachment of outside influences.

No.	Date	Denomination	Mintmark	Metal	Mintage	Ref.
SR9	*1900*	5 Cents	H	0.800 Silver	200,012	Y9
SR10		10 Cents	H	0.800 Silver	150,010	Y10
SR11		20 Cents	H	0.800 Silver	75,007	Y11
SR12		50 Cents	H	0.800 Silver	40,004	Y12
SR10	*1906*	10 Cents	H	0.800 Silver	50,000	Y10
SR11		20 Cents	H	0.800 Silver	25,000	Y11
SR12		50 Cents	H	0.800 Silver	10,000	Y12
	1908					
SR9	m1907	5 Cents	H	0.800 Silver	40,000	Y9
SR10	*1910*	10 Cents	H	0.800 Silver	50,000	Y10
SR11		20 Cents	H	0.800 Silver	25,000	Y11
SR9	*1911*	5 Cents	H	0.800 Silver	40,000	Y9
SR10		10 Cents	H	0.800 Silver	100,000	Y10
SR11		20 Cents	H	0.800 Silver	15,000	Y11
SR9	*1913*	5 Cents	H	0.800 Silver	100,000	Y9
SR10		10 Cents	H	0.800 Silver	100,000	Y10
SR11		20 Cents	H	0.800 Silver	25,000	Y11
SR9	*1915*	5 Cents	H	0.800 Silver	100,000	Y9
SR10		10 Cents	H	0.800 Silver	100,000	Y10
SR11		20 Cents	H	0.800 Silver	25,000	Y11

In 1917 Charles Brooke was succeeded by his son Charles Vyner Brooke, the third and last White Rajah of Sarawak, whose principal contribution to the coinage was the gradual shift away from silver. The debased silver coinage of 1920 was the last order placed by the Borneo Co. Ltd. Henceforth the Sarawak Government placed its orders directly through its London office.

SR13

No.	Date	Denomination	Mintmark	Metal	Mintage	Ref.
SR13	*1920*	1 Cent	H	Copper–Nickel	3,264,000	Y15
SR13	m1921	1 Cent	H	Copper–Nickel	1,736,000	Y15
SR14		5 Cents	H	0.400 Silver	100,000	Y18
SR20	m1921	5 Cents	H	Copper–Nickel	400,000	Y16

Catalogue

No.	Date	Denomination	Mintmark	Metal	Mintage	Ref.

SR16

No.	Date	Denomination	Mintmark	Metal	Mintage	Ref.
SR15	1920	10 Cents	H	0.400 Silver	150,000	Y19
SR21	m1921	10 Cents	H	Copper–Nickel	800,000	Y17
SR16		20 Cents	H	0.400 Silver	25,000	Y20

SR17

No.	Date	Denomination	Mintmark	Metal	Mintage	Ref.
SR19x	1927	1 Cent	H	Copper	5,000,000	Y14
SR20		5 Cents	H	Copper–Nickel	600,000	Y16
SR21		10 Cents	H	Copper–Nickel	1,000,000	Y17
SR16		20 Cents	H	0.400 Silver	250,000	Y20
SR17		50 Cents	H	0.400 Silver	200,000	Y21

Half of the 1927 1 cent pieces were made by King's Norton Mint (ICI), but bear the H mintmark.

Although all of the coins of Sarawak from 1891 to 1941 bear the H mintmark, a part of most of the succeeding coinages was produced by ICI under sub-contract to THE MINT. The mintage figures shown below are in each case the total issue quantity, with that portion produced by ICI indicated parenthetically.

SR19

No.	Date	Denomination	Mintmark	Metal	Mintage	Ref.
SR19x	1929	1 Cent	H (Half were produced by ICI)	Copper	2,000,000	Y14
SR19x	1930	1 Cent	H (Half were produced by ICI)	Copper	3,000,000	Y14
SR18x	1933	½ Cent	H (All were produced by ICI)	Copper	2,000,000	Y13

Coinage Issues of The Birmingham Mint

No.	Date	Denomination	Mintmark	Metal	Mintage	Ref.
SR21	1934	10 Cents	H	Copper–Nickel	986,000	Y17
SR21	m1935	10 Cents	H	Copper–Nickel	1,014,000	Y17
SR19x	1937	1 Cent	H	Copper	2,844,000	Y14
SR19x	m1938	1 Cent	H	Copper	156,000	Y14
		(Half were produced by ICI)				
SR19x	1941	1 Cent	H	Copper	2,016,000	Y14
SR19x	m1942	1 Cent	H	Copper	984,000	Y14
		(ICI produced 18,227 of the 1942 strikes)				

Due to the war the last issue was recalled before being sent to Sarawak. Relatively few copies have since shown up.

And so, eighty years and a million dollars later, the coinage of Sarawak ended where it began – with the issue of a 1 cent piece. During World War II Sarawak was occupied by the Japanese, and afterwards was ceded to the British by the Brooke family. It next became part of Malaya and British Borneo, and later of the Federation of Malaysia. In both of these circumstances it continued to be provided with coins manufactured by THE MINT, although no longer solely so.

SAUDI ARABIA During the 1902–24 period the sheikdoms of Nedj and Hedjaz were gradually consolidated under Ibn Sa'ud, becoming in 1932 the Kingdom of Saudi Arabia. After Hedjaz was absorbed in 1924, the first coinage was produced in Mecca, but thereafter until about 1940 all issues were struck in England by London and THE MINT.

SA3

	AH1346(1927/8)					
SA1x	m1927	¼ Ghirsh	None	Copper–Nickel	1,250,000	Y6
SA1x	m1928	¼ Ghirsh	None	Copper–Nickel	1,750,000	Y6
SA2x	m1927	½ Ghirsh	None	Copper–Nickel	1,112,000	Y7
SA2x	m1928	½ Ghirsh	None	Copper–Nickel	1,888,000	Y7
SA3x	m1927	1 Ghirsh	None	Copper–Nickel	1,258,000	Y8
SA3x	m1928	1 Ghirsh	None	Copper–Nickel	1,742,000	Y8
SA4	m1927	¼ Riyal	None	0.830 Silver	100,000	Y12
SA4	m1928	¼ Riyal	None	0.830 Silver	300,000	Y12
SA5	m1927	½ Riyal	None	0.830 Silver	50,000	Y13
SA5	m1928	½ Riyal	None	0.830 Silver	150,000	Y13
SA6	m1927	1 Riyal	None	0.830 Silver	200,000	Y14
SA6	m1928	1 Riyal	None	0.830 Silver	600,000	Y14

The 1927 and 1928 BMRs list these issues under Hedjaz. The coins carry the legend "King of Hedjaz, Nedj and its Dependencies." THE MINT's Orderbook for 1927 includes a note saying that the issues are "... urgently needed for the pilgrim season." ICI produced half of the above copper–nickel issues.

Catalogue

No.	Date	Denomination	Mintmark	Metal	Mintage	Ref.

SA6

	AH*1354*(1935)					
SA10	m1936	¼ Riyal	None	0.917 Silver	100,000	Y18
SA10	m1937	¼ Riyal	None	0.917 Silver	800,000	Y18
SA11	m1936	½ Riyal	None	0.917 Silver	150,000	Y19
SA11	m1937	½ Riyal	None	0.917 Silver	800,000	Y19
SA12x	m1936	1 Riyal	None	0.917 Silver	1,900,000	Y20
SA12x	m1937	1 Riyal	None	0.917 Silver	2,400,000	Y20
SA12x	m1938	1 Riyal	None	0.917 Silver	1,310,698	Y20
SA12x	m1939	1 Riyal	None	0.917 Silver	389,302	Y20

SA12

The 1940 BMR states that: "The coinage of riyals, piastres, half and quarter piastres for Saudi-Arabia had hitherto been undertaken by The Mint, Birmingham. In view, however, of the pressure on the Royal Mint, and the greater convenience in present circumstances of transporting this coin from India, it was arranged that any further orders during the war should be entrusted to the Indian Mints." For a while after the war, however, the coinage reverted to THE MINT.

SA9

No.	Date	Denomination	Mintmark	Metal	Mintage	Ref.
	AH*1354*(1935)					
SA12x	m1948	1 Riyal	None	0.917 Silver	5,500,000	Y20
SA12x	m1949	1 Riyal	None	0.917 Silver	14,500,000	Y20
	AH*1356*(1937)					
SA7	m1938	¼ Ghirsh	None	Copper–Nickel	1,000,000	Y9
SA8	m1938	½ Ghirsh	None	Copper–Nickel	1,000,000	Y10
SA9	m1937	1 Ghirsh	None	Copper–Nickel	2,360,000	Y11
SA9	m1938	1 Ghirsh	None	Copper–Nickel	1,640,000	Y11

These pieces were struck with plain edges. Similar pieces, but with reeded edges, were struck by the Philadelphia Mint in the years 1944–9.

Serbia (Now YUGOSLAVIA)   Without its own mint, Serbia had to procure its coinage from various world mints. Vienna produced most of Serbia's coins, but in 1879 and again in 1884 the Serbian Government asked the Royal Mint in London to supervise a coinage being made by Heatons in Birmingham.

SE2

	1879					
SE1	m1880	5 Para	None	Bronze	6,000,000	Y7
SE2	m1880	10 Para	None	Bronze	9,000,000	Y8
SE4s	1883	10 Para	H	Copper–Nickel	Unknown	Y15

This specimen, in The Mint collection, was probably struck for approval purposes.

SE4

SE3	1884	5 Para	H	Copper–Nickel	3,000,000	Y14
SE4		10 Para	H	Copper–Nickel	6,500,000	Y15
SE5		20 Para	H	Copper–Nickel	6,000,000	Y16

Siam (Now THAILAND)   The beginning of modern struck coinage of Siam probably goes back to the year 1857, at which time Queen Victoria presented to King Mongkut, as a State gift, a small hand-operated minting plant. The

206   *Catalogue*

No.   Date   Denomination   Mintmark   Metal   Mintage   Ref.

machinery, made by the firm that is now Taylor and Challen Ltd., consisted of a screw coining press, a punch press for blanks, a marking machine, and various related equipment. This was inadequate for Mongkut's purposes, and so the next year he ordered from Taylor & Challen a complete minting plant, including two lever presses of the Uhlhorn type. With this plant Siam produced most of its own coinage for several decades.

With the plant given by Victoria was a set of dies which were probably made by Heaton. The Heaton book of Testimonials[54] pictures six coins, from 1/16 Baht to 4 Baht (excluding only the 1 Baht), which undoubtedly were die trials from those original dies. Unfortunately, neither dies nor specimen coins of this type are to be found today in THE MINT collection. The designs of all six pieces are alike, involving on the obverse the Royal Crown flanked by two Royal Umbrellas, and on the reverse an elephant encircled by a Chakra (symbol of the God Vishnu). All are undated. It is likely that any presently available specimens were actually struck in the Bangkok Mint.

During the ensuing years several coinage orders were executed in England for Siam, probably all by James Watt & Co., but in 1890 an order was placed on THE MINT for a bronze coinage. This was the first Siamese issue to be dated in the Ratanakosind-soc Era system.

SM3

	RS*109*(1890)					
SM1	m1890/91	½ Att	None	Bronze	10,240,100	Y21
SM2	m1890/91	1 Att	None	Bronze	10,240,100	Y22
SM3	m1890/91	2 Atts	None	Bronze	5,120,100	Y23
	RS*114*(1895)					
SM2	m1896	1 Att	None	Bronze	5,120,000	Y22

SM6

[54]Ralph Heaton & Sons, *Testimonials*, 1st Edition, *ca.* 1879.

Coinage Issues of The Birmingham Mint 207

No.	Date	Denomination	Mintmark	Metal	Mintage	Ref.

In 1898, by Royal Decree dated 21 August 1898, Siam introduced new denominations in a new metal. In anticipation, an order had been placed on THE MINT dated 16 February 1898 for the entire issue.

	RS*116*(1897)					
SM4	m1898	2½ Satangs	H	Copper–Nickel	5,080,238	Y24
SM5	m1898	5 Satangs	H	Copper–Nickel	5,080,238	Y25
SM6	m1898	10 Satangs	H	Copper–Nickel	3,810,178	Y26
SM7	m1898	20 Satangs	H	Copper–Nickel	3,126,300	Y27

This series turned out to be unpopular with the Siamese and was withdrawn in 1908. (This is Siam's only issue with a foreign mintmark.)

In 1900 THE MINT received an order for a complete minting plant capable of producing 100,000 ticals per day, plus dies for three denominations of silver coinage. Trial strikes from these dies are in THE MINT cabinet.

SM8 SM9

SM10

	No date					
SM8x	m1900	1 Fuang	None	Silver	Unknown	Y32
SM9x	m1900	1 Sal'ung	None	Silver	Unknown	Y33
SM10x	m1900	1 Baht	None	Silver	Unknown	Y34

The 1900–3 BMRs report emissions in the above denominations from the Bangkok Mint, along with bronze coinages from the Hamburg and Birmingham Mints. The Bangkok issues were undated. In 1903 THE MINT received a request for new dies of the above types, with the complaint that the 1900 dies had neither dates nor room for same.

	RS*121*(1902)					
SM2x	m1903	1 Att	None	Bronze	11,251,200	Y22
SM3x	m1903	2 Atts	None	Bronze	2,796,800	Y23
	RS*122*(1903)					
SM2	m1904	1 Att	None	Bronze	4,108,800	Y22
SM3	m1904	2 Atts	None	Bronze	2,323,200	Y23

208 · *Catalogue*

No.	Date	Denomination	Mintmark	Metal	Mintage	Ref.

In 1908 the Siamese Government enacted a Gold Standard law, establishing a new decimal system. The new subsidiary coins, of 1 Satang, and 5 and 10 Satangs, were thereafter issued without reign identification. These were used until about 1939, when new designs were adopted. The total quantities shown below are correct, but it is not certain that the breakdown by coin dates in the years 1919–21 are accurate, since existing records are not explicit in relating annual mintages to coin dates.

No.	Date	Denomination	Mintmark	Metal	Mintage	Ref.
	BE*2458*(1915)					
SM11	m1915	1 Satang	None	Bronze	1,640,000	Y35
SM11	m1916	1 Satang	None	Bronze	1,840,000	Y35
SM11	m1917	1 Satang	None	Bronze	1,520,000	Y35
	BE*2462*(1919)					
SM11x	m1919	1 Satang	None	Bronze	6,400,000	Y35
SM12x	m1920	5 Satangs	None	Nickel	2,000,000	Y36
SM13x	m1920	10 Satangs	None	Nickel	773,500	Y37
	BE*2463*(1920)					
SM11x	m1920	1 Satang	None	Bronze	17,240,000	Y35

SM13

	BE*2464*(1921)					
SM11x	m1921	1 Satang	None	Bronze	6,360,000	Y35
SM12	m1921	5 Satangs	None	Nickel	5,220,000	Y36
SM12	m1922	5 Satangs	None	Nickel	7,780,000	Y36
SM13	m1921	10 Satangs	None	Nickel	5,475,000	Y37
SM13	m1922	10 Satangs	None	Nickel	16,251,500	Y37

Relations between Thailand and THE MINT continued to exist, although not involving Birmingham coinages. Both blanks and dies have been sent out from THE MINT, and in 1934 THE MINT produced large quantities of branding irons for use in Siam.

SIERRA LEONE Formerly a part of British West Africa, Sierra Leone achieved independence in 1961. THE MINT's participation in their first distinctive coinage continued a relationship of long standing. Michael Rizzello was the designer.

| SL1x | *1964* | 1 Cent | None | Bronze₄ | 35,000,000 | Y2 |

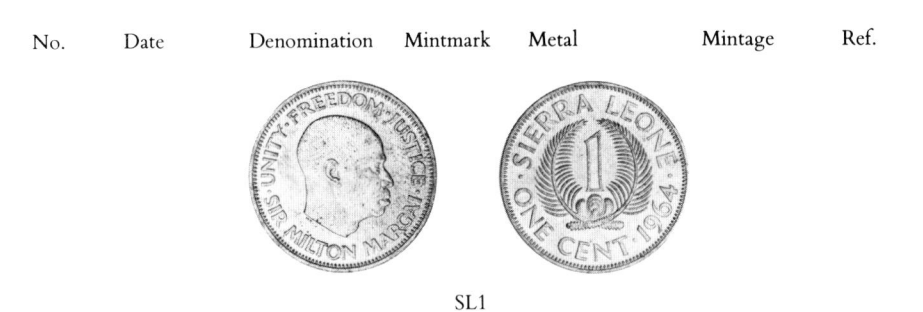

Coinage Issues of The Birmingham Mint 209

| No. | Date | Denomination | Mintmark | Metal | Mintage | Ref. |

SL1

SOMALI British Somaliland was the first country to leave the East Africa Protectorate, joining with Italian Somaliland in 1960 to form the Somali Republic. Its first national coinage was dated 1967. Michael Rizzello also designed this issue.

SO1

No.	Date	Denomination	Mintmark	Metal	Mintage	Ref.
SO1	1967	10 Centesimi	None	Brass	8,400,000	Y7
SO1	m1968	10 Centesimi	None	Brass	6,600,000	Y7
SO1a	m1967?	10 Centesimi	None	Aluminium	Unknown	–

Specimens of this trial piece are in THE MINT cabinet.

SOUTH AFRICA Well before the Pretoria Mint was opened, President Burgers commissioned the first true South African coin. Unfortunately, his Council rejected it, and no subsequent issues of it were made.

SF1c

No.	Date	Denomination	Mintmark	Metal	Mintage	Ref.
SF1	1874	1 Pond	None	0.917 Gold	837	Fr1

SF1a
SF1b Prior to the final coinage, patterns in bronze (a) and aluminium (b) were prepared for approval purposes, several different such pieces being known. Die trials in copper (c) were
SF1c also struck; both gold-plated and unplated specimens are in THE MINT cabinet.

The gold for this coinage was shipped to England from South Africa and delivered to Johnson Matthey & Co. for refining. L. C. Wyon was commissioned to produce the master dies, which he did from photographs of President Burgers and sketches from South Africa. Records in THE MINT show that one gold bar of 256.25 ounces was received for the coinage. On Friday, 24 June 1874, Heatons

210   *Catalogue*

No.	Date	Denomination	Mintmark	Metal	Mintage	Ref.

produced the first lot of 695 pieces. The second and final lot of 142 pieces was struck on 14 August. 40.3 ounces of gold were returned to South Africa. Sixteen dies were required for this small coinage, an unusually large number which came about because Wyon's die design caused excessive pressure concentrations during striking, and frequent die breakage.[55]

South Vietnam (Now VIETNAM)

SV1

| SV1 | 1963 | 50 Xu | None | Aluminium | 20,000,000 | Y6 |

SV3

	1964					
SV2x	m1965	1 Dong	None	Copper–Nickel	24,000,000	Y7
SV2x	m1967	1 Dong	None	Copper–Nickel	20,000,000	Y7
SV3x	m1967	10 Dong	None	Copper–Nickel	15,000,000	Y9

SRI LANKA – *see* Ceylon

Straits Settlements (Now part of MALAYSIA, q.v.) Most of the Straits Settlements coinage was produced by the Royal Mint, but Heatons made an important contribution at those times when the Royal Mint was otherwise occupied. In contrast with other Colonial coinages produced by THE MINT, most of their Straits Settlements orders were for silver coinages.

SS1	1872	¼ Cent	H	Copper	9,240,000	Y7
SS2		½ Cent	H	Copper	5,610,000	Y8
SS3		1 Cent	H	Copper	5,770,000	Y9

[55] Matthy Esterhuysen, *South Africa's First Gold Coin*, Pretoria, 1976.

Coinage Issues of The Birmingham Mint

No.	Date	Denomination	Mintmark	Metal	Mintage	Ref.

SS3

No.	Date	Denomination	Mintmark	Metal	Mintage	Ref.
SS5	1872	10 Cents	H	0.800 Silver	230,000	Y14
SS6		20 Cents	H	0.800 Silver	40,000	Y15
SS3	1874	1 Cent	H	Copper	10,000,000	Y9
SS4		5 Cents	H	0.800 Silver	60,000	Y13
SS5		10 Cents	H	0.800 Silver	180,000	Y14
SS6		20 Cents	H	0.800 Silver	45,000	Y15
SS4	1876	5 Cents	H	0.800 Silver	40,000	Y13
SS5		10 Cents	H	0.800 Silver	120,000	Y14
SS6		20 Cents	H	0.800 Silver	30,000	Y15
SS4	1879	5 Cents	H	0.800 Silver	100,000	Y13
SS5		10 Cents	H	0.800 Silver	250,000	Y14
SS6		20 Cents	H	0.800 Silver	50,000	Y15
SS4	1880	5 Cents	H	0.800 Silver	90,000	Y13
SS5		10 Cents	H	0.800 Silver	235,000	Y14
SS6		20 Cents	H	0.800 Silver	85,000	Y15
SS4	1882	5 Cents	H	0.800 Silver	120,000	Y13
SS4	m1883	5 Cents	H	0.800 Silver	260,000	Y13
SS5		10 Cents	H	0.800 Silver	430,000	Y14
SS6		20 Cents	H	0.800 Silver	105,000	Y15
SS6	m1883	20 Cents	H	0.800 Silver	140,000	Y15
SS5	1883	10 Cents	H	0.800 Silver	610,000	Y14
SS4	1890	5 Cents	H	0.800 Silver	440,000	Y13
SS5		10 Cents	H	0.800 Silver	730,000	Y14
SS6		20 Cents	H	0.800 Silver	270,000	Y15
SS7		50 Cents	H	0.800 Silver	42,000	Y16
SS4	1897	5 Cents	H	0.800 Silver	440,000	Y13

SS8
(courtesy Krause Publications)

No.	Date	Denomination	Mintmark	Metal	Mintage	Ref.
SS5	*1897*	10 Cents	H	0.800 Silver	390,000	Y14
SS6		20 Cents	H	0.800 Silver	185,000	Y15
SS7		50 Cents	H	0.800 Silver	44,000	Y16
SS4	*1900*	5 Cents	H	0.800 Silver	400,000	Y13
SS5		10 Cents	H	0.800 Silver	1,000,000	Y14
SS6		20 Cents	H	0.800 Silver	300,000	Y15
SS7		50 Cents	H	0.800 Silver	40,000	Y16

SS9
(courtesy British Museum)

No.	Date	Denomination	Mintmark	Metal	Mintage	Ref.
SS8	*1907*	50 Cents	H	0.900 Silver	2,666,667	Y24
SS9		1 Dollar	H	0.900 Silver	4,000,000	Y26
SS8	*1908*	50 Cents	H	0.900 Silver	In above	Y24

These last two issues were recoinages in which old 416 grain dollars (Y25) were converted into new 312 grain dollars and 156 grain 50 cents.

SYRIA The coinage of Syria had previously been produced by the Paris Mint, and this became the first time that a mint in the British Empire was used for a Syrian coinage. ICI also struck some 10 piastres dated 1948, and the Pakistan Mint in Lahore struck the issue of 1956 in these same denominations.

SY1   SY2 rev.

	AH*1367/1948*					
SY1	m1948	2½ Piastres	None	Copper–Nickel	2,500,000	Y12
SY2	m1948	5 Piastres	None	Copper–Nickel	4,000,000	Y13
SY2	m1949	5 Piastres	None	Copper–Nickel	4,000,000	Y13

TANZANIA In 1964 the United Republic of Tanzania was formed by the consolidation of Tanganyika (formerly German East Africa) and the islands of Pemba and Zanzibar. Previously THE MINT had struck two coinages for Zanzibar (q.v.) in 1887 and 1908.

Coinage Issues of The Birmingham Mint

No.	Date	Denomination	Mintmark	Metal	Mintage	Ref.

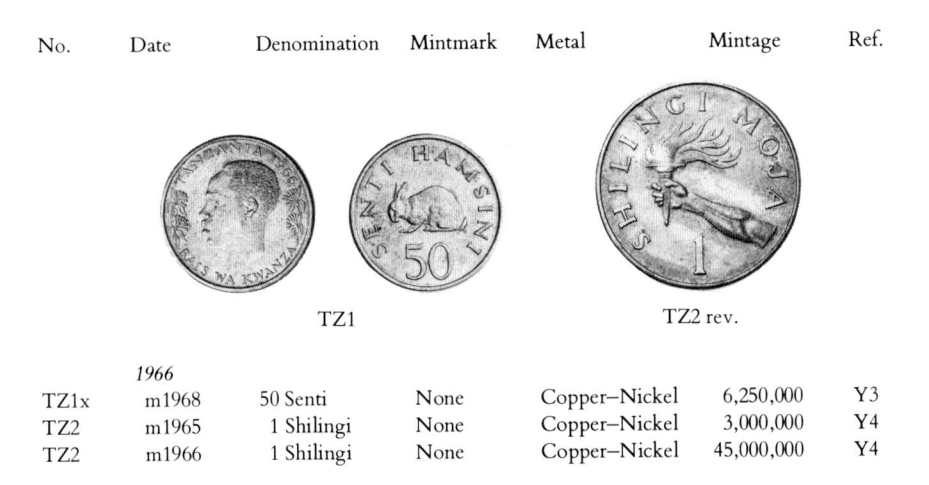

TZ1

TZ2 rev.

	1966					
TZ1x	m1968	50 Senti	None	Copper–Nickel	6,250,000	Y3
TZ2	m1965	1 Shilingi	None	Copper–Nickel	3,000,000	Y4
TZ2	m1966	1 Shilingi	None	Copper–Nickel	45,000,000	Y4

The 1966 issues were designed by Christopher Ironside.

Tarim This desert community in Southeastern Arabia, now in the People's Republic of Yemen, has had three separate coinage issues. These were dated AH1258 (AD1842), AH1270 (AD1853), and AH1315 (AD1897). At least the last issue was produced by THE MINT, the first time in 1898 to the order of Sheik Abou Bakar Bin Mohammed Ba Yusef.

TA3

	AH*1315*(1897)					
TA1	m1898	6 Chomsihs	None	0.900 Silver	16,800	Y1
TA1	m1899	6 Chomsihs	None	0.900 Silver	16,800	Y1
TA1	m1900	6 Chomsihs	None	0.900 Silver	33,600	Y1
TA1	m1902	6 Chomsihs	None	0.900 Silver	33,600	Y1
TA1	m1904	6 Chomsihs	None	0.900 Silver	33,600	Y1
TA1	m1924	6 Chomsihs	None	0.900 Silver	100,094	Y1
TA1	m1926	6 Chomsihs	None	0.900 Silver	100,094	Y1
TA2	m1898	12 Chomsihs	None	0.900 Silver	8,400	Y2
TA2	m1899	12 Chomsihs	None	0.900 Silver	8,400	Y2
TA2	m1900	12 Chomsihs	None	0.900 Silver	16,800	Y2
TA2	m1902	12 Chomsihs	None	0.900 Silver	16,800	Y2
TA2	m1904	12 Chomsihs	None	0.900 Silver	16,800	Y2
TA2	m1924	12 Chomsihs	None	0.900 Silver	49,945	Y2
TA2	m1926	12 Chomsihs	None	0.900 Silver	49,945	Y2
TA3	m1898	24 Chomsihs	None	0.900 Silver	4,200	Y3
TA3	m1899	24 Chomsihs	None	0.900 Silver	4,200	Y3
TA3	m1900	24 Chomsihs	None	0.900 Silver	8,400	Y3
TA3	m1902	24 Chomsihs	None	0.900 Silver	8,400	Y3

No.	Date	Denomination	Mintmark	Metal	Mintage	Ref.
	AH*1315*(1897)					
TA3	m1904	24 Chomsihs	None	0.900 Silver	8,400	Y3
TA3	m1924	24 Chomsihs	None	0.900 Silver	24,923	Y3
TA3	m1926	24 Chomsihs	None	0.900 Silver	24,923	Y3

THAILAND – *see* Siam

Travancore – *see* Indian Native States

TRINIDAD AND TOBAGO These two islands in the Caribbean achieved their independence in 1962, and issued their first distinctive coinage in 1966, most of which was produced by THE MINT. The designs are by Geoffrey Colley.

TT4

TT1	*1966*	1 Cent	None	Bronze$_4$	24,500,000	Y1
TT2		5 Cents	None	Bronze$_4$	7,500,000	Y2
TT3		25 Cents	None	Copper–Nickel	5,700,000	Y4
TT3	m1967	25 Cents	None	Copper–Nickel	1,500,000	Y4
TT4		50 Cents	None	Copper–Nickel	600,000	Y5
TT4	m1967	50 Cents	None	Copper–Nickel	375,000	Y5
TT1	*1967*	1 Cent	None	Bronze$_4$	4,000,000	Y1
TT2		5 Cents	None	Bronze$_4$	3,000,000	Y2
TT3		25 Cents	None	Copper–Nickel	1,800,000	Y4
TT4		50 Cents	None	Copper–Nickel	750,000	Y5
TT1x	*1968*	1 Cent	None	Bronze$_4$	3,000,000	Y1
TT1x	m1969	1 Cent	None	Bronze$_4$	2,000,000	Y1

Tunis (Now TUNISIA) During the period when Turkey was in nominal control of Tunis, Heatons were commissioned by the Bey to supply a new coinage.

TU6

Coinage Issues of The Birmingham Mint 215

No.	Date	Denomination	Mintmark	Metal	Mintage	Ref.

The design depicted Tunis's dual allegiance; the obverse bore the title Sultan Abdul Aziz Lord, signifying the Turkish suzerainty, and the reverse the name of the Tunisian Bey Muhammed es Sadik.

AH*1281*(1864/5)

No.	Date	Denomination	Mintmark	Metal	Mintage	Ref.
TU1	m1864	¼ Kharub	None	Copper	3,200,000	C161
TU2	m1864	½ Kharub	None	Copper	3,200,000	C162
TU3	m1864	1 Kharub	None	Copper	5,600,000	C163
TU4	m1864	2 Kharubs	None	Copper	12,000,000	C164
TU5	m1864	4 Kharubs	None	Copper	12,000,000	C165
TU6	m1864	8 Kharubs	None	Copper	10,000,000	C166

In addition to the above coinage, Heatons also prepared the master dies for a coinage of gold and silver, all dated AH1281. Die trials in copper and specimen strikes in gold are in the cabinet of THE MINT, as follows:

AH*1281*(1864/5)

No.	Date	Denomination	Mintmark	Metal	Mintage	Ref.
TU7s	m1864	2 Piastres	None	0.900 Silver	Unknown	C178
TU8s	m1864	5 Piastres	None	0.900 Gold	Unknown	C181
TU8a	m1864	5 Piastres	None	Copper	Unknown	–
TU9s	m1864	10 Piastres	None	0.900 Gold	Unknown	C182
TU9a	m1864	10 Piastres	None	Copper	Unknown	–
TU10s	m1864	25 Piastres	None	0.900 Gold	Unknown	C183
TU10a	m1864	25 Piastres	None	Copper	Unknown	–
TU11s	m1864	50 Piastres	None	0.900 Gold	Unknown	C184
TU11a	m1864	50 Piastres	None	Copper	Unknown	–
TU12s	m1864	100 Piastres	None	0.900 Gold	Unknown	C185
TU12a	m1864	100 Piastres	None	Copper	Unknown	–

TU12

Mint records contain a copy of the Authority from the Bey to Emile Erlanger et Cie, dated 5 April 1864, to strike gold coins of 5 million piastres nominal value, silver coins of 2 million piastres, and bronze coins of 10 million piastres. The copper mintage above has a value of 10 million piastres, and is referred to in an 1866 article[56] by Ralph Heaton III. No reference in that article is made to silver or gold issues for Tunis, and so it is assumed that Erlanger had the silver and gold business strikes produced in the Paris Mint from Heaton dies.

[56] Ralph Heaton, *Birmingham Coinage*, Industrial History of the Birmingham and Midland Hardware District, London, 1866.

216   *Catalogue*

No.   Date   Denomination   Mintmark   Metal   Mintage   Ref.

"That the Bey clearly liked the coin designs is indicated by the expression of appreciation contained in his letter of 12 February 1865:

16 Ramazan 1281

"Praise be to God alone! From the servant of God glorified (upon Whom rest all hopes, and to His Divine Will all things are resigned), El Musheer Muhammed Sadik Pasha Bey, and Supreme Lord of the Kingdom of Tunis, to the worthy and respected Signor Heaton, principal of the Mint of Birmingham: May God preserve him!

That, at the request of our Prime Minister and the Minister of Foreign Affairs, in respect to the faithful discharge of public service, we confer upon you this decoration bearing our inscription of the Third Class Officer of honour of our institution, with our grateful and best wishes."

TURKEY   Abdul Aziz became ruler of Turkey on about 26 June 1861, just before the end of AH1277. A copper coinage of three denominations (5, 10, and 20 para) was struck dated AH1277 Year 1. Whether or not this issue was struck in Birmingham is not known, but correspondence in THE MINT files, and the existence of specimen strikes in THE MINT cabinet, clearly confirm the provenance of the following issue – the second and last copper issue during the sixteen years reign of Abdul Aziz.

TY4

	AH*1277*/Yr *4*(1864/65)					
TY1	m1864?	5 Para	None	Copper	16,000,000	Y4
TY2	m1864?	10 Para	None	Copper	8,000,000	Y5
TY3	m1864?	20 Para	None	Copper	4,000,000	Y6
TY4	m1864?	40 Para	None	Copper	2,000,000	Y7

Tuscany – *see* ITALY

UGANDA   Continuing its minting activities for the people of what was previously East Africa, THE MINT struck some of the first coins for Uganda four years after it became an independent country.

Coinage Issues of The Birmingham Mint

No.	Date	Denomination	Mintmark	Metal	Mintage	Ref.
UG1	1966	10 Cents	None	Bronze₄	18,000,000	Y2
UG1	m1967	10 Cents	None	Bronze₄	1,100,000	Y2
UG2	1968	1 Shilling	None	Copper–Nickel	10,000,000	Y5

URUGUAY The 1869 coinage listed below is sometimes improperly credited to the La Rochelle Mint, which also used an H mintmark, but which ceased operations some years earlier. The order for this coinage was placed through the firm of Chas. J. Shaw Co., who wrote to Heatons on 23 July 1878, saying: "We have much pleasure in certifying that the Contracts for Bronze Coinages we entrusted to your firm in the year 1870 [sic], for the Oriental Republic of Uruguay and the Republic of Paraguay were executed most efficiently, and gave satisfaction to the Governments of the respective countries."

No.	Date	Denomination	Mintmark	Metal	Mintage	Ref.
UR1	1869	1 Centesimo	H	Bronze	1,000,000	Y7
UR1a		1 Centesimo	H	Silver	Unknown	KM6
UR1b		1 Centesimo	H	Gold	Unknown	KM8
UR2		2 Centesimos	H	Bronze	2,000,000	Y8
UR2a		2 Centesimos	H	Silver	Unknown	KM10
UR2b		2 Centesimos	H	Gold	Unknown	KM12
UR2p		2 Centesimos	H	Bronze	Unknown	–
UR3		4 Centesimos	H	Bronze	6,250,000	Y9
UR3a		4 Centesimos	H	Silver	Unknown	KM14
UR3b		4 Centesimos	H	Gold	Unknown	KM16
UR3p		4 Centesimos	H	Bronze	Unknown	–
UR4p		4 Centesimos	None	Bronze	Unknown	–

The off-metal strikes shown above are listed in Krause,[57] but have not been

---

[57] Chester L. Krause et al., *Standard Catalog of World Coins*, 1980 Edition.

No.	Date	Denomination	Mintmark	Metal	Mintage	Ref.

observed by the author. The UR2p and UR3p patterns differ from the regular issues in lacking the engraver's name (Tasset), and having smaller H mintmarks and a different sunface. Proof specimens were offered as Lots 3618 and 3619 in the NASCA 8 December 1977 auction. UR4p relates to the die trials sold as Lot 3620 in the same auction.

No.	Date	Denomination	Mintmark	Metal	Mintage	Ref.
UR5x	1953	2 Centesimos	None	Copper–Nickel	16,880,000	Y29
UR5x	m1954	2 Centesimos	None	Copper–Nickel	33,120,000	Y29
UR6x	m1954	5 Centesimos	None	Copper–Nickel	17,500,000	Y30
UR7	1959	10 Centesimos	None	Copper–Nickel	10,000,000	Y31

UR7

The 1953–9 issues were modelled by Mr. T. H. Paget. Both the Royal Mint and ICI participated in the production of 1953 two and five centesimos.

VENEZUELA Heatons' second national coinage contract (following their 1851 issue for Chile) was also Venezuela's second national issue – their first having been an 1843 copper coinage, produced by the British Royal Mint and signed by Wyon. The Heaton issues were identical, save for date and signature.

VE3

No.	Date	Denomination	Mintmark	Metal	Mintage	Ref.
VE1	1852	¼ Centavo	H	Copper	2,000,000	Y1
VE2		½ Centavo	H	Copper	500,000	Y2
VE3		1 Centavo	HEATON	Copper	250,000	Y3
VE3m		1 Centavo	None	Copper	Unknown	–
VE3ma		1 Centavo	None	Copper–Nickel	Unknown	–

VE3m is a double-reverse mule; a specimen was offered as Lot 3656C in the NASCA 5 December 1977 auction. VE3ma is similar, but of a different metal.

| No. | Date | Denomination | Mintmark | Metal | Mintage | Ref. |

VE3ma is in THE MINT cabinet, and also was Lot 3656B in the same NASCA auction.

The second 1852 issues (VE4–6) are about 5% smaller than the old 1852 issues, and there are minor but clearly discernible differences in design details. All three of the new series, plus the 1 centavo (VE3) of the old series, are illustrated in Heatons' book of Testimonials,[58] and are in the cabinet of THE MINT. Their cabinet also contains obverse dies of both the $\frac{1}{4}$ centavo (VE4) and the 1 centavo (VE6) of 1852, thus definitely identifying these as Heaton emissions. The minutes of the First General Meeting of the Manchester Numismatic Society, which took place on 17 June 1864, record that Ralph Heaton presented to the Society the following items (among others): "Venezuela – Old coinage; six copper proofs, one, half, and quarter cents, 1852; new ditto; two bronze proofs of one cent piece."

VE6
(courtesy Krause Publications)

No.	Date	Denomination	Mintmark	Metal	Mintage	Ref.
VE4	1852	$\frac{1}{4}$ Centavo	None	Copper	4,000,000	Y4
VE5		$\frac{1}{2}$ Centavo	None	Copper	1,000,000	Y5
VE5m		$\frac{1}{2}$ Centavo	None	Copper	Unknown	–
VE6		1 Centavo	None	Copper	500,000	Y6
VE6a		1 Centavo	None	Bronze	Unknown	–
VE6m		1 Centavo	None	Copper	Unknown	–
VE6ma		1 Centavo	None	Copper–Nickel	Unknown	–

The above mintages are as shown by Krause in the *Standard Catalog of World Coins*. The VE5m and VE6m are double-reverse mules; both are in THE MINT collection, as well as the VE6ma which also was Lot 3656A in the above referenced NASCA auction.

VE7

---

[58] Ralph Heaton & Sons, *Testimonials*, 1st Edition, ca. 1879.

No.	Date	Denomination	Mintmark	Metal	Mintage	Ref.

A Venezuelan Resolution dated 15 March 1857 authorized an issue of 20,000 pesos in ¼, ½, and 1 centavos, but this was changed in 1859 to eliminate the fractional centavos.

VE7	1858 m1859	1 Centavo	HEATON	Bronze	2,000,000	Y7

The word LIBERTAD appears in both incuse and relief on varieties of this issue.

VE8p	1858	1 Centavo	HEATON	Copper	Unknown	–

This pattern, which appeared as Lot 3657 in the December 1977 NASCA auction, has a VE7 reverse, but an obverse differing from VE7 in several details, notably in the additional drapery at the base of the bust. It is probably the specimen pattern required by the March 1857 Resolution.

VE8a
VE8b

THE MINT collection contains a plain-edge bronze specimen, as well as a copper–nickel specimen. The 1857 Resolution specified a copper issue; the 1859 Amendment changed the metal to bronze.

VE9

VE9	1862	1 Centavo	HEATON	Bronze	5,000,000	Y7.1
VE9p		1 Centavo	HEATON	Bronze	Unknown	–

Except for the date, VE9p is identical with the 1858 VE8p. Specimens exist in THE MINT cabinet with both plain and engrailed edges.

VE9	1863	1 Centavo	HEATON	Bronze	1,000,000	Y7.1
VE9a		1 Centavo	None	Copper–Nickel	Unknown	–

VE9a was offered as Lot 225 in the Freeman Craig auction of 22 April 1979.

VE10

VE10x	1967 m1969	1 Bolivar	None	Nickel	5,240,000	Y42

Coinage Issues of The Birmingham Mint 221

No.　　Date　　Denomination　Mintmark　Metal　　　Mintage　　Ref.

This is another of the several instances where a century intervened between successive issues by THE MINT for a single country.

VIETNAM – *see* South Vietnam

YEMEN – *see* Ghurfah and Tarim

ZAIRE – *see* Belgian Congo; Congo

ZAMBIA This was the first coinage struck by THE MINT for this part of Africa.

ZA1

| ZA1x | 1968 | 2 Ngwee | None | Bronze$_4$ | 2,070,000 | Y10 |
| ZA1x | m1967 | 2 Ngwee | None | Bronze$_4$ | 16,930,000 | Y10 |

Norman Sillman produced the obverse portrait design for this coin.

Zanzibar (Now part of TANZANIA) Although an independent nation, Zanzibar in 1877 came under the administrative rule of the British East Africa Association as the result of an agreement by the Sultan of Zanzibar. This led to the first distinctive coinage for the country being produced by Brussels in 1882, followed by the Heaton issue of twelve tons of copper coins in 1887.

ZZ1

| | AH*1304*(1887) | | | | | |
| ZZ1x | m1887 | 1 Pysa | None | Copper | 627,000 | Y2 |

The balance scale design on the reverse of the above coin was also used for the 1888 Mombasa issue that Heatons struck for the Imperial East Africa Company. The Zanzibar pysas were ordered by Smith Mackenzie & Co. of Zanzibar through the English firm of Gray Dawes & Co.

222   *Catalogue*

No.	Date	Denomination	Mintmark	Metal	Mintage	Ref.

ZZ3

No.	Date	Denomination	Mintmark	Metal	Mintage	Ref.
ZZ2	1908	1 Cent	None	Bronze	1,000,000	Y8
ZZ3		10 Cents	None	Bronze	100,000	Y9
ZZ4		20 Cents	None	Nickel	100,000	Y10

According to Remick[59] these coins were never released into circulation. He estimates that only 20 to 60 pieces of each denomination are extant.

---

[59] Jerome Remick et al., *British Commonwealth Coins*, p. 552.

Appendix I

The Marseilles Affaire

Note: This account of Heatons' operation of the Marseilles Mint in 1852–6 is presented in some detail, because it illustrates several points:

(1) The entrepreneurial spirit of the Heaton family,
(2) The state of the minting art at that time, and
(3) The contract mintage system then in use in France.

Material for this appendix has been excerpted from letters, diaries, account books, etc. directly related to the event. In other words, the account is authentic — any speculation by the author is so identified.

It all came about quite by surprise. The Heatons had been in the minting business only two years when the opportunity to participate in the new French coinage was offered them. George Heaton described the circumstances in a 30 August 1852 letter to his brother Ralph:

"This afternoon before starting out to the railroad station to see the Queen, Mr. Wragge at the Grenfells Copper Warehouse brought a French gentleman, M. Ritterbandt, who after rather a long explanation and after I had shewed him our presses and drawbenches etc. dictated to me whilst I wrote down as follows (The French Government have passed a law to call in all the old Copper coin and sell all the Bell Metal of which a great part is made in the revolution times.)

"M. Ritterbandt proposes to join 2 of the Directors of France — *viz* at Bordeaux and Lyons for the manufacture of two sixths of the new French Copper Coins — the amount of such manufacture will be fifteen hundred tons — the time for making to extend over four years.

"The price agreed upon to be paid by the French Government is $1\frac{1}{4}$ francs per Kilogramme — $6\frac{1}{4}$d per lb. Government will supply Directors with 105 tons of the best old Copper coin and the Directors are to return 100 tons of coin.

"The Directors require a person with the capital necessary for putting the Mints and machinery (at Lyons, Bordeaux & Marseilles) in effective order (there is already engines etc. but M. R could not say on what principle they worked) and supply such machinery as may be necessary — this is calculated not to exceed £4000.

"This outlay is to be repaid from the first profits, i.e. on about 214 tons – the profit on the remainder of the quantity to be equally divided between the Directors and ourselves – less the agency."

It was a proposition they could not refuse, and so a few weeks later Ralph Heaton III, then only 25 years old, was sent to France to tie down the details. After a brief visit to the Paris Mint, he went on to Marseilles where on 22 October 1852 he executed a contract with M. A. J. Beaussier, Director of the Marseilles Mint, for the production of one-eighth of the total issue. Ralph Heaton & Sons were to install the necessary equipment (which they could afterwards sell) in the Marseilles Mint, and proceed with the manufacture at their own expense. M. Beaussier would deposit a surety bond of 60,000 francs with the Government, and would supervise the operation. The Government would purchase the coinage at the following prices:

```
312,500 kilos of 10 Centimes @ 0.92 francs = 287,500 francs
250,000 kilos of  5 Centimes @ 1.32 francs = 330,000 francs
 31,250 kilos of  2 Centimes @ 2.24 francs =  70,000 francs
 31,250 kilos of  1 Centimes @ 3.00 francs =  93,750 francs
 31,250 kilos of additional  @ 2.00 francs =  62,500 francs
```

The total of 656,250 kilos would be purchased for 843,750 francs, then equal to £33,415. After deduction of costs, the profit would be divided 87% for Heatons and 13% for M. Beaussier.

The contract signed, Heaton set about to equip the mint. He had found in the mint little that could be used: ". . . six brass coining presses out of order – these will be taken out and sold, five rusty old milling machines, four decent cutting-out presses, etc." Four lever-type coining presses were ordered from Paris. From the local sugar refinery he bought two second-hand boilers, 7 × 1.45 metres, for £72. From a salvage yard in Marseilles he bought an old steamboat engine "30 h.p. double-engine, high pressure, with two cylinders 14 inch bore, 42 inch stroke, oscillating". The engine and boilers were sent to a local machinery shop for repairs and eventual installation in the Mint, all of which was completed five months later. Some equipment had to be sent over from the Birmingham shop, including a screwing-machine and a drawing-through or raising machine. Nine rolling mills were also procured from Birmingham. The French Government offered to forgive the import duty on the drawing machine if scale drawings were furnished to the French Mint at Paris, but Heaton rejected this offer. New equipment foundations were put in place, and a new chimney stack 20 metres high was built. When it was all done, the total cost of equipping the Mint came to £3700.

Rather than set up to make his own dies, Heaton contracted to have them made in Paris. The fuel for the boilers had to be coke ". . . to prevent a smoke nuisance", and this was obtained on favourable terms from the Marseilles Gas Works where ". . . the Manager, being an Englishman, has fraternised a little." Water was obtained from the Canal Company on a five year agreement to deliver one module of 8,640 litres every 24 hours. Casting pots were purchased locally. Metal for the coins was to be furnished by the French Government from obsolete coinage that had been called in: "Laid centimes, Royal sous, and sous Head of Liberty".

Common labour was hired locally, but the skills essential to successful operation of a mint were brought over from The Birmingham Mint. The first to come (and the last to leave) was Leonard Brierley, brought over as a clerk and an assistant to Heaton at £4 per week. Others included Moses Howlett, a machinist, and his apprentice son Tom; Edward Wyon, a member of the great Wyon family of Royal Mint fame, but himself then only starting out in the minting trade; Jonathon Newey, a caster; Woodward, a roll-mill operator; and Edwards, a furnace operator. The contract that was signed with Newey was probably typical:

> "Ralph Heaton & Son of Birmingham, Brassfounders etc., hereby agree to employ and Jonathon Newey agrees to give his best and entire services as a Caster of metals or at any other work which he may be required to do at their works in Marseilles, Bouches du Rhone, France, during and until the end of their French contract (3 to 4 years) and they agree to give him in return for his services, Fifty Shillings per week of sixty hours work, all time over or under to be paid or deducted at the same rate; they also agree to pay his passage to Marseilles.
>
> "Jonathon Newey also agrees to accept no other engagement during the said term unless by mutual consent of the parties hereto.
>
> "This agreement is not intended to prevent payment for work by the piece if mutually thought more desirable.
>
>   Signed: Ralph Heaton & Son
>   Signed: Jonathon Newey
>   Witness: George Heaton".

Minting operations finally started up in June of 1853, and although very respectable mintage rates were eventually attained, it was not without difficulties along the way. First, there was the matter of coin colour. The French were extremely particular that the right colour be attained because ". . . the pieces were so much smaller than the old ones that the people might complain unless they had something to look at." Heaton experimented with a variety of processes, but was never able to get consistent results. Finally M. Beaussier learned and passed along the method used by the Paris Mint, and this was adopted at Marseilles.

There was trouble with the casting pots. The English were used to much thicker-walled pots than the French employed, and so breakage was a significant problem. English pots were ordered, but the delivery time was excessive and so in the meantime a French Caster was hired to teach Newey how to use the thin pots. Newey resented this — even threatened to quit — but he finally did learn to use the French pots.

Another bothersome problem showed up in the rolling operation. Of two ingots from a single melt, one might roll out very satisfactorily, and the other might split and streak badly in the rolling process. This eventually worked itself out also, but only after a month of trial and error experimentation, including a suggestion from M. Beaussier to include a little lead in the melt as some of the other mints had done when confronted with the same problem.

The dies from Paris also gave trouble. M. Barre, the Paris Mint die-maker, opined that the fault was with Heaton's use of the dies, a criticism that Heaton summarily rejected. Heaton concluded that the dies needed hardening, but the French officials absolutely forbade it. Nevertheless, Heaton secretly heat-treated a pair of dies, and the results were what he had anticipated. Grudgingly, the French then agreed to heat-treatment when necessary.

As if the technical problems were not enough, cholera broke out in July of 1854. The death toll in Marseilles was huge, and the Heaton group certainly contributed its share. Moses Howlett lost his baby son – only shortly after his wife had died of brain fever, and both the Newey and Woodward families lost a child. Several of the adults were quite ill, but all recovered.

Despite all the problems, real progress in the execution of the coinage contract was being made. During the four weeks of June 1855, the coinage rate averaged a healthy 4.12 million pieces a week. Their best performance in a single sixty-hour week was 5,588,000 pieces.

In February 1856 Ralph Heaton returned to Birmingham, confident that he could safely leave matters in Leonard Brierley's capable hands. Within a year the Order came down from Paris that the mintage was to be completed by the end of March. Accordingly, Brierley turned over the last shipment to the French in late March, sent the Englishmen back to Birmingham, and closed up shop on 31 March 1857.

In the period between June 1853 and March 1857 Heatons had produced 101 million coins of all four denominations, according to Harris.[1] By comparison, the other French mints produced as follows:

Paris	194 million
Bordeaux	90 million
Lille	110 million
Strasbourg	89 million
Lyon	90 million
Rouen	113 million

At the end of April 1857, Ralph Heaton III made his last trip back to Marseilles – to dispose of the plant. This he did to a French manufacturer named Figueron for 27,000 francs, equivalent to £1080 at the time.

Thus ended the French adventure.

---

[1] Robert P. Harris, *A Guidebook of Modern European Coins*, Racine, Wisc., 1965.

Appendix II

Edward Wyon

To most numismatists, the name *Wyon* is inextricably linked with the skilful exercise of the engraving art in the British Royal Mint. It is deservedly so, with names like Leonard Wyon and William Wyon gracing some of the finest products of that venerable institution.

Few know, however, that a member of that illustrious family was closely associated with the mint of Ralph Heaton & Sons. Edward Wyon was a Birmingham native. In about 1852 he was apprenticed to the firm, and almost immediately joined the cadre from Birmingham that operated the Marseilles Mint during the years 1852–7. Wyon chose to concentrate on the business and technical aspects of operating a mint, and his career followed this path — as can be seen from his obituary which appeared in the *Birmingham Daily Post* of 24 August 1906.

"The late Mr. E. Wyon of Canton, China, who died suddenly while on a visit to Kobe, Japan, on the 16th inst., was a Birmingham man, whose career was a remarkably interesting and eventful one. At the time of his death he held the position of Chief of the Operative Department in the Imperial Mint at Canton. Mr. Wyon commenced his business life about 1857 [*sic*] when he was apprenticed to the late Mr. Ralph Heaton of the Birmingham Mint, who, in that year, sent out a mint to Marseilles to strike bronze coins, having received a contract from the French Government to convert the copper coin into bronze. In the early part of 1864, Mr. Wyon was sent out to Burmah[1] on behalf of his employers to superintend the erection and equipment of a mint for the Burmese Government. That the work was satisfactorily performed may be gathered from the following quaint testimonial which Messrs. Heaton subsequently received, the 'foreman' referred to being the late Mr. Wyon.[2]

'We, the Atween Woon, Yah-Bhat-Myingi Woon, Yaw Myoza-Min, and

---

[1] The Burma contract was handled by an agent of the Government of Burma — an English firm known as Wallace Brothers. Wyon signed a three-year contract with Wallace to supervise the installation and initial operation of the Burma Mint.

[2] This translation of the original letter in Burmese also appeared in the Heaton book of Testimonials. A corrected translation, by Mr. J. W. Okell, Lecturer in Burmese at the London Shcool of Oriental and African Studies, appears in Chapter III of the text.

Mingee-Miulha-Maha-Sec, Burmese Ministers of State, do hereby certify that the great merchant and his deputy undertook, in the name of the most powerful God (on oath), to purchase for us instruments with which to coin money, and that they arrived in this heaven-like country in February 1864. The said merchant also sent out a foreman to manage our mint, and he has proved himself a most capable and able man in his business, and the ministers are therefore most thankful to God.'

"After a considerable stay in this 'heaven-like' country Mr. Wyon went to Japan and worked at the Imperial Mint there for a brief period.[3] From Japan he journeyed to Egypt where he managed a cotton mill at Nikla, but he subsequently returned to the service of Messrs. Heaton. Shortly afterwards, his employers received an enquiry from the Republic of Colombia and a contract was entered into for the erection of a mint at Bogota. Mr. Wyon was entrusted with the superintendance of the erection of the machinery and the instruction of the Colombians how to use it. That was in 1881[4] and he remained there for five or six years and taught the new staff every branch of the work. In 1888 Messrs. Heaton erected a mint for the Chinese Government at Canton which was, at that time, the largest Mint in the world. It was a great undertaking but Mr. Wyon was equal to it, and he erected machinery capable of striking 2,700,000 coins per day. He was accompanied by a large staff of men from Birmingham, including a chief cashier, a roller, a coiner and a die-maker. They remained at Canton for two years and after instructing the Chinese in the manufacture of money, the party returned to England with the exception of Mr. Wyon who entered the service of the Chinese Government as Chief of the Operative Department. So completely satisfied were the Chinese authorities with the work done that in October 1893, the following communication was addressed to Mr. Ralph Heaton from the Imperial Mint, Canton.

'To: Mr. Ralph Heaton Esq., The Manager of The Mint, Birmingham, (Limited), Dear Sir, this large mint which our late Viceroy Chang in the 12th year of Kwang Su, ordered from you through the late Minister Lew is working to the satisfaction of our present Viceroy Li, by whose permission the accompanying gold badge, as a token of your good work, is presented to you through Mr. Wyon. It has four Chinese characters thereon, signifying

---

[3] In 1870 Japan purchased the equipment from the defunct Hong Kong Mint, which included several ancient screw presses of the type used by Boulton in his Soho Mint. Recognizing that these would not be adequate for their needs, the Japanese ordered ten lever presses from Heatons; two in 1872 and eight in 1874. The initial equipping and operation of their new mint in Osaka was assisted by a group of English consultants under Thomas Kinder, former Master of the Hong Kong Mint, who was appointed Director of the Imperial Mint in Osaka. The European contingent included Edward Wyon, who was seconded there by Heatons from 1871 until Kinder handed the mint over to Japanese management in February 1875. Wyon served as foreman of the Coining Decpartment in Osaka, and from 1872 was assisted by Thomas Howlett, who was also sent out by Heatons and stayed on until February 1878.

[4] The agreement between Wyon and the Colombian Government was actually signed in December 1883.

that you have "no rival in the world as constructors of minting machinery". Hoping that you will give us the pleasure of accepting same.'

"Mr. Wyon was held in high esteem by the Chinese Government and his services were recognized by the conferment upon him of a distinguished order. While at Canton, he went to Pekin[5] on behalf of Messrs. Heaton to conduct some negotiations in connection with the proposed establishment of a mint there. This was during the Boxer disturbances and Mr. Wyon who was accompanied by his wife entered Pekin shortly before the European Legations were besieged. He and his wife were locked up in the city through-out the siege and Mrs. Wyon died during that trying time. Mr. Wyon escaped without injury although on one occasion he was reported as dead and his death was recorded in the home press.

"He returned to England about eighteen months ago and married a daughter of Mr. Hugh Middleton[6] of Birmingham. They returned to China shortly afterwards. A few months ago a letter was received from Mr. Wyon saying that he intended to retire to England but before doing so he wished to spend a holiday in Japan, a country which had always held a great attraction to him. He had apparently commenced the tour with his wife and sister, but was taken ill at Kobe and died suddenly on Thursday of last week. He was related to the late Mr. Leonard Wyon, the famous engraver at the Royal Mint in London. The news of Mr. Wyon's death was received with great regret at the Birmingham Mint where he was held in the highest esteem and where his exceptional abilities were appreciated to the full."

---

[5] In 1899 Peking decided to establish an Imperial Mint in the capital, and Kann (*Illustrated Catalog of Chinese Coins*) states that a new mint at Hangchow (with machinery from Germany), which had been in operation only since the beginning of the year, was ordered dismantled and shipped to Peking. The question of the origin of the Peking Mint continues to be somewhat of a Chinese mystery, since records in The Mint show that an order for mint equipment for Peking was received in Birmingham in March 1900. It is doubtful that this could have been shipped in time to reach Peking before the Boxer Rebellion caused the destruction of whatever had been put in place using the Hangchow equipment. Wyon may indeed have been looking out for the Mint's interests during his visit to Peking, but we learn from the *Peking and Tientsin Times* of 9 September 1899 that he may have had a more immediate reason for being there. That issue noted that the Canton Mint manager had been recommended to take charge of the new Peking Mint..

[6] Mr. Hugh Middleton was a long-time employee of Heatons, and a top manager of The Birmingham Mint in the period about 1895–1902.

Appendix III

The Heaton Family

The chart opposite shows all of the direct descendants of the several Ralph Heatons who have been, in one way or another, associated with The Birmingham Mint. Only the capitalized names on the chart were directly involved in the operations of The Mint. As it stands, the chart is believed to be reasonably correct, having been compiled from records such as wills, obituary notices, gravestones, etc., and having been checked with several surviving members of the Heaton family. In addition to the information on the chart, there is a parish record of a Ralph Heaton marrying Ann Clowes at Leek, Staffordshire on 6 December 1753. No proof has been found that these were the parents of the Ralph Heaton (I) shown below, but the coincidence of dates and names is certainly striking.

231

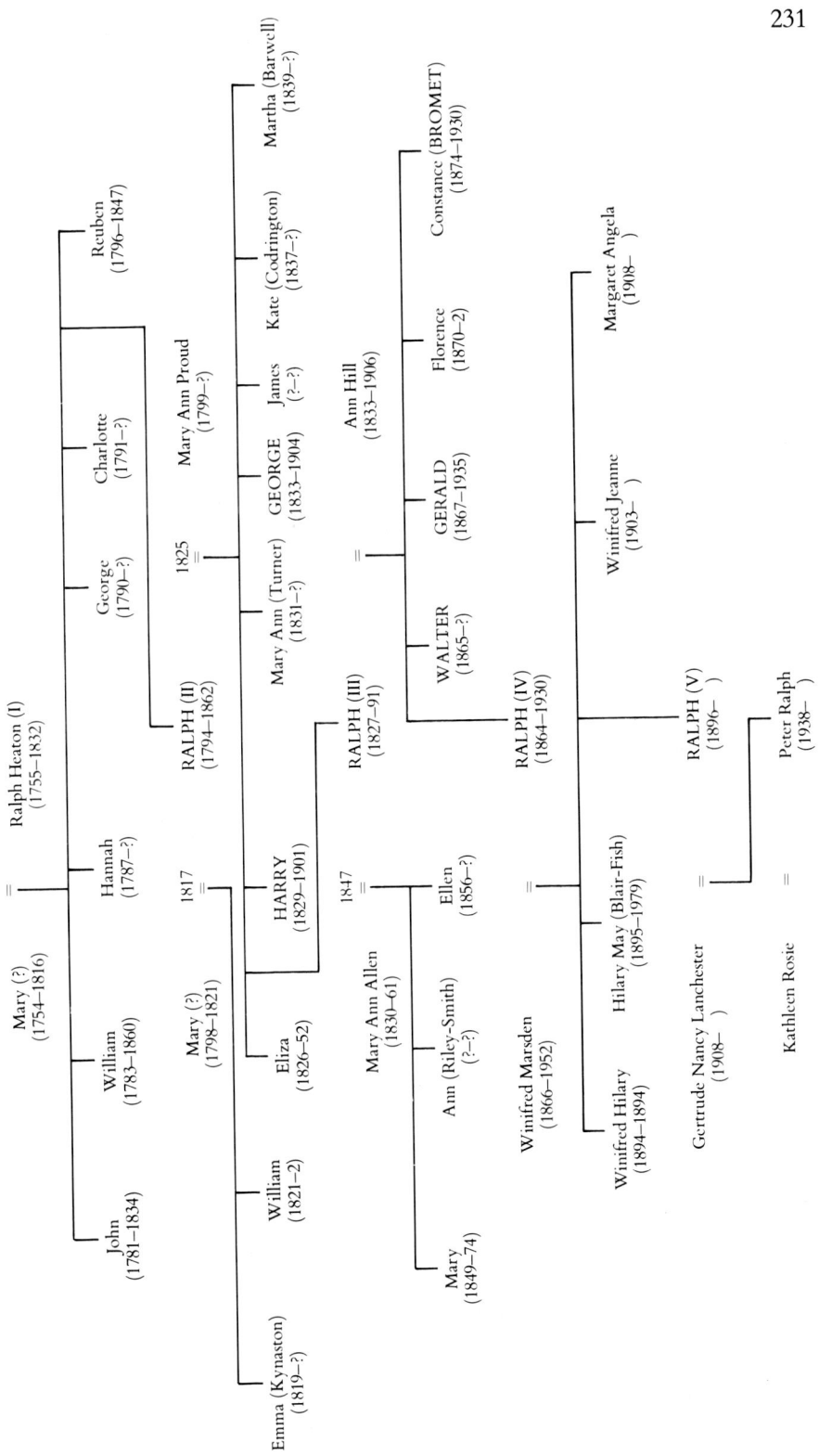

```
                                    Ralph Heaton (I)
Mary (?)              ══════════    (1755–1832)
(1754–1816)

┌──────────────┬──────────────┬─────────────────────────┬──────────────┬──────────────┬──────────────┐
John           William        Hannah                    George         Charlotte      Reuben
(1781–1834)    (1783–1860)    (1787–?)                  (1790–?)       (1791–?)       (1796–1847)
               ═══════        ══════ 1817                    1825 ═══════
               Mary (?)       RALPH (II)                     Mary Ann Proud
               (1798–1821)    (1794–1862)                    (1799–?)

        ┌──────────────┬──────────────┐          ┌──────────────┬──────────────┬──────────────┐
Emma    William        HARRY          Eliza      Mary Ann       GEORGE         James          Kate (Codrington)   Martha (Barwell)
(Kynaston) (1821–2)    (1829–1901)    (1826–52)  (Turner)       (1833–1904)    (?–?)          (1837–?)            (1839–?)
(1819–?)               ═══════ 1847                              ═══════
                       Mary Ann Allen                            Ann Hill
                       (1830–61)                                 (1833–1906)

            ┌──────────────┐                     ┌──────────────┬──────────────┬──────────────┐
Mary        Ann (Riley-Smith)  Ellen             RALPH (IV)     WALTER         GERALD         Florence          Constance (BROMET)
(1849–74)   (?–?)              (1856–?)          (1864–1930)    (1865–?)       (1867–1935)    (1870–?)          (1874–1930)
                               RALPH (III)       ═══════
                               (1827–91)         Hilary May (Blair-Fish)
                                                 (1895–1979)

                    ┌──────────────┬──────────────┐
                    Winifred Marsden  Winifred Hilary  Winifred Jeanne   RALPH (V)      Margaret Angela
                    (1866–1952)       (1894–1894)      (1903– )          (1896– )       (1908– )
                                                                         ═══════
                                                                         Gertrude Nancy Lanchester
                                                                         (1908– )

                                                        Peter Ralph        ═══════   Kathleen Rosie
                                                        (1938– )
```

Appendix IV

The Soho Sale of 1850

The auction of the contents of the Soho Mint in 1850 was broken up into two parts: the mint machinery and miscellaneous equipment were sold on 29 April 1850; the coins and dies forming the Soho collection were auctioned separately the next day. The author has so far been unable to locate an annotated sale catalogue of the machinery auction, but Mr. David Vice (of Peter Ireland (Format) Ltd., Birmingham) has kindly furnished the following information regarding the auction of 30 April 1850.

An annotated copy of the auction catalogue shows that Heatons bought the following lots at the auction sale itself:

174 – containing 63 Gilt Copper Blanks for penny pieces
17 Gilt Copper Blanks for dollars
3 Gilt Copper Blanks for small coin   Cost 6/6d
218 – Hudsons Bay Company Medal, obv. bust Geo III, rev. the arms of the company. Finely executed by Kuchler.
1 pr dies.   Cost 18/-d
220 – Charleville Forest. obv. specimen token
1 pr dies, 1 extra die of rev.
1 punch of obv. and steel collar   Cost 10/-d
256 – Copper Company of Upper Canada ½d 1796
1 pr dies and 1 extra obv. die   Cost 18/-d

Based on cardboard die impressions contributed by The Birmingham Mint to the Birmingham City Museum and Art Galleries, Heatons also acquired all of the dies bought by a Mr. Price at the auction. These were as follows, along with the successful bids made by Mr. Price:

215 – Prince and Princess of Wales on their marriage. O. Busts of Prince of Wales and Caroline. R. Hymen, with Torch in left hand; the right hand holding a Nuptial Knot, uniting the Shields of England and Brunswick, London in the distance. Beautifully executed by Kuchler.
One pair dies and steel collar.   Cost £2,15.0d
216 – Marquis Cornwallis, on the peace with Tippoo. O. Bust of Cornwallis.

232

The Soho Sale of 1850 233

        R. The General receiving as hostages, the Children of Tippoo Saib at his tent. Finely executed by Kuchler.
        One pair dies, punch for reverse and steel collar.   Cost £3.17.6d

\# 222 – Empress Catherine of Russia. O. Bust of the Empress. R. The Imperial arms of Russia. By Kuchler.
        One pair dies, one punch for obverse and steel collar   Cost 18.0d

\# 238 – Three Medals. St. Alban's Female Friendly Society, Ipswich Theatre, and Welsh Society.
        Three pair dies and steel collar.   Cost 13.0d

Again, based on the cardboard die impressions, it would appear that Heatons also acquired a lot that the catalogue indicates was repurchased at the sale by Boulton. The lot, and Boulton's cost, was:

\# 252 – Geo III proposed ½d 1788, a wreath round the edge by Droz, beautifully executed.
        1 pr. dies and steel collar with sexagon cheeks.   Cost £1.6

Of all these, the only dies known to remain in the possession of THE MINT are the reverse die of the Hudsons Bay Company Medal (Lot No. 218), and the obverse die of the marriage medal of the Prince and Princess of Wales (Lot No. 215). What has happened to all the rest is a mystery. At the beginning of World War II some fifty tons of old dies were scrapped as a contribution to the war effort. It is possible that the Boulton sale dies were tragically included in that sacrificial offering.

Appendix V

The Ubiquitous "H"

By no means did the Heaton Mint enjoy a monopoly on the use of the letter H on coins. When Ralph Heaton II decided to use the initial letter of his family name as an identification for coins struck by his firm, he probably did not know that others before him had made the same decision. Indeed, others were still using the H to designate their mints – and thus a certain degree of confusion was created by his decision. His selection is understandable, although other choices might have created less confusion in later years – but that is the way it was. Those other users of an H on coins were as follows.

France (La Rochelle)

At least in modern times the French were the first. In 1540 Francis I, to bring about a more orderly identification system, issued a Royal Decree dated 14 January which, among other things, stipulated that henceforth the H would be used on coins emanating from the La Rochelle Mint. This mint had been in operation since as early as 1400, and had used an R mintmark during part of that time. Thereafter, until it closed, it was to use the H mintmark.

Francis I also introduced another coinage custom that later involved the letter H in a different way than as a mintmark. At least the gold coins during his reign had an F (for Francis) worked into the reverse design. This caused no immediate problems, since no French mints were then authorized to use an F mintmark, but in starting this custom he did not foresee that he would be succeeded by Henry II. Henry caused his own monogram to be used on coins during his reign, as did

1731H Isles du Vent 12 Sols
(courtesy British Museum)

1722H Colonies Françoises 9 Deniers
(courtesy British Museum)

234

Henry III and Henry IV later in the same century. Thus the coins of the Henrys that were struck at La Rochelle had the H used in two ways, and in style and size the several Hs were alike. The crowned Hs to right and left of the shield are Henrys. The H below signifies La Rochelle.

The La Rochelle Mint operated off and on until early in the nineteenth century, striking gold and silver coins with an H mintmark for the many governments of France. In addition, in 1731/32 La Rochelle struck silver coins for the Windward Isles (Isles du Vent) in the West Indies, and in 1700/1800 struck bronze coins for the French Colonies. All bore the H mintmark. Finally, in 1837 the La Rochelle Mint was closed, since which time no French coins have displayed the H mintmark. Because its closure preceded the opening of the Heaton Mint, there should be no confusion between La Rochelle and Heaton coins. Such has not been the case, however. In 1869 Heaton struck a series of coins for Uruguay using dies prepared in the Paris Mint. Due to the Paris privy mark (a bee) on these coins, and the Heaton H, they have occasionally been mis-attributed to the La Rochelle Mint.

Holy Roman Empire

During most of the eighteenth century, the Holy Roman Empire was a rather loose confederation of Central European States – with the House of Hapsburg providing the leadership in the form of the Emperor. The individual States enjoyed a high degree of independence, including the right to mint. There was little attempt at unification, and so it is not surprising that mintmarks were not completely the distinguishing devices that they were intended to be.

1788H Austrian Netherlands ¼ Kronenthaler
(courtesy Krause Publications)

In the Tyrol near Innsbruck was the city of Hall. The mint for the Princely County of Tyrol was in Hall, which mint bears the distinction of having struck, in 1484, the first dollar-sized silver coin – the famous Joachimsthaler. During the period 1746–65, Hall emissions were identified by the letters H–A, and thereafter by a variety of marks, including an H on the coins of Maria Theresa and Francis I until 1765. The death of Francis in 1765 generated another interesting use of the letter H as a minting year designator. After 1765 the Francis I coins continued to be struck with the 1765 date, but with letters (starting with A = 1766) to indicate the actual year of mintage. Thus the 3 Kreuzer (Craig[1] 113) was struck in 1773, as

---

[1] William D. Craig, *Coins of the World 1750–1850*, 3rd Edition, Whitman Publishing Co., Racine, Wisc.

indicated by the letter H, as was the 20 Kreuzer (Craig 116) and the 1 Ducat (Craig 55). In no case, however, were these Year H coins also struck with an H mintmark. To make matters yet more confusing, another Austrian mint also used the H mintmark in the same period. The Gunzburg Mint, near Ulm, struck coins for the County of Burgau from 1768 to 1788 with a G indicating Burgau or an H mintmark. In addition, coins for Further Austria with the H mintmark were produced by Gunzburg until 1804, as were coins for the Duchy of Austria and the Austrian Netherlands. In 1805 Gunzburg became part of Bavaria, and minting ceased.

Saxony

1813H Saxony 1 Heller
(courtesy British Museum)

In the short unsettled period between the fall of the Holy Roman Empire and the establishment of the German Confederation, the mint at Dresden used the letter H as a mintmark. This lasted only during the years 1804 through 1813, before and after which other mintmarks were employed. Even within the period other marks were also used; the gold and silver coins of 1804–12 bore the identifying letters SGH.

Switzerland

1817H Geneva 1 Sol
(courtesy British Museum)

For a short time, cantonal mints used the H on limited coinage issues. In 1810 and 1811 the Schwyz Mint struck 4 Batzen with H marks, and in 1817 the Geneva Mint struck 1 and $1\frac{1}{2}$ Sols, also with an H mintmark.

Netherlands

Between 1814 and 1826 a mint in Amsterdam struck a large number of coins for the Dutch East Indies, identifying itself as the source of these coins with an H mark.

The H employed by Amsterdam has a different character than has been elsewhere used.

1815H Batavia 1 Duit
(courtesy British Museum)

Germany

1877H Hesse-Darmstadt 2 Mark
(courtesy Krause Publications)

In the late nineteenth century most of the states of Germany operated their own mints. For a period of time, the mint in Darmstadt in the Grand Duchy of Hesse used the H mark on both state and federal issues. This started with the beginning of Imperial coinage, and continued until 1882, after which an A mintmark was used. The following table includes all issues having an H for Hesse–Darmstadt.

	1872	1873	1874	1875	1876	1877	1878	1879	1880	1881	1882
1 Pfennig				H	H	H					
2 Pfennig				H	H	H					
5 Pfennig				H	H						
10 Pfennig			H	H	H	H					
20 Pfennig			H	H	H	H					
50 Pfennig				H	H	H					
1 Mark			H	H	H				H	H	H
2 Mark						H	H				
5 Mark				H	H						
5 Mark Gold						H					
10 Mark Gold	H	H		H	H	H	H	H	H		
20 Mark Gold	H	H	H								

Essentially the same observation can be made in the case of the Hesse emissions as was made for La Rochelle. This use of the H mintmark should lead to no confusion, because Hesse struck no non-German coins, and Heatons struck no German coins.

Mexico

1881H̊ Mexico 1 Centavo
(courtesy British Museum)

The Mexican mints, of which as many as fourteen operated at one time or another during the nineteenth century, used a simple but effective system of mintmarks. Generally, the mintmark consisted of a principal letter which was the first letter in the name of the mint city, and a subordinate letter which was the last letter of the city's name. Thus the mint at Hermosillo used on its rather sparse coinage either an H̊ or an H°. The former was more frequently used in its earlier years, and the latter more in its later years. This mint began operations in about 1832, and at first issued minor state copper coinage. In 1835 and 1836 it struck an issue of silver 8 reales from unauthorized dies with an H̊ mintmark, but these were caused to be recalled. A new mint was constructed starting in 1860, and from 1861 until 1895 the Hermosillo Mint regularly produced a full range of the current denominations, although not all in every year. In fact, its output was among the smallest of all the Mexican mints then operating, and consequently its issues are today among the rarest and most expensive of the coinage of the Republican period. As in most of the preceding cases, the Hermosillo Mint struck no non-Mexican coins, and Heatons struck no coins for Mexico with an H "marca de la ceca".

Finland

1951H Finland 500 Markkaa
(courtesy M. Rogozinsky)

Since 1864 the Finnish Mint in Helsinki has used a mintmark (on coins 20 Pennia and larger) which was the last initial of the name of the current Director of the Mint. This has caused some interesting cases of repetitive marks, since of the total of six Directors from 1864 to 1975, three (including Mr. Soiniemi from 1958 to 1975) have had names starting with S, two with L, and one with H. From 1948 to 1958 the Director was Mr. P. U. Helle, and so the H mark appears on Finnish coinage of that period. All of the Finnish coins of 1948–58 were struck in Helsinki. The Mint did strike coins for Finland in 1921 with the H mintmark, but only in that year. No foreign coins were struck by Helsinki during the time they were using the H mintmark.

One might question whether a mark signifying the name of the Mint Director can properly be considered a mintmark. In some respects it more nearly approaches the function of the assayer's marks used on Spanish-American coins. However, it is the only identifying mark on Finnish coins, and the Finnish Mint considers it a mintmark. So be it. These marks since 1864 are as follows:[2]

Mark	Period	Mint Director
S	1864–85	A. F. Soldan
L	1885–1912	C. Lihr
S	1912–47	I. G. Sundell
L	1948	V. Liuto
H	1948–58	P. U. Helle
S	1958–75	A. Soiniemi

[2] Courtesy of Mr. Soiniemi.

Appendix VI

Australasian Tokens

No documentary records have been so far located which clearly define the part that the Heaton firm played in the extensive issues of tokens used in Australia and New Zealand in the period 1850–75. That they were involved has long been recognized, if only because of the fact that two of the tokens bear the Heaton signature. However, a much more extensive participation is inferred from study of a group of die impressions on cardboard which are in the keeping of the Birmingham City Museum, having been placed in their care by The Birmingham Mint in about 1968. Included among the some 146 die impressions making up the whole group are 25 imprints which clearly and definitely relate to the Australasian tokens – strongly suggesting (but certainly, without more, not proving) a Heaton provenance.

Of the 146 imprints, 13 are of dies which were produced before 1850, which was the first year Heaton & Son began actual minting operations. Twelve of these are of dies apparently acquired by Heatons at the Soho Mint auction (see Appendix IV), and one is dated 1846 and signed RH. Ralph Heaton II was himself a diesinker, and so it can be postulated that the 1846 die (for a RUTHERFORD BROS., HARBOR GRACE, NEWFOUNDLAND token) was engraved by Heaton, but used elsewhere to strike that issue. All of the remainder of the die impressions can be assumed to represent products of the Heaton Mint; no evidence has been seen to indicate otherwise, and positive evidence exists in quite a number of cases. Thus the impressions of the 25 Australasian token dies support in greater or lesser degree the attribution of many tokens to Heatons, as is shown in the trial listing to follow.

In the following listings, references are used as assigned by Clarke[1] (T numbers) and Andrews[2] (A numbers). Note that where a token was issued in both halfpenny and penny denominations, both are here attributed to Heatons, even though the die impressions include only one of the denominations. Unless otherwise stated, the

---

[1] Robert A. Clarke, *The Coins and Tokens of British Oceania*, 5th Edition (San Clemente, CA, Malter-Westerfield Publishing Co. Inc., 1971).
[2] Dr. Arthur Andrews, *Australasian Tokens and Coins* (Sydney, William Applegate Gulick, 1921).

Australasian Tokens

illustrations which follow are photographs of the actual die impressions (used through the courtesy of the Birmingham City Museum).

Tokens for which die impressions of both obverse and reverse exist.

Obverse   Reverse

T15/A189	½d	HANKS AND LLOYD	THE SYDNEY RAILWAY	1855
T16/A188	1d	HANKS AND LLOYD	THE SYDNEY RAILWAY	1855
T17/A193	½d	HANKS AND LLOYD	PEACE & PLENTY	1857
T18/A190	1d	HANKS AND LLOYD	PEACE & PLENTY	1857

T165/A246	½d	HIDE & DE CARLE	MELBOURNE V./Justice seated	1858
167/A236	1d	HIDE & DE CARLE	MELBOURNE V./Justice seated	1858

T18/A497	1d	M. SOMERVILLE	NEW ZEALAND Rose, thistle, and shamrock	1857

Appendix VI

Tokens for which impressions of both obverse and reverse exist, but with dates differing from those on the die impressions.

Obverse   Reverse

T85/A2	½d	LEWIS ABRAHAMS	TASMANIA/Emu and kangaroo	1855
T86/A54	1d	LEWIS ABRAHAMS	TASMANIA/Emu and kangaroo	1855

T142/A650	1d	PEACE & PLENTY ND	MELBOURNE V./Justice seated	1858
T164/A232	½d	HIDE & DE CARLE	MELBOURNE V./Justice seated	1858
T166/A227	1d	HIDE & DE CARLE	MELBOURNE V./Justice seated	1857

Tokens with the Heaton signature. (The Annand Smith token photograph is from The Mint cabinet.)

T19/A291	1d	IREDALE & CO.	BRITANNIA/Britannia seated	ND
T149/A18	1d	ANNAND SMITH	BRITANNIA/Britannia seated	ND

Australasian Tokens

Tokens for which there are die impressions of only obverse or reverse. Dates may be different from die impression dates.

Obverse   Reverse

T6/A61	½d	JAMES CAMPBELL	AUSTRALIA/Justice standing	ND
T7/A59	1d	JAMES CAMPBELL	AUSTRALIA/Justice standing	ND
T10A31	1d	BATTLE & WEIGHT	Justice standing	ND
T13/A186	½d	HANKS and COMPY.	PEACE & PLENTY	1857
T14/A184	1d	HANKS and COMPY.	PEACE & PLENTY	1857
T20/A292	1d	IREDALE & CO.	AUSTRALIA/Justice standing	ND
T37/A616	½d	WEIGHT & JOHNSON	Justice standing	ND
T38/A615	1d	WEIGHT & JOHNSON	Justice standing	ND
T69/A368	½d	T. F. MERRY	PEACE & PLENTY	ND
T70/A366	1d	T. F. MERRY	PEACE & PLENTY	ND
T71/A364	1d	MERRY & BUSH 1863	PEACE & PLENTY	ND
T84/A226	1d	SAMUEL HENRY	TASMANIA/Emu and kangaroo	1857

T88/A137	½d	I. FRIEDMAN	TASMANIA/Justice seated	1857
T89/A133	1d	I. FRIEDMAN	TASMANIA/Justice seated	1857
T95/A279	½d	G. HUTTON	Emu and kangaroo	ND
T96/A278	1d	G. HUTTON	Emu and kangaroo	ND

Appendix VI

		Obverse		Reverse	
T102/A356	1d	R. ANDREW MATHER	TASMANIA/Justice standing		ND
T114/A310	½d	R. JOSEPHS	VAN DIEMEN'S LAND Justice seated		1855
T115/A309	1d	R. JOSEPHS	VAN DIEMEN'S LAND Justice seated		1855
T116/A621	½d	THOMAS WHITE	TASMANIA/Emu and kangaroo		1855
T117/A620	1d	THOMAS WHITE	TASMANIA/Emu and kangaroo		1855
T118/A622	1d	THOMAS WHITE	TASMANIA/Emu and kangaroo		1857

T132/A51	1d	T. BUTTERWORTH	WINE & SPIRIT MERCHANTS	ND
T133/A54	1d	T. BUTTERWORTH	Justice seated	1859
T141/A409	1d	R. PARKER	AUSTRALIA/Justice standing	ND
T143/A655	1d	PEACE & PLENTY 1859	Justice seated	1859
T176/A281	½d	ROBERT HYDE	PEACE & PLENTY	1857
T177/A285	½d	ROBERT HYDE	PEACE & PLENTY	1861
T178/A280	1d	ROBERT HYDE	PEACE & PLENTY	1857
T179/A283	1d	ROBERT HYDE	PEACE & PLENTY	1861
T196/A464	1d	G. & W. H. ROCKE	MELBOURNE V./Justice seated	1859
T252/A30	1d	W. BATEMAN JUN^r 1855	AUSTRALIA/Justice standing	ND

T7/A64	1d	ARCHIBALD CLARK	NEW ZEALAND/Justice seated	1857
T9/A131	½d	T. S. FORSAITH	NEW ZEALAND/Justice seated	1858
T10/A130	1d	T. S. FORSAITH	NEW ZEALAND/Justice seated	1858

T58/A10	½d	D. ANDERSON	Justice standing		ND
T59/A9	1d	D. ANDERSON	Justice standing		ND

T65/A666	½d	PROFESSOR HOLLOWAY	Hygeia seated	1857
T66/A672	½d	PROFESSOR HOLLOWAY	Hygeia seated	1858
T67/A660	1d	PROFESSOR HOLLOWAY	Hygeia seated	1857
T68/A668	1d	PROFESSOR HOLLOWAY	Hygeia seated	1858

Tokens with either obverse or reverse identical with any of the preceding tokens, but for which there are no corresponding die impressions.

		Obverse	Reverse	
T11/A123	1d	FLAVELLE BROS.	Emu and kangaroo	ND
T12/A125	1d	FLAVELLE BROS.	Emu and kangaroo	ND
T63/A305	1d	T. H. JONES	AUSTRALIA/Justice standing	ND
T77/A349	1d	JOHN MARTIN	AUSTRALIA/Justice standing	ND
T78/A349	1d	MARTIN & SACH	AUSTRALIA/Justice standing	ND
T81/A567	1d	ALFRED TAYLOR	AUSTRALIA/Justice standing	ND
T187/A391	1d	MOUBRAY, LUSH & CO.	AUSTRALIA/Justice standing	ND
T230/A604	½d	WARNOCK BROS.	PEACE & PLENTY	1861
T231/A603	1d	WARNOCK BROS.	PEACE & PLENTY	1861
T2/A19	½d	H. ASHTON	NEW ZEALAND/Justice seated	1858
T3/A20	½d	H. ASHTON	NEW ZEALAND/Justice seated	1859
T44/A98	1d	DAY & MIEVILLE	NEW ZEALAND/Justice seated	1857
T46/A308	1d	JONES & WILLIAMSON	NEW ZEALAND/Justice seated	1858
T49/A639	1d	A. S. WILSON	NEW ZEALAND/Justice seated	1857

In this trial listing, no account has been taken of the possibility that Heatons prepared the dies for striking elsewhere. This may well have been the case, for instance, with the Professor Holloway tokens, which have been sometimes attributed to a London source. It should also be noted that this listing has been prepared based solely on perusal of various catalogues; the actual tokens have not been compared directly with the die impressions. Thus some inaccuracies may have crept in due to the limitations of the photographic reproductions.

Regardless, it becomes clear that Heatons participated in the production of the Australasian merchant tokens to a much greater degree than has heretofore been recognized.